本书得到了以下项目的支持和资助：国家社科基金重点项目（No. 12&ZD217），国家自然科学基金项目（No.71671118，No.71702156，No. 71772025），四川省科技厅项目（No.2019JDR0026），四川省教育厅项目（No.18SB0400），四川省教育厅重点研究基地川酒发展研究中心项目（No.CJZ17-02），四川轻化工大学人才引进项目（No. 2017RCSK21，No.2018RCSK01），教育部人文社科项目（No.17YJC630098，No.19YJC630222），四川省社会科学重点研究基地项目（No. Xq18C07）。

蒋相岚 著

白酒可持续供应链研究
决策模型及其应用

Research on Chinese Baijiu Sustainable
Supply Chain Management
Decision Making Model and Its Application

中国社会科学出版社

图书在版编目（CIP）数据

　　白酒可持续供应链研究：决策模型及其应用/蒋相岚著.—北京：中国社会科学出版社，2019.12
　　ISBN 978-7-5203-5776-0

　　Ⅰ.①白… Ⅱ.①蒋… Ⅲ.①白酒工业—工业企业管理—供应链管理—研究—中国 Ⅳ.①F426.82

　　中国版本图书馆 CIP 数据核字（2019）第 287937 号

出 版 人	赵剑英
责任编辑	王　衡
责任校对	朱妍洁
责任印制	王　超
出　　版	中国社会科学出版社
社　　址	北京鼓楼西大街甲 158 号
邮　　编	100720
网　　址	http://www.csspw.cn
发 行 部	010-84083685
门 市 部	010-84029450
经　　销	新华书店及其他书店
印　　刷	北京明恒达印务有限公司
装　　订	廊坊市广阳区广增装订厂
版　　次	2019 年 12 月第 1 版
印　　次	2019 年 12 月第 1 次印刷
开　　本	710×1000　1/16
印　　张	14.5
字　　数	216 千字
定　　价	79.00 元

凡购买中国社会科学出版社图书，如有质量问题请与本社营销中心联系调换
电话：010-84083683
版权所有　侵权必究

摘　　要

随着经济全球化和知识经济的快速发展，市场竞争越来越激烈。企业之间的竞争已经逐步发展为供应链之间的竞争。近年来，随着对环境保护、经济绩效和社会影响的关注，供应链之间的竞争又演变成了可持续供应链之间的竞争。可以看出，构建一条高效率的可持续供应链已经成为企业发展的核心和重点，由此产生了一种新型的管理模式——可持续供应链管理。白酒行业是中国国民经济的重要物质生产部门，对中国经济的发展起着举足轻重的作用，但中国白酒行业也存在产能过剩、结构失衡、物流成本居高不下、废弃物较多和社会影响有待提高等问题。随着全球化的发展，国外洋酒不断蚕食白酒企业的市场份额，葡萄酒、啤酒、果酒等加剧了白酒市场的竞争。在这样的环境下，中国白酒企业应如何在激烈的市场竞争中立足成为需要思考的问题。在供应链管理思想给企业创造巨大价值的前提下，作为供应链管理与可持续发展研究的新领域，可持续供应链管理将经济、环境和社会三个维度进行集成思考。可持续供应链上的网络设计、供应商选择、风险管控和供应链绩效评价在理论研究上和企业实践上均得到了越来越多学者专家的关注，并且取得了丰硕的研究成果。因此，如何将可持续供应链理论研究和白酒企业实践结合起来，并有效解决相关决策问题是一项很有价值的研究。

可持续供应链研究涉及多个不同的管理目标。一般情况下，经济目标是企业最关注的衡量标准之一，因此降低任何运营成本，提高任何绩效水平，都可以提高决策者的满意度。同时，众所周知，白酒企业的生产和销售活动对环境会产生一定的影响。另外，企业管理者还需平衡协调劳动者工作环境、股东权益等社会管理目标。这些相互关联，有时甚至相互冲突的管理目标需要在供应链管理的优化决策问题中深入探讨。运用可持续供应链管理的思想可以帮助白酒行业的决策者实现多个管理目标、优化资源配置，从而实现企业竞争力的提升。

一般而言，可持续供应链管理具有不确定性、模糊性和动态性的特点。一方面，白酒行业可持续供应链往往受到经济、环境和社会等不确定因素的影响；另一方面，白酒行业供应链管理中的相关指标不能用精确的数字表示，但能用模糊语言变量进行很好的度量。另外，白酒行业可持续供应链管理具有动态变化的特点。随着时代的发展，可持续供应链不断发展变化。这种不确定的动态可持续供应链管理给决策者进行定量和精确分析带来了很大的挑战。

本书在广泛吸收和借鉴已有研究的基础上，以随机不确定理论、多目标理论以及模糊理论为研究工具，对模糊随机环境下的白酒行业可持续供应链管理问题进行了研究。第一章为引言，介绍了研究背景，可持续供应链、白酒行业、供应链网络设计、供应商选择、风险管控、供应链评价的研究现状，并给出了本书的研究框架。第二部分为理论基础，概述了涉及的多目标规划理论、模糊理论、随机不确定理论和可持续供应链基础知识。主体内容为第三章到第六章，第七章是结论部分。以下分别概述第三章到第六章的内容。

第三章以某一白酒企业的网络布局为原型，研究了白酒行业可持续供应链网络设计优化问题。这涉及多个不确定性研究。比如配送中心选择的随机不确定性、配送中心的配送量的不确定性、从酒厂到配送中心的运输模式的不确定性、从配送中心到需求点路径的不确定性，管理者需要通过模型和算法进行优化决策，实现最小化供应链总体成本、最小化碳排放以及最大化社会影响力的目标，由此提出了一个多目标多阶段的集成优化决策模型。通过 R 语言求出了最优解决方案。随后，将模型和算法应用到了四川一家白酒企业的可持续供应链网络布局实际案例中，对结果进行了分析和讨论，说明了模型和算法的科学性和有效性。

第四章针对模糊环境下的白酒可持续供应链供应商选择问题做了进一步研究。当产品出现问题时，一般会追根溯源，找到供应商。因此，供应商选择已经成为企业关注的重要方面。针对供应商可持续发展的要求，提出了经济维度、环境维度和社会维度三个可持续维度的15个供应商选择指标。考虑到面对的决策环境具有模糊不确定性，运用模糊 DEMATEL 算法对供应商选择指标进行了重要度分析和原因结果分析。随后，将模型和算法应用到四川一家白酒企业的可持续供应链选择案例中，验证了模型和方法的有效性和实际可操作性。

第五章鉴于供应链风险管理的重要影响，探讨了白酒可持续供应链中的风险管控问题。对风险的维度、管理方法和白酒风险进行了介绍。在经济全球化的前提下，企业面临的环境越来越复杂，相应面对的各项风险也越来越多。通过风险识别，确定了经济、环境和社会三个维度30个风险因子，通过 FMEA 方法进行衡量、评估，用算出的风险顺序数进行分析，结合相应环境给出了风险应对策略。随后，将模型和算法应用到了白酒企业的风险控制项目中来验证方法的有效性和实用性。

第六章在综合考虑白酒行业供应链特点的基础上，深入研究了可持续供应链的绩效评价问题。由于企业、消费者、政府、非政府组织等诸多利益相关者的影响，现代企业都会定期不定期地对所处的供应链进行评价。随着时代的发展，人们对环境和社会的关注也越来越重视，因此，对供应链的可持续性进行评价也越来越受到企业的关注。这里构建了基于经济、环境和社会三个可持续维度的15个供应链评价指标。考虑到评价问题的模糊性，将模糊理论与层次分析法和 TOPSIS 方法结合起来，用模糊 AHP 方法求解指标权重，用模糊 TOPSIS 方法进行方案选择。随后，将模型和算法应用到四川一家白酒企业的可持续供应链评价案例中来验证其有效性和科学性。

综上所述，针对白酒行业供应链的现有问题，对白酒行业可持续供应链优化及其应用进行了深入研究。依次探讨了白酒可持续供应链环境下的网络设计优化问题、供应商选择问题、风险控制问题和供应链绩评价问题。首先，对这四类问题，分别建立了相应的多目标决策模型，并分析了这四类问题中的模糊随机不确定性。其次，基于该问题的复杂性和模型的特点，分别设计了相应的算法。最后，针对这四类可持续供应链问题进行了案例应用研究，进一步验证了方法的有效性和实用性。提出的决策模型和算法能够帮助决策者根据不同的决策环境制定出更加合理有效的决策方案，对于白酒行业可持续供应链研究问题有着一定的指导意义。对于多目标理论、模糊理论和随机不确定理论以及算法研究也有着积极的推动作用。

Abstract

With the rapid development of economic globalization and knowledge economy, the market competition is becoming more and more fierce. The competition among enterprises has gradually developed into the competition among supply chains. In recent years, with the concern of environmental protection, economic performance and social responsibility, supply chain competition has evolved into sustainable supply chain competition. It can be seen that the construction of a highly efficient and sustainable supply chain has become the core and focus of enterprise development. Chinese Baijiu industry is an important material production sector of China's national economy, which plays an important role in the development of China's economy. However, there are many problems in Chinese Baijiu industry, such as overcapacity, structural imbalance, high logistics costs, waste and social responsibility. With the development of globalization, the market share of Baijiu companies has been eroded by foreign liquor. Wine, beer, fruit wine intensifies the competition. In such an environment, how can Chinese Baijiu enterprises stand in the fierce market competition? Supply chain management creates huge value to the enterprise. As a new research field of sustainable development and supply chain management, sustainable supply chain management integrates the three dimensions of economic, environmental and social thinking. Through the research on the network design, supplier selection, risk management and supply chain performance evaluation in sustainable supply chain, more and more scholars pay attention to both theoretical research and business practice, and achieved fruitful results. Therefore, it is a valuable research how to combine the theory of sustainable supply chain with the practice of Chinese Baijiu enterprises, and effectively solve the related decision-making problems.

Sustainable supply chain research involves a number of different management objectives. In general, the economic goal is one of the most concerned measures of the enterprise. Therefore, reducing any operating costs and improving any performance levels can improve the satisfaction of decision makers. At the same time, it is well known that the Chinese Baijiu production and sales activities will have a certain impact on the environment. In addition, business managers also face the social management objectives such as the working environment and the rights of shareholders. These interrelated and sometimes conflicting management objectives need to be explored in the optimization of supply chain management. The sustainable supply chain management thinking can help the decision-makers in Chinese Baijiu industry to achieve multiple management objectives, optimize the allocation of resources, and enhance the competitiveness of enterprises.

Generally speaking, sustainable supply chain management is characterized by uncertainty, ambiguity and dynamism. On one hand, due to the economic situation, environmental conditions and social factors will be unpredictable, Chinese Baijiu industry sustainable supply chain is often affected by various uncertainties. On the other hand, the relevant indicators of the supply chain management in the Chinese Baijiu industry can not be accurately expressed, but can be measured with fuzzy linguistic variables. In addition, the Chinese Baijiu industry sustainable supply chain management has the characteristics of dynamic change. With the development of the times, the sustainable supply chain is constantly evolving. This kind of uncertain dynamic sustainable supply chain management has brought great challenge to decision makers.

This book researches on sustainable supply chain management of Chinese Baijiu industry based on existing research and with the research tools of stochastic uncertainty theory, multi-objective theory and fuzzy theory. The organization of this paper is as follows: Chapter 1 is an introduction for research background, literature review for sustainable supply chain, Chinese Baijiu industry, supply chain network design, supplier selection, risk management and supply chain performance evaluation, and research framework. Chapter 2 reviews the theoretical foundations related to this book, including multi-objective programming theory, fuzzy theory, stochastic uncertainty theory and sustainable supply chain management theory. Chapter 3—6 are the main contents of this paper. Chapter 7 concludes with a summary. The following is an over view of the main content.

The research discusses the optimization of the sustainable supply chain network design in Chinese Baijiu industry with the network layout of a Chinese Baijiu enterprise in Chapter 3. This involves multiple uncertainty studies, such as the stochastic uncertainty of the distribution center selection, the uncertainty of the distribution volume of the distribution center, the uncertainty of the transportation mode from the distillery to the distribution center, the uncertainty path from the distribution center to the demand point. Managers need to optimize the decision-making model and algorithm by minimizing the total cost of the supply chain, minimizing carbon emissions and maximizing the social impact goals, which proposes a multi-objective and multi-stage integrated optimization decision model. The optimal solution is obtained by R language. Finally, this chapter applies the model and algorithm to the practical case of network design of Chinese Baijiu in Sichuan to show the scientific and efficiency of the methodology.

Chapter 4 makes the further research on the supplier selection of sustainable supply chain in the fuzzy environment. If products have problems, it will be traced to suppliers. Therefore, supplier selection has become an important aspect of corporate concern. In order to meet the requirements of sustainable development of suppliers, it puts forward three dimensions of sustainable development, the economic dimension, the environmental dimension and the social dimension, and develops 15 supplier selection criteria. Considering the uncertainty of decision making environment, fuzzy DEMATEL method is used to analyze the importance of supplier selection criteria and the cause analysis. Finally, the model and method are applied to the case study of a sustainable supply chain in a Chinese Baijiu company in Sichuan, and efficiency and feasibility of the model are verified.

In view of the important influence of supply chain risk management, the risk control in Chinese Baijiu sustainable supply chain is discussed. This chapter introduces risk dimension, management method and Chinese Baijiu risk. In the premise of economic globalization, enterprises are facing more and more complex environment, the corresponding risks are more and more complex. Through the risk identification, the three dimensions of economy, environment and society are identified, and the risk factors are measured by FMEA method. The risk sequence is analyzed by using RPN. Finally, the risk response strategies are is given according to the corresponding environment. Finally, the model and algorithm are applied to the risk control project of a Chinese Baijiu company to verify the efficiency and practicability of the method.

Considering the Chinese Baijiu industry supply chain, this chapter studies the performance evaluation of sustainable supply chains. Modern enterprises have to evaluate their supply chain regularly or irregularly due to pressures from enterprises, consumers, governments, non-governmental organizations and many other stakeholders. With the development of the times, people pay more and more attention to the environment and society. Therefore, the evaluation of the sustainability of the supply chain is more and more concerned by enterprises. This chapter establishes 15 supply chain evaluation criteria based on three sustainable dimensions of economy, environment and society. Considering the ambiguity of the evaluation problem, the fuzzy theroy and the analytic hierarchy process and the TOPSIS method are combined. The fuzzy AHP method is used to solve the criteria weight, and the fuzzy TOPSIS is used to select the alternatives. Finally, the model and algorithm are applied to the sustainable supply chain evaluation of a Chinese Baijiu enterprise to verify the effectiveness and scientificity.

In conclusion, this book studies the Chinese Baijiu sustainable supply chain optimization problem in a fuzzy random environment and its applications. It discusses network design optimization, supplier selection, risk control and supply chain evaluation. First, multi-objective programming model is established respectively for these four problems, and fuzzy random uncertain decision environment and its processing method are introduced. Then, based on the complex characteristics of the optimization problems and models, corresponding solution algorithms are designed respectively. Finally, the results and an analysis of a practical example at a Chinese Baijiu enterprise demonstrate the practicality and efficiency of the proposed model and optimization method for these four sustainable supply chain problems. The proposed decision models and solution algorithms can help decision makers clarify decision-making levels and make a more reasonable and effective decision scheme, which is a practical significance to Chinese Baijiu sustainable supply chain research, and is also benefit to the theoretical research of multi-objective programming theory, fuzzy theory, stochastic uncertainty theory and sustainable supply chain management theory.

目 录

第一章 引言 …………………………………………… (1)
  一 研究背景 ………………………………………… (2)
  二 研究现状 ………………………………………… (10)
    (一)文献整理 …………………………………… (10)
    (二)综合分析 …………………………………… (36)
  三 研究框架 ………………………………………… (39)
    (一)研究思路 …………………………………… (39)
    (二)技术路线 …………………………………… (40)
    (三)研究内容 …………………………………… (41)

第二章 理论基础 ……………………………………… (44)
  一 模糊理论 ………………………………………… (44)
    (一)基本概念 …………………………………… (44)
    (二)期望算子 …………………………………… (50)
  二 随机不确定理论 ………………………………… (54)
  三 多目标规划理论 ………………………………… (56)
    (一)基本概念 …………………………………… (56)
    (二)求解方法 …………………………………… (58)
  四 可持续供应链 …………………………………… (59)

第三章 白酒可持续供应链网络设计模型及应用 ……… (62)
  一 问题描述 ………………………………………… (63)

（一）网络维度 ………………………………………… (64)
　　　（二）关键问题 ………………………………………… (68)
　二　模型构建 ……………………………………………… (70)
　　　（一）模型符号 ………………………………………… (71)
　　　（二）经济模型 ………………………………………… (72)
　　　（三）环境模型 ………………………………………… (74)
　　　（四）社会模型 ………………………………………… (74)
　　　（五）总体模型 ………………………………………… (75)
　三　案例分析 ……………………………………………… (76)
　　　（一）现实背景 ………………………………………… (76)
　　　（二）优化建模 ………………………………………… (80)
　　　（三）结果讨论 ………………………………………… (82)
　四　本章小结 ……………………………………………… (88)

第四章　白酒可持续供应链供应商选择模型及应用 ……… (90)
　一　维度模型 ……………………………………………… (91)
　　　（一）选择维度 ………………………………………… (91)
　　　（二）模型方法 ………………………………………… (101)
　二　指标体系 ……………………………………………… (106)
　　　（一）经济指标 ………………………………………… (106)
　　　（二）环境指标 ………………………………………… (112)
　　　（三）社会指标 ………………………………………… (114)
　三　模糊决策实验与评价实验室方法 …………………… (115)
　四　实际应用 ……………………………………………… (119)
　　　（一）选择方法 ………………………………………… (120)
　　　（二）讨论分析 ………………………………………… (127)
　五　本章小结 ……………………………………………… (129)

第五章　白酒可持续供应链风险管控模型及应用 ………… (130)
　一　维度方法 ……………………………………………… (131)
　　　（一）风险维度 ………………………………………… (131)

　　　　（二）管理方法 …………………………………………（137）
　　　　（三）白酒风险 …………………………………………（140）
　　二　风险辨析 ………………………………………………（142）
　　　　（一）经济风险 …………………………………………（143）
　　　　（二）环境风险 …………………………………………（147）
　　　　（三）社会风险 …………………………………………（149）
　　三　失效模式与影响分析方法 ……………………………（151）
　　四　案例探讨 ………………………………………………（155）
　　　　（一）风险识别 …………………………………………（157）
　　　　（二）风险衡量 …………………………………………（157）
　　　　（三）风险评估 …………………………………………（160）
　　　　（四）风险控制 …………………………………………（163）
　　　　（五）结果分析 …………………………………………（163）
　　五　本章小结 ………………………………………………（167）

第六章　白酒可持续供应链绩效评价模型及应用 ……………（168）
　　一　评价研究 ………………………………………………（169）
　　　　（一）评价维度 …………………………………………（169）
　　　　（二）评价方法 …………………………………………（173）
　　　　（三）白酒评价 …………………………………………（176）
　　二　框架研究 ………………………………………………（180）
　　　　（一）框架结构 …………………………………………（181）
　　　　（二）指标确定 …………………………………………（181）
　　　　（三）方法概述 …………………………………………（189）
　　三　应用实例 ………………………………………………（193）
　　　　（一）指标方案 …………………………………………（194）
　　　　（二）绩效权重 …………………………………………（194）
　　　　（三）方案排序 …………………………………………（199）
　　　　（四）评价结果 …………………………………………（202）
　　四　本章小结 ………………………………………………（208）

第七章 结语	（209）
一 主要工作	（209）
二 本书创新	（212）
三 后续研究	（214）

致谢	（215）

第一章 引言

可持续供应链管理的概念近年来引起了学术界和企业界的极大兴趣，这是由于人们对经济目标、环境保护和社会福利的意识提高的缘故[①]。同时，由于来自各利益相关者，特别是客户、政府、非政府组织（NGO）的压力和日益激烈的全球竞争，可持续发展已成为21世纪一项极具挑战性的重要任务[②]。白酒酿造在中国属于一个较为传统的行业，有着悠久的历史。白酒作为中国人情感交流的载体，是中华民族的文化符号之一[③]。白酒行业虽然创造了巨大的经济效益，但随着人们环境保护意识的增强和企业社会责任的不完善，这个行业的发展也受到一定影响。在国际国内竞争不断加剧、环境保护意识增强、社会责任越来越受关注的今天，白酒行业如何实现可持续发展已成为理论界和企业界

---

① Seuring, S., Müller, M., "From a Literature Review to a Conceptual Frame-Work for Sustainable Supply Chain management", *Journal of Cleaner Production*, 16 (15), 2008: 1699 – 1710; Hassini, E., Surti, C., Searcy C., "A Literature Review and a Case Study of Sustainable Supply Chains with a Focus on Metrics", *International Journal of Production Economics*, 140 (1), 2012: 69 – 82; O'Rourke, D., "The Science of Sustainable Supply Chains", *Science*, 344 (6188), 2014: 1124 – 1127; Glaser, G., "Policy: Base Sustainable Development Goals on Science", *Nature*, 491 (7422), 2012: 35; Seuring, S., "A Review of Modeling Approaches for Sustainable Supply Chain Management", *Decision Support Systems*, 54 (4), 2013: 1513 – 1520; Linton, J. D., Klassen, R., Jayaraman, V., "Sustainable Supply Chains: An Introduction", *Journal of Operations Management*, 25 (6), 2007: 1075 – 1082.

② Berning, A., & Venter, C., "Sustainable Supply Chain Engagement in a Retail Environment", *Sustainability*, 7 (5), 2015: 6246 – 6263.

③ 赵凤琦：《我国白酒产业可持续发展研究》，博士学位论文，中国社会科学院，2014年。

关注的重点。白酒行业可持续供应链是一个具有不确定性的多目标决策问题。对它的研究贯穿整个白酒供应链，涉及可持续网络设计、供应商选择、风险管理及供应链评价。在白酒供应链研究中，如何实现经济、环境和社会的最优化是行业能否实现可持续发展的关键。如何在白酒行业中实现物流配送中心布局的成本最小化，在环境影响最小的同时使社会影响达到最大；对风险管理进行可持续性评估并给出相应的策略；对供应链绩效的可持续性进行全面、客观的评价，已成为理论界、企业界、政府、消费者共同关注的焦点。对白酒行业可持续供应链优化决策模型的研究既有利于白酒行业实现降低成本、减小环境负面影响、增进社会福利的可持续发展目标，又有利于其他领域的专家和企业借鉴其经验进行相关研究，提高中国学者在可持续供应链研究方面的水平。

一　研究背景

随着经济全球化，负面事件将对公司的生存和发展产生越来越大的影响，如温州资金链断裂、中国三聚氰胺奶污染事件、富士康不健康的工作条件等。这些事件反映了失业、环境污染和不人道的工作条件等问题。由于这些影响，供应链企业越来越多地通过达成经济绩效、环境保护和社会福利三个目标来实现可持续发展。可持续发展被定义为"既能满足当代人的需要，又不对后代人满足其需要的能力构成危害的发展"[1]。根据Elkington，经济、环境、社会的三维框架被称为三重底线原则（Triple Bottom line Principle，TBL），也称为三个支柱：profit（利润）、planet（地球）和people（人）[2]。关于可持续供应链管理的研究已经得到理论界和企业界的广泛关注，取得了大量研究成果。但国内关于可持续供应链管理的研究成果还比较少，和国外相比存在较大差距。

---

[1] Brundtland, G. H., Khalid, M., Agnelli, S., Al-Athel, S. Chidzero, B., *Our Common Future*, New York, 1987: 8.

[2] Elkington, J., "Partnerships from Cannibals with Forks: The Triple Bottom Line of 21st-Century Business", *Environmental Quality Management*, 8 (1), 1998: 37–51.

供应链管理（Supply Chain Management, SCM）的定义为从物料采购到终端客户产品的交付过程中对物流、资金流和信息流的管理[1]。Linton 等将可持续性和供应链联系起来，认为可持续性必须整合超越供应链管理核心的问题和流程[2]。Seuring 和 Müller 将可持续供应链管理定义为物质、信息和资本流动的管理，以及供应链各公司之间的合作，同时从经济、环境和社会三个方面来考虑客户和利益相关者的要求。可持续供应链中的成员需要实现环境和社会标准来将自己保持在供应链中，同时通过满足客户预期需求来维持竞争力[3]。Carter 和 Rogers 将可持续供应链管理定义为实现组织的社会、环境和经济目标并协调系统关键的业务流程，以提高公司的长期经济绩效[4]。可持续供应链管理是通过对供应链运营、资源、信息和资金的管理，最大限度地提高供应链的盈利能力，同时最大限度地减少环境影响，并使社会福利最大化。基于三重底线的可持续供应链管理表明，在社会、环境和经济绩效的交叉点，组织参与的活动不仅对自然环境和社会有积极影响，还会给企业带来长期的经济效益和竞争优势[5]。

白酒在中国文化和人们的日常生活中起着重要的作用[6]。白酒文化

---

[1] Cooper, M. C., Lambert, D. M., & Pagh, J. D., "Supply Chain Management: More Than a New Name for Logistics", *The International Journal of Logistics Management*, 8 (1), 1997: 1–14.

[2] Linton, J. D., Klassen, R., Jayaraman, V., "Sustainable Supply Chains: An Introduction", *Journal of Operations Management*, 25 (6), 2007: 1075–1082.

[3] Seuring, S., Müller, M., "From a Literature Review to a Cnceptual Framework for Sustainable Supply Chain Management", *Journal of Cleaner Production*, 16 (15), 2008: 1699–1710.

[4] Carter, C. R., & Rogers, D. S., "A Framework of Sustainable Supply Chain Management: Moving Toward New Theory", *International Journal of Physical Distribution & Logistics Management*, 38 (5), 2008: 360–387.

[5] Elkington, J., "Partnerships from Cannibals with Forks: The Triple Bottom Line of 21st-Century Business", *Environmental Quality Management*, 8 (1), 1998: 37–51.

[6] Wang, H. Y., Gao, Y. B., Fan, Q. W., & Xu, Y., "Characterization and Comparison of Microbial Community of Different Typical Chinese Liquor Daqus by PCR-DGGE.", *Letters in Applied Microbiology*, 53 (2), 2011: 134–140; Zheng, X. W., Yan, Z., Han, B. Z., Zwietering, M. H., Samson, R. A., Boekhout, T., & Nout, M. R., "Complex Microbiota of a Chinese 'Fen' Liquor Fermentation Starter (Fen-Daqu), Revealed by Culture-Dependent and Culture-Independent Methods", *Food Microbiology*, 31 (2), 2012: 293–300.

是中国传统文化的重要组成部分,被赋予礼仪、尊重、英雄、吉祥、情义等多重象征意义。中国人对于白酒的感情也是世代相传,根深蒂固[①]。中国白酒是世界上最古老的蒸馏酒精饮料之一,它通常使用大曲发酵起始物获得。中国白酒的年产量近年来稳步增长,目前超过1000万吨[②]。白酒通常由谷物(主要是高粱)通过发酵、蒸馏和成熟来制备。中国是世界三大酒文化的起源地之一。中国白酒、白兰地、威士忌、杜松子酒、朗姆酒和伏特加酒是世界上最著名的六种蒸馏酒[③]。基于酵母的固态发酵(中国大曲)是中国白酒的主要特征。根据香型,中国白酒主要包括酱香型(茅台风味)、浓香型(泸州风味)和清香型(汾酒风味)三种类型。在酒精饮料行业中,白酒行业占据较大比例。据2014年的销售统计数据,白酒的销售额占酒精饮料行业的60%,啤酒占21%,红葡萄酒占5%,其他果酒、健康酒、鸡尾酒等占14%(如图1.1所示)。

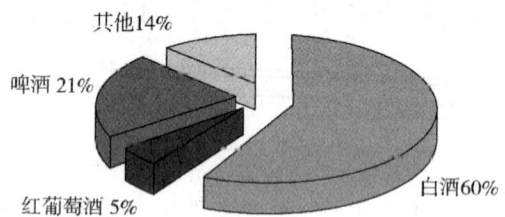

图1.1　2014年酒精饮料行业销售分析

2015年白酒总产量约为131.28亿升,同比增长4.43%。总销售收入为5559亿元,比2014年增长5.22%。产量从2006年的39.71

---

① 赵凤琦:《我国白酒产业可持续发展研究》,博士学位论文,中国社会科学院,2014年。

② Han, Y., Huang, B., Liu, S., Zou, N., Yang, J., Zhong, Z., & Pan, C., "Residue Levels of Five Grain-Storage-Use Insecticides During the Production Process of Sorghum Distilled Spirits", *Food Chemistry*, 206, 2016: 12–17.

③ Shi, J. H., Xiao, Y. P., Li, X. R., Ma, E. B., Du, X. W., & Quan, Z. X., "Analyses of Microbial Consortia in the Starter of Fen Liquor", *Letters in Applied Microbiology*, 48 (4), 2016: 478–485.

亿升增加到 2015 年的 131.28 亿升，年均增长率为 23%。销量从 2006 年的 38.39 亿升增加到 2015 年的 121.30 亿升。近年来，由于产业结构调整，供需不平衡越来越严重。2006—2012 年，白酒行业进入公认的黄金时代，由高端消费者驱动，产业的生产和销售也持续增长。2012 年起，叠加的政策因素和产业发展周期因素使得白酒行业进入了长时间的调整期。加上"塑化剂"风波的影响，白酒行业进入"冬季"，2013 年利润率开始出现负增长。但是，来自饮食业大规模消费市场转型的支持，使得白酒行业在 2013 年触底后，2014 年开始呈现稳步上升趋势。由此可见饮食业和烈酒之间的相关性非常高，其在促进酒类消费上具有直接作用。

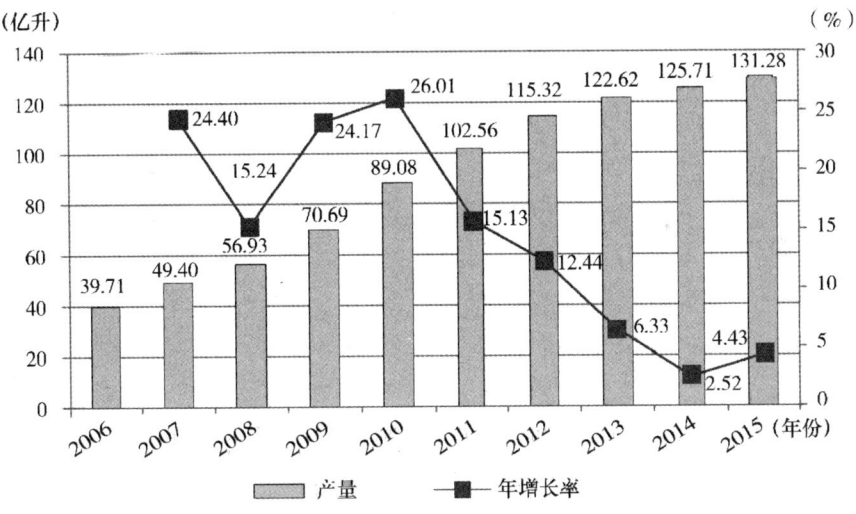

图 1.2　2006—2015 年中国白酒产量变化

2015 年中国白酒总产量为 131.28 亿升，其中四川为 37.09 亿升，占 28%，是产量最高的区域。此外，2015 年十大生产省份是四川、山东、河南、江苏、河北、内蒙古、吉林、黑龙江、安徽和辽宁（如图 1.6 所示）。受益于悠久的酿酒历史、得天独厚的地域性酿酒资源以及良好的原料供应和区域消费环境，再加上较为宽松的地方产业政策环境

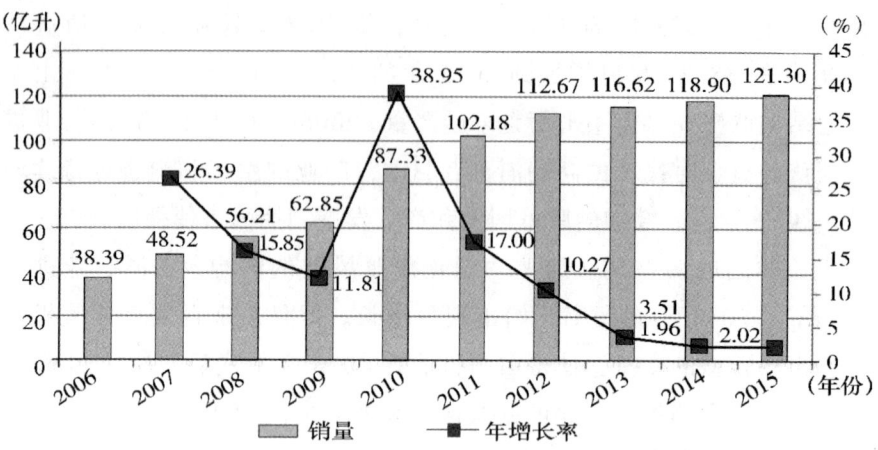

图1.3 2006—2015年中国白酒销量变化

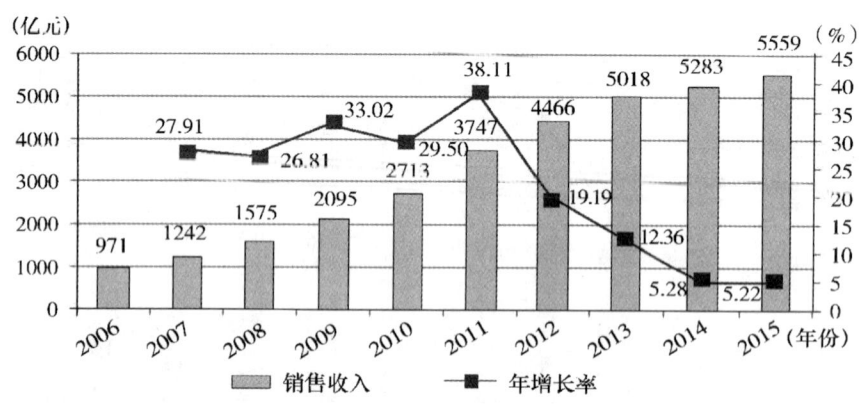

图1.4 2006—2015年中国白酒销售收入变化

等,四川省白酒行业在中国一直占据着重要地位。川酒的泸州老窖、五粮液、剑南春、全兴、郎酒、沱牌曲酒"六朵金花"享誉中外①。

从图1.5可看出,虽然中国白酒行业的总产值在逐年增加,但白酒行业的利润空间越来越小,说明白酒行业的成本没有得到很好的控制,白酒供应链有优化的必要。中国白酒行业存在结构不合理(产能过剩现象

---

① 方美燕:《四川省白酒产业区际竞争力研究》,博士学位论文,西南财经大学,2009年。

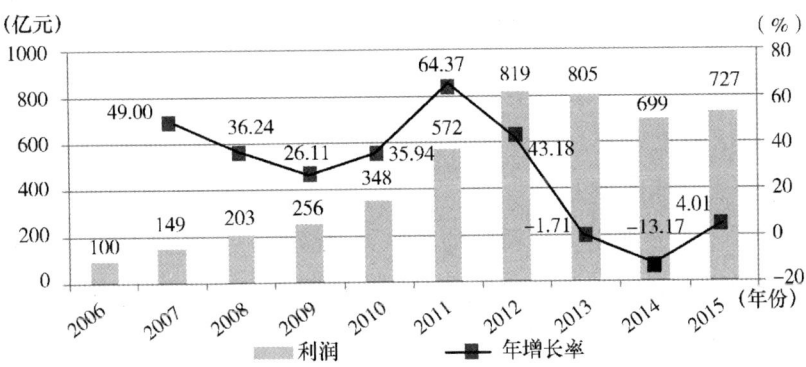

图 1.5　2006—2015 年中国白酒销售利润变化

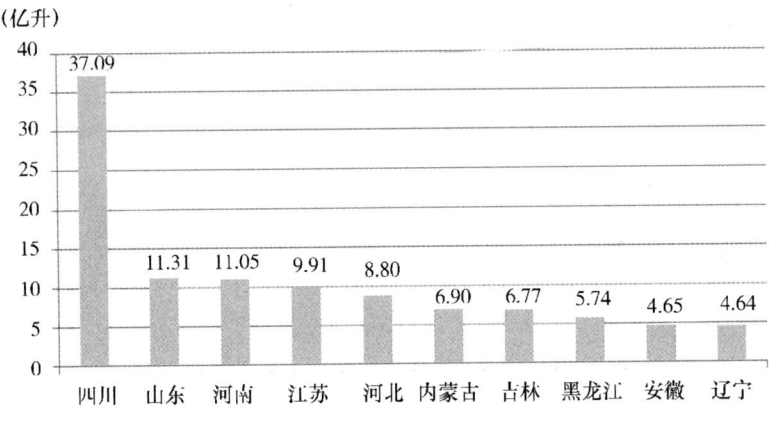

图 1.6　2015 年中国白酒前十省份

突出，低端过剩，高端不足）、行业运营成本增加（人工、原材料、物流等成本增加）、利润面临压缩、行业资源重构、竞争不断加剧、环境保护压力增大、社会责任要求越来越高等问题。这些问题的解决迫切需要对白酒行业的供应链进行可持续性研究，以降低经济成本、减小环境负面影响、增强企业责任。在经济快速发展和行业改革的冲击下，市场环境动态地发生着剧烈的变化，而传统的管理模式已经不能适应环境的变化，在供应链管理给制造业带来巨大价值的推动下，可持续供应链管理理论在白酒行业的应用为提高白酒行业绩效提供了较好的途径。可持续供应链管理也应当得到各界专家学者的足够关注和重视，从而为中国制造业和国民经济的发展带来一定的经济效益和生态社会价值。白酒作为中国传统行业，存在以下问题。

第一，产能过剩。白酒行业产能过剩突出，存在供过于求的现象。去库存、去产能的压力加大。

第二，竞争加剧。白酒市场竞争异常激烈。一是白酒行业由于厂家众多，产能过剩，竞争趋于白热化。二是随着葡萄酒、啤酒和果酒的发展，白酒的发展空间进一步缩小。三是全球化进程中洋酒占领了部分白酒市场，大部分白酒企业基本上处于微利状态；白酒的国际化道路却相当艰难。中国是蒸馏酒的最大生产国，约占世界产量的38%。然而，销量仅占不到1%的国际市场份额，远低于其他国际烈性酒品牌。四是行业资源重构、并购整合成为新常态，竞争进一步加剧。

第三，结构失衡。在白酒行业中，一是存在着企业规模发展不均衡的问题，市场集中度低。2015年中国规模以上酒类企业（营业额2000万元以上）有1263家，其中大型企业30家，中型企业159家，小型企业1074家，占比分别为2.38%、12.59%和85.03%。如果包括小酒厂，全国白酒企业有3万多家。小酒厂盲目发展，数量众多，企业结构严重不合理。二是白酒行业自身存在高端固态产能不足，低端液态产能过剩的结构失衡问题。

第四，转型压力加大。整体装备水平仍然较低。除一些大中型企业外，其余多数企业仍是手工作坊，进行粗放型生产，产品质量很难得到保障。在"互联网+"、大数据、云计算等新技术、新模式的带动下，企业亟须对从采购到营销的全过程进行深刻变革，转型发展压力大。白酒企业集团化、规模化发展仍需引导。

第五，运输模式和碳排放的相关性。白酒生产销售季节性强。每年9月到次年6月，由于自然气温较低，有利于酵母等微生物的培养繁殖，可以保证酿造的质量，因此这段时间是生产白酒的旺季。白酒销售和传统节日有非常密切的关系。白酒的销售旺季是从每年9月到次年3月

(中秋节、国庆节、元旦、春节、元宵节等带动销售被称为节日效应)。超过 2/3 的烈酒销售在销售旺季完成。近年来,中国的雾霾日益严重。雾霾通常出现在秋季和冬季,而这个季节也是白酒的生产和销售旺季。据统计,机动车尾气是雾霾颗粒最重要的组成部分。最新数据显示,北京雾霾颗粒中机动车尾气占 22.2%,煤占 16.7%,扬尘占 16.3%,工业占 15.7%。其中大型柴油车辆的使用是雾霾颗粒排放中的重要因素。因此,我们可以通过控制碳排放量来控制空气污染,并减少雾霾天数。客户愿意为环保产品支付更高的价格,也有利于当地社区发展[①]。现有配送模式大多是汽车运输,而公路运输的碳排放量是最高的,因此合理采用铁路和水路配送将对降低碳排放量产生一定的积极作用。

第六,成本增高。人工、原材料、物流、运营等成本增加,利润面临压缩。配送中心布局影响企业的营销绩效。据统计,中国物流的总成本占 GDP 的比重约为 18%,酒类行业单位经营成本的物流成本率高达 20%。公司的运营成本太高,会对企业利润提升产生巨大压力。企业必须降低成本,提高业务效率。通过优化配送中心结构和优化运输模式可以获得供应链的最低成本。

第七,低经济增长。中国经济增长放缓。随着宏观经济增长放缓,经济增长率将逐步放缓。在这个阶段,促进就业和提高居民的生活水平是非常重要的。

第八,废弃物处理。"三废"治理仍需加强。特别是酒糟和废水问题,有些企业未严格采取工业化处理措施,对环境造成了严重污染。

第九,诚信问题。如仿照名酒品牌包装,误导消费者;勾兑酒冒充高档纯粮酿造酒;产品质量不合格;一些小酒厂、批发商、零售商以瞒报产销量、不开或者少开发票的方式偷税漏税;等等。

第十,文化危机。白酒文化面临危机,"塑化剂"风波和政策调整给白酒行业带来了严重的影响。洋酒、果酒、葡萄酒等对白酒文化产生

---

① Valenzuela, L., & Maturana, S., "Designing a Three-dimensional Performance Measurement System (SMD3D) for the Wine Industry: A Chilean Example", *Agricultural Systems*, 142, 2016: 112-121.

一定的冲击。需要挖掘白酒健康文化，倡导健康饮酒。同时，人口老龄化也会影响白酒文化的传承。

二 研究现状

为了更好地分析白酒行业可持续供应链的研究现状和研究热点，以下分别对可持续供应链、白酒行业、供应链网络设计、供应商选择、风险管理、供应链评价的现有文献进行归纳分析。为了客观、全面、准确地分析国内外学者在相关领域的研究情况，主要选用了两个重要的数据库：Web of Science（SCI）核心集合数据库和 CNKI 核心期刊数据库来检索现有中英文文献。在 Web of Science 数据库中，分别选用"sustainable supply chain""supply chain network design""supply chain supplier selection""distilled spirits supply chain""supply chain evaluation""supply chain risk management"等作为检索词。在 CNKI 数据库中，选用"可持续供应链""白酒行业""供应链网络设计""供应链评价"等作为检索词。所有文献检索结果截止时间是 2017 年 2 月 15 日。采用 NoteExpress 软件导入题录，为了保证文献与主题有较大的相关性和适当的数据量，删掉其中的重复题录以及与主题相关性不大的题录，得到关键词的数据库。并运用 NoteExpress 与 NodeXL 软件的系统化文献研究方法（NN-SRM）对文献进行系统整理与汇总，该文献研究方法分析流程如图 1.7 所示。

（一）文献整理

以下分别从可持续供应链、白酒行业、供应链网络设计、供应商评估选择、供应链风险管理和供应链绩效评估六个方面进行文献梳理。

1. 可持续供应链

我们在 Web of Science 数据库中输入检索词"sustainable supply chain""sustainability + supply chain"，为了保证较高的相关性和避免过多的文献，只选取检索词在"title"中出现"sustainable supply chain""sustainability +

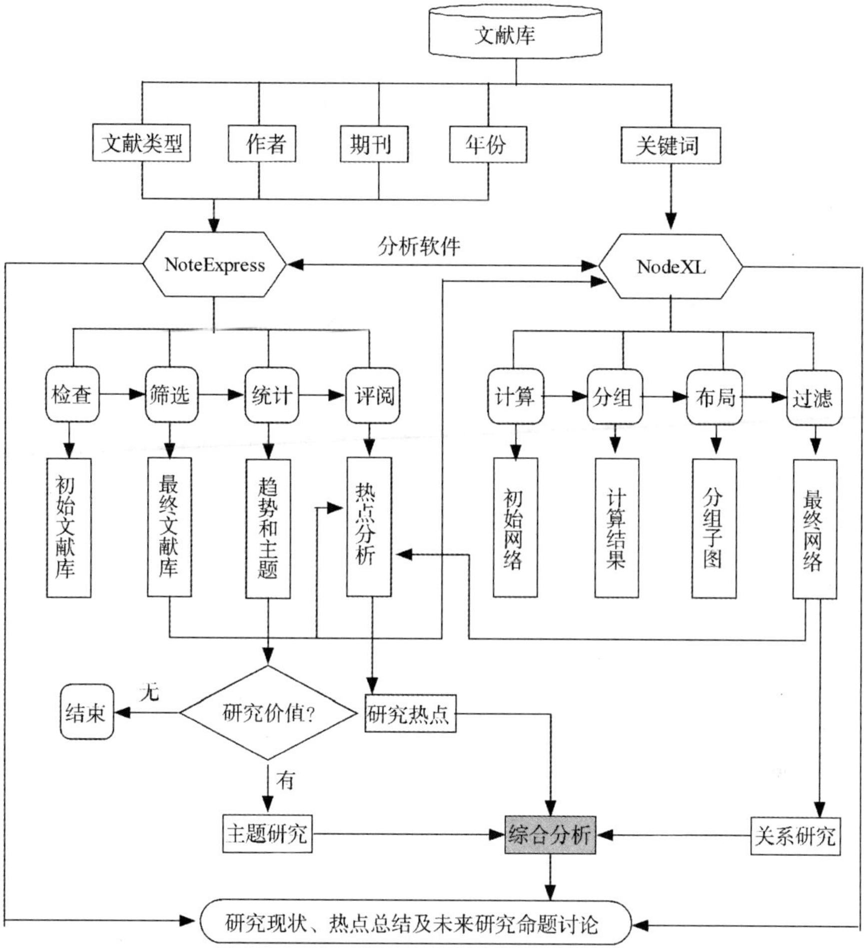

图 1.7 基于 NoteExpess 与 NodeXL 软件的系统化文献研究方法

supply chain"的文献，总共得到 747 条记录。在 CNKI 数据库中输入检索词"可持续供应链"，得到 70 条记录。从两个数据库中总共得到了 817 条记录，采用 NoteExpress 软件导入题录，查找重复题录，重复判定字段设置为"题录类型""期刊""年份""标题""关键字"和"作者"等。删掉其中的重复题录，得到记录数为 734 的可持续供应链的数据库，如图 1.8 所示。然后选择"文件夹统计信息"，分别对"年份""期刊""作者"进行统计，如图 1.9、图 1.10 和图 1.11 所示。

从图 1.9 中可以清楚地看出，关于可持续供应链问题的研究文献数量呈逐年递增的趋势。1999—2006 年，随着时间的推移，可持续供应链越来越受到专家学者的重视。2007—2013 年研究文献数量稳步上升。2014—2016 年达到数量巅峰。学者们提出了一系列的理论体系和研究框架。

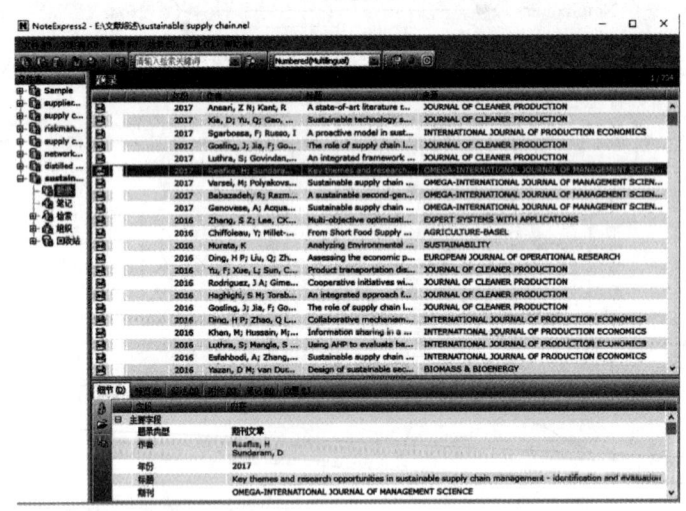

图 1.8　可持续供应链研究文献在 NoteExpress 中的汇总

根据对相关文献的汇总，表 1.1 展示了题录中论文的发表年份、论文发表的杂志和作者的统计结果。从表 1.1 中可以看出，重要的可持续供应链管理杂志包括 *Journal of Clear Production*、*International Journal of Production Economics*、*Supply Chain Management—An International Journal*、*Sustainability* 和《WTO 经济导刊》。在研究学者方面，Seuring、Govindan、Gunasekaran 和 Walker 等在可持续供应链管理领域做出了巨大的贡献。Seuring 在可持续供应链理论和应用研究方面做出了突出贡献[①]，有

[①] Seuring, S., Müller, M., "From a Literature Review to a Conceptual Framework for Sustainable Supply Chain Management", *Journal of Cleaner Production*, 16 (15), 2008: 1699–1710; Seuring, S., " A Review of Modeling Approaches for Sustainable Supply Chain Management", *Decision Support Systems*, 54 (4), 2013: 1513–1520.

12 篇文章。Govindan 在可持续供应链绩效、优化模型方面有所创新①，有 10 篇文章。Gunasekaran 重点研究了可持续供应链中的社会责任维度、网络设计等问题②。Walker 则重点研究了可持续供应链的理论和应用③。

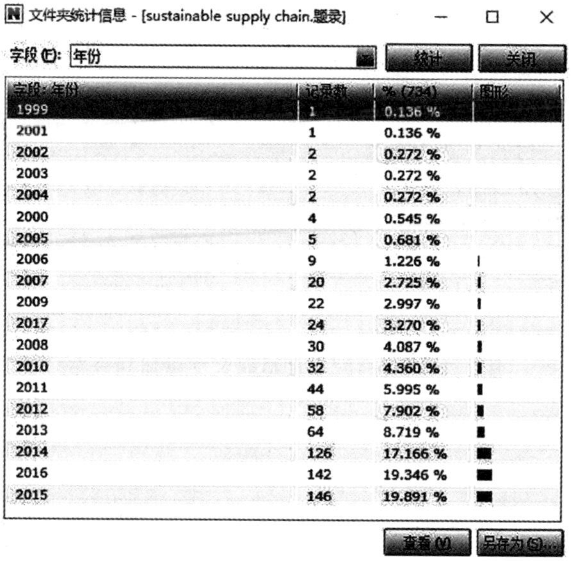
文件夹统计信息 - [sustainable supply chain.题录]

字段(F): 年份 统计 关闭

字段: 年份	记录数	% (734)	图形
1999	1	0.136 %	
2001	1	0.136 %	
2002	2	0.272 %	
2003	2	0.272 %	
2004	2	0.272 %	
2000	4	0.545 %	
2005	5	0.681 %	
2006	9	1.226 %	
2007	20	2.725 %	
2009	22	2.997 %	
2017	24	3.270 %	
2008	30	4.087 %	
2010	32	4.360 %	
2011	44	5.995 %	
2012	58	7.902 %	
2013	64	8.719 %	
2014	126	17.166 %	
2016	142	19.346 %	
2015	146	19.891 %	

查看(V) 另存为(S)...

图 1.9　可持续供应链研究文献年份分布

---

① Govindan, K., Azevedo, S. G., Carvalho, H., & Cruz-Machado, V., "Impact of Supply Chain Management Practices on Sustainability", *Journal of Cleaner Production*, 85, 2014: 212-225; Govindan, K., Jha, P. C., & Garg, K., "Product Recovery Optimization in Closed-loop Supply Chain to Improve Sustainability in Manufacturing", *International Journal of Production Research*, 54 (5), 2016: 1463-1486.

② Mani, V., Gunasekaran, A., Papadopoulos, T., Hazen, B., & Dubey, R., "Supply Chain Social Sustainability for Developing Nations: Evidence from India", *Resources, Conservation and Recycling*, 111, 2016: 42-52; Dubey, R., Gunasekaran, A., & Childe, S. J., "The Design of a Responsive Sustainable Supply Chain Network under Uncertainty", *The International Journal of Advanced Manufacturing Technology*, 80 (1-4), 2015: 427-445.

③ Alexander, A., Walker, H., & Naim, M., "Decision Theory in Sustainable Supply Chain Management: A Literature Review", *Supply Chain Management: An International Journal*, 19 (5/6), 2014: 504-522; Cucchiella, F., Koh, L., Walker, H., & Jones, N., "Sustainable Supply Chain Management across the UK Private Sector", *Supply Chain Management: An International Journal*, 17 (1), 2012: 15-28.

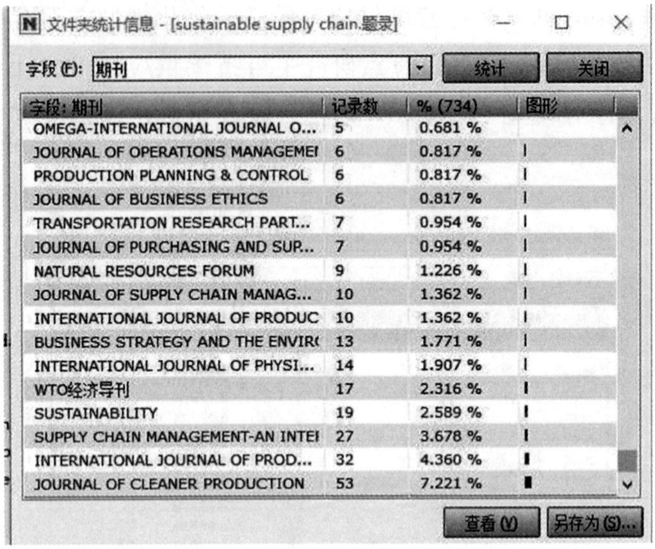

字段：期刊	记录数	% (734)
OMEGA-INTERNATIONAL JOURNAL O...	5	0.681 %
JOURNAL OF OPERATIONS MANAGEMEI	6	0.817 %
PRODUCTION PLANNING & CONTROL	6	0.817 %
JOURNAL OF BUSINESS ETHICS	6	0.817 %
TRANSPORTATION RESEARCH PART...	7	0.954 %
JOURNAL OF PURCHASING AND SUP...	7	0.954 %
NATURAL RESOURCES FORUM	9	1.226 %
JOURNAL OF SUPPLY CHAIN MANAG...	10	1.362 %
INTERNATIONAL JOURNAL OF PRODUC	10	1.362 %
BUSINESS STRATEGY AND THE ENVIRC	13	1.771 %
INTERNATIONAL JOURNAL OF PHYSI...	14	1.907 %
WTO经济导刊	17	2.316 %
SUSTAINABILITY	19	2.589 %
SUPPLY CHAIN MANAGEMENT-AN INTEI	27	3.678 %
INTERNATIONAL JOURNAL OF PROD...	32	4.360 %
JOURNAL OF CLEANER PRODUCTION	53	7.221 %

图 1.10　可持续供应链研究文献期刊分布

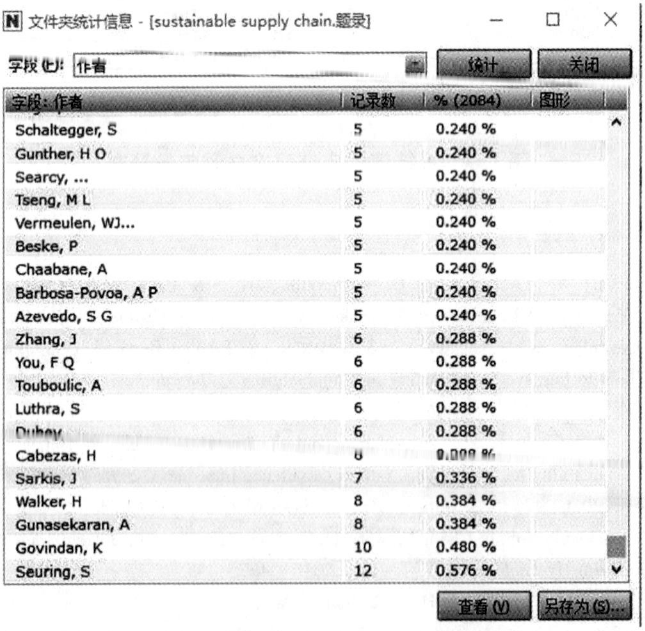

字段：作者	记录数	% (2084)
Schaltegger, S	5	0.240 %
Gunther, H O	5	0.240 %
Searcy, ...	5	0.240 %
Tseng, M L	5	0.240 %
Vermeulen, W J...	5	0.240 %
Beske, P	5	0.240 %
Chaabane, A	5	0.240 %
Barbosa-Povoa, A P	5	0.240 %
Azevedo, S G	5	0.240 %
Zhang, J	6	0.288 %
You, F Q	6	0.288 %
Touboulic, A	6	0.288 %
Luthra, S	6	0.288 %
Dubey	6	0.288 %
Cabezas, H	6	0.288 %
Sarkis, J	7	0.336 %
Walker, H	8	0.384 %
Gunasekaran, A	8	0.384 %
Govindan, K	10	0.480 %
Seuring, S	12	0.576 %

图 1.11　可持续供应链研究文献作者分布

表1.1　　　　　　　　　　可持续供应链文献总体统计

项目	结果
时间	1999—2010 年：130 篇（17.639%） 2011 年：44 篇（5.995%） 2012 年：58 篇（7.902%） 2013 年：64 篇（8.791%） 2014 年：126 篇（17.166%） 2015 年：146 篇（19.891%） 2016 年：142 篇（19.346%） 2017 年：24 篇（3.270%）
期刊	*Journal of Clear Production*：53 篇（7.221%） *International Journal of Production Economics*：32 篇（4.360%） *Supply Chain Management—An International Journal*：27 篇（3.678%） *Sustainability*：19 篇（2.589%） 《WTO 经济导刊》：17 篇（2.316%）
作者	Seuring, S.：12 篇（0.576%）；Govindan, K.：10 篇（0.480%）；Gunasekaran, A.：8 篇（0.384%）；Walker, H.：8 篇（0.384%）；Sarkis, J.：7 篇（0.336%）

2. 白酒行业

我们在 Web of Science 数据库中输入检索词 "liquor（distilled spirits, alcohol, white spirits, baijiu）industry" "liquor（distilled spirits, alcohol, white spirits, baijiu）supply chain" "wine supply chain" "beer supply chain"。为了保证较高的相关性和避免过多的文献，只选取检索词在 "title" 中出现 "liquor（distilled spirits, alcohol, white spirits）industry" "liquor（distilled spirits, alcohol, white spirits）supply chain" 的文献，共得到 381 条记录。在 CNKI 数据库中输入检索词 "白酒行业" "白酒产业" "白酒供应链" 得到 442 条记录。从两个数据库中总共得到了 822 条记录，采用 NoteExpress 软件导入题录，查找重复题录，重复判定字段设置为 "题录类型" "期刊" "年份" "标题" "关键字" 和 "作者" 等。删掉其中的重复题录、会议纪要、通知、工作报告、刊讯、访谈等 172 条，得到记录数为 650 的白酒行业的数据库（如图 1.12 所示）。然后选择 "文件夹统计信息"，分别对 "年份" "期刊" "作者" 进行统计，如图 1.13、图 1.14 和图 1.15 所示。文献总体统计结果如表 1.2 所示。从年份分布可以看出，关于白

酒行业的研究文献数量呈一个递增的趋势，同时可以看到在 1995—2010 年发表的文章约占 60%。2014 年文章数最多。也就是说，白酒是一个经久不变的话题，是一个长久的研究主题。同时从这里也得到启发，白酒行业定性研究持续的时间远远多于白酒行业定量研究的时间。从期刊分布来看，《酿酒科技》、*Addiction*、《酿酒》、*BMI-British Medical Journal* 和 *Drug and Alcohol Review* 等是白酒研究领域的重要杂志。可以看出，在研究学者方面，McCambridge、Babor、Hawkins、Kypri 和 Roche 等在蒸馏酒行业方面做出了巨大的贡献。如果水质处理、污水排放问题和酒糟处理不当，易造成可利用资源的严重浪费及环境污染。白酒属于食品饮料行业，据统计，到 2017 年 2 月中旬，关于食品业的可持续供应链研究文献有 81 篇，占总文献的 11.04%。

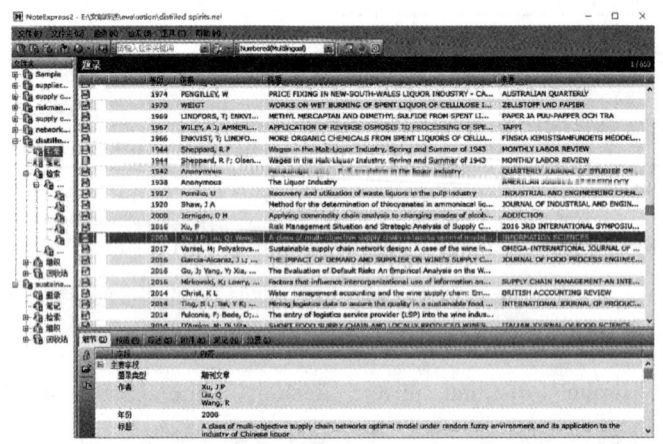

图 1.12　白酒行业研究文献在 NoteExpress 软件中的汇总

蒋玉石等基于 CSSCI 数据库白酒企业经济领域的相关文献，利用 Cite Space 科学计量工具，探讨了相关白酒企业经济研究者的阶段性研究规律、白酒企业经济的研究热点主题演变路径和研究机构的演变特征。他们以 CSSCI 数据库中 1990—2015 年 112 篇白酒企业经济文献为研究数据，利用 Cite Space 科学计量工具绘制了白酒企业经济研究学者、研究机构和研究主题的知识图谱，用数据可视化的方法还原了近

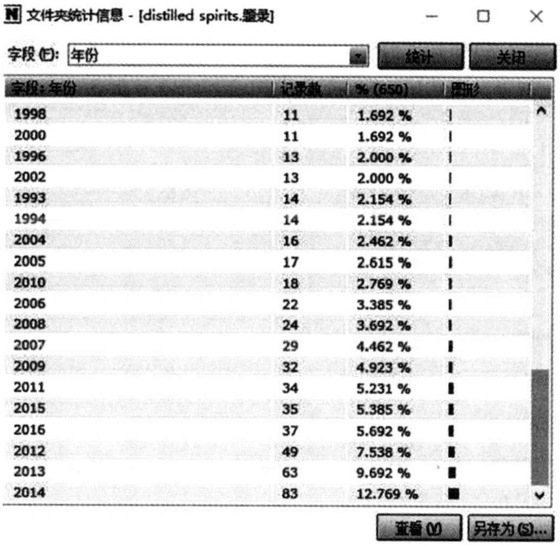

图 1.13　白酒行业研究文献年份分布

15 年来中国白酒企业经济研究的发展历程①。李桂英以沱牌舍得酒业为例，从白酒企业新形势下所面临的经营状况出发，论述了供应链整合管理对白酒企业参与行业竞争的重要性。在此基础上，从渠道管理和供应链整合等方面出发，对提升沱牌舍得酒业的竞争力提出了一定的政策建议②。卢琳主要研究供应链整合对宜宾白酒业竞争力的提升问题，通过选取宜宾市 74 家白酒生产企业样本研究数据进行实证分析，结果证明了供应链整合与企业竞争力存在正向影响关系③。并针对宜宾目前供应链现状，针对各个要素提出了整合白酒企业供应链的重要性，以此来提升宜宾白酒企业整体竞争力④。严娜以白酒茅台供应链为例，得出优化供应链结构的可行措施是调整生产者与经销商之间的关系，形成利益共

---

① 蒋玉石、宋红娟、罗霄：《我国白酒企业经济研究（1991—2015 年）的可视化分析》，《四川理工学院学报》（社会科学版）2016 年第 4 期。

② 李桂英：《供应链物流管理下的白酒企业竞争策略研究——以沱牌舍得酒业的发展为例》，《时代金融旬刊》2012 年第 3 期。

③ 卢琳：《供应链整合对宜宾白酒企业竞争力提升的关系研究》，《中国商贸》2011 年第 12 期。

④ 卢琳：《宜宾白酒企业供应链整合的必要性分析》，《中国商贸》2011 年第 32 期。

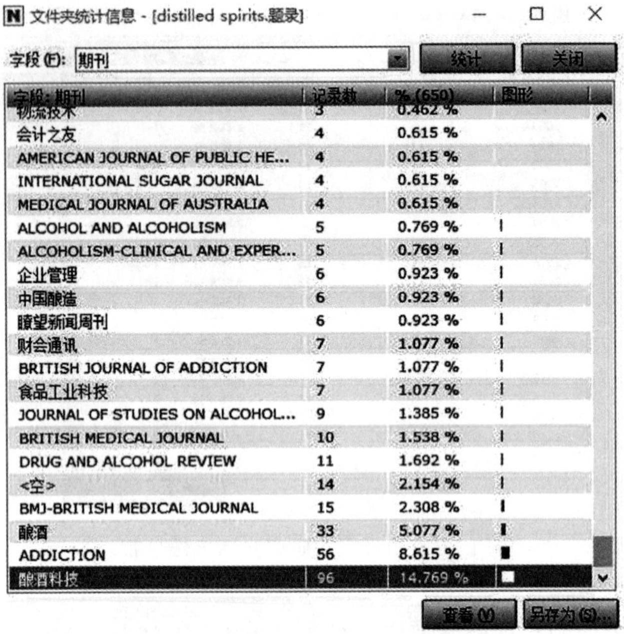

N 文件夹统计信息 - [distilled spirits.题录]

字段(F): 期刊 统计 关闭

字段：期刊	记录数	% (650)	图形
物流技术	3	0.462 %	
会计之友	4	0.615 %	
AMERICAN JOURNAL OF PUBLIC HE...	4	0.615 %	
INTERNATIONAL SUGAR JOURNAL	4	0.615 %	
MEDICAL JOURNAL OF AUSTRALIA	4	0.615 %	
ALCOHOL AND ALCOHOLISM	5	0.769 %	
ALCOHOLISM-CLINICAL AND EXPER...	5	0.769 %	
企业管理	6	0.923 %	
中国酿造	6	0.923 %	
瞭望新闻周刊	6	0.923 %	
财会通讯	7	1.077 %	
BRITISH JOURNAL OF ADDICTION	7	1.077 %	
食品工业科技	7	1.077 %	
JOURNAL OF STUDIES ON ALCOHOL...	9	1.385 %	
BRITISH MEDICAL JOURNAL	10	1.538 %	
DRUG AND ALCOHOL REVIEW	11	1.692 %	
<空>	14	2.154 %	
BMJ-BRITISH MEDICAL JOURNAL	15	2.308 %	
酿酒	33	5.077 %	
ADDICTION	56	8.615 %	
酿酒科技	96	14.769 %	

查看(V) 另存为(S)...

图 1.14 白酒行业研究文献期刊分布

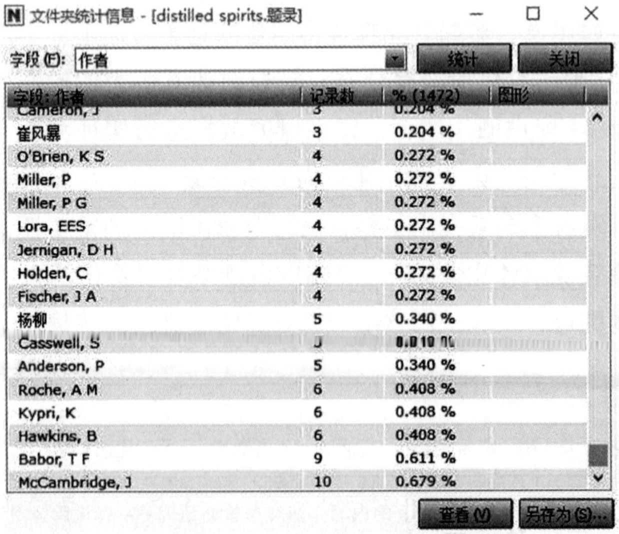

N 文件夹统计信息 - [distilled spirits.题录]

字段(F): 作者 统计 关闭

字段：作者	记录数	% (1472)	图形
Cameron, J	3	0.204 %	
崔风暴	3	0.204 %	
O'Brien, K S	4	0.272 %	
Miller, P	4	0.272 %	
Miller, P G	4	0.272 %	
Lora, EES	4	0.272 %	
Jernigan, D H	4	0.272 %	
Holden, C	4	0.272 %	
Fischer, J A	4	0.272 %	
杨柳	5	0.340 %	
Casswell, S	5	[illegible]	
Anderson, P	5	0.340 %	
Roche, A M	6	0.408 %	
Kypri, K	6	0.408 %	
Hawkins, B	6	0.408 %	
Babor, T F	9	0.611 %	
McCambridge, J	10	0.679 %	

查看(V) 另存为(S)...

图 1.15 白酒行业研究作者分布

同体，优化供应链①。祝进城等将酒业园区与供应链理论结合起来，对泸州酒业集中发展区供应链现状及供应链发展趋势进行了研究②。

表1.2　　　　　　　白酒行业研究文献总体统计结果

项目	结果
时间	1905—2010 年：347 篇（53.38%） 2011 年：34 篇（5.231%） 2012 年：49 篇（7.538%） 2013 年：63 篇（9.692%） 2014 年：83 篇（12.769%） 2015 年：35 篇（5.385%） 2016 年：37 篇（5.692%） 2017 年：2 篇（0.308%）
期刊	《酿酒科技》：96 篇（14.769%） *Addiction*：56 篇（8.615%） 《酿酒》：33 篇（5.077%） *BMI-British Medical Journal*：15 篇（2.308%） *Drug and Alcohol Review*：11 篇（1.692%）
作者	McCambridge, J.：10 篇（0.679%）；Babor, T. F.：9 篇（0.611%）；Hawkins, B.：6 篇（0.408%）；Kypri, K.：6 篇（0.408%）；Roche, A. M.：6 篇（0.408%）

3. 供应链网络设计

企业界和学术界在过去几十年一直对供应链设计和操作的优化模型和方法十分感兴趣③。在 Web of Science 数据库和 CNKI 数据库中，将"供应链网络设计"（supply chain network design）作为关键词，并考虑中英文的不同表达形式，在主题中进行检索。将检索结果导入 NoteExpress 软件，依次查重和分析题目类型，剔除重复题录，选择期刊文章，

---

① 严娜：《茅台供应链的优化问题探究——以经销商的角度》，《黑河学院学报》2016 年第 5 期。

② 祝进城、帅斌、孙朝苑：《泸州酒业集中发展区供应链现状及发展趋势研究》，《物流技术》2010 年第 15 期。

③ Sunil, C., & Peter, M., "Supply Chain Management: Strategy, Planning and Operation", *Pearson Education International*, 34（2），2010：221 - 222；Eskandarpour, M., Dejax, P., Miemczyk, J., & Péton, O., "Sustainable Supply Chain Network Design: An Optimization-oriented Review", *Omega*, 54, 2015：11 - 32.

最终确定 421 条文献记录。其中，Web of Science 数据库筛选出 337，CNKI 数据库筛选出 84 篇。供应链网络设计数据库如图 1.16 所示。然后选择“文件夹统计信息”，分别统计“年份”“期刊”“作者”信息，如图 1.17、图 1.18 和图 1.19 所示。文献总体统计结果如表 1.3 所示。从图 1.17 来看，关于供应链网络设计的研究文献数量呈逐年递增的趋势。从表 1.3 可以看出，*International Journal of Production Research*、

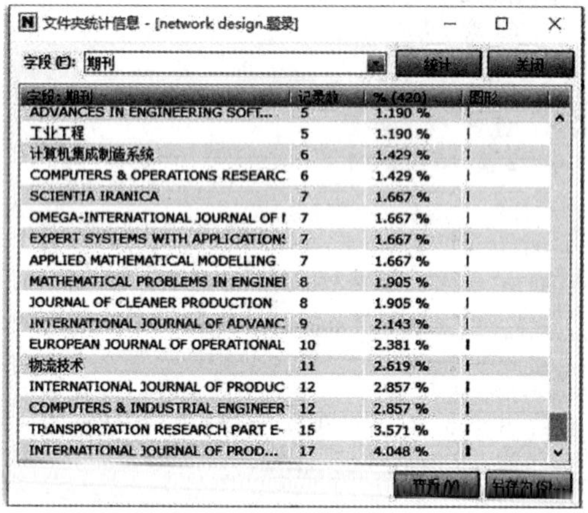

字段：期刊	记录数	% (420)	图形
ADVANCES IN ENGINEERING SOFT...	5	1.190 %	
工业工程	5	1.190 %	
计算机集成制造系统	6	1.429 %	
COMPUTERS & OPERATIONS RESEARC	6	1.429 %	
SCIENTIA IRANICA	7	1.667 %	
OMEGA-INTERNATIONAL JOURNAL OF I	7	1.667 %	
EXPERT SYSTEMS WITH APPLICATION!	7	1.667 %	
APPLIED MATHEMATICAL MODELLING	7	1.667 %	
MATHEMATICAL PROBLEMS IN ENGINEI	8	1.905 %	
JOURNAL OF CLEANER PRODUCTION	8	1.905 %	
INTERNATIONAL JOURNAL OF ADVANC	9	2.143 %	
EUROPEAN JOURNAL OF OPERATIONAL	10	2.381 %	
物流技术	11	2.619 %	
INTERNATIONAL JOURNAL OF PRODUC	12	2.857 %	
COMPUTERS & INDUSTRIAL ENGINEER	12	2.857 %	
TRANSPORTATION RESEARCH PART E-	15	3.571 %	
INTERNATIONAL JOURNAL OF PROD...	17	4.048 %	

图 1.16　供应链网络设计研究文献在 NoteExpress 软件中的汇总

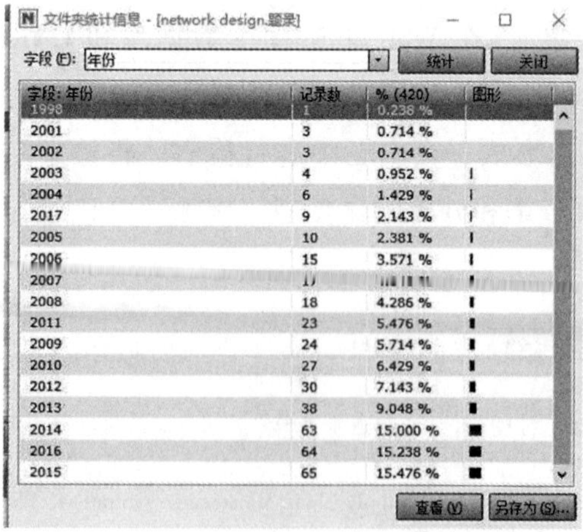

字段：年份	记录数	% (420)	图形
1998	1	0.238 %	
2001	3	0.714 %	
2002	3	0.714 %	
2003	4	0.952 %	
2004	6	1.429 %	
2017	9	2.143 %	
2005	10	2.381 %	
2006	15	3.571 %	
2007	17	[illegible]	
2008	18	4.286 %	
2011	23	5.476 %	
2009	24	5.714 %	
2010	27	6.429 %	
2012	30	7.143 %	
2013	38	9.048 %	
2014	63	15.000 %	
2016	64	15.238 %	
2015	65	15.476 %	

图 1.17　供应链网络设计研究文献年份分布

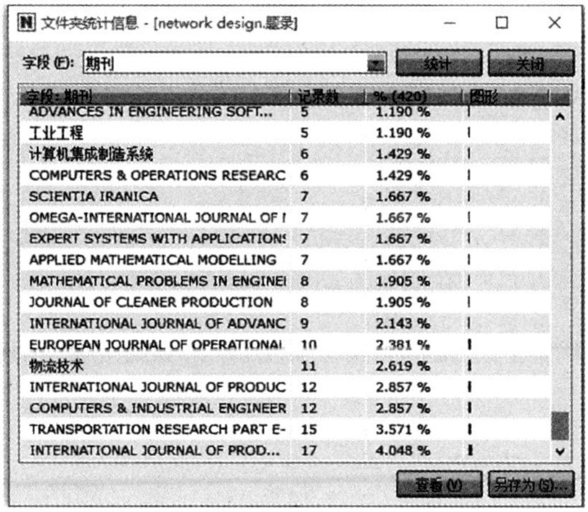

文件夹统计信息 - [network design.题录]

字段 (F): 期刊　统计　关闭

字段: 期刊	记录数	% (420)	图形
ADVANCES IN ENGINEERING SOFT...	5	1.190 %	
工业工程	5	1.190 %	
计算机集成制造系统	6	1.429 %	
COMPUTERS & OPERATIONS RESEARC	6	1.429 %	
SCIENTIA IRANICA	7	1.667 %	
OMEGA-INTERNATIONAL JOURNAL OF I	7	1.667 %	
EXPERT SYSTEMS WITH APPLICATION:	7	1.667 %	
APPLIED MATHEMATICAL MODELLING	7	1.667 %	
MATHEMATICAL PROBLEMS IN ENGINEI	8	1.905 %	
JOURNAL OF CLEANER PRODUCTION	8	1.905 %	
INTERNATIONAL JOURNAL OF ADVANC	9	2.143 %	
EUROPEAN JOURNAL OF OPERATIONAL	10	2.381 %	
物流技术	11	2.619 %	
INTERNATIONAL JOURNAL OF PRODUC	12	2.857 %	
COMPUTERS & INDUSTRIAL ENGINEER	12	2.857 %	
TRANSPORTATION RESEARCH PART E-	15	3.571 %	
INTERNATIONAL JOURNAL OF PROD...	17	4.048 %	

查看 (V)　另存为 (S)...

图 1.18　供应链网络设计研究文献期刊分布

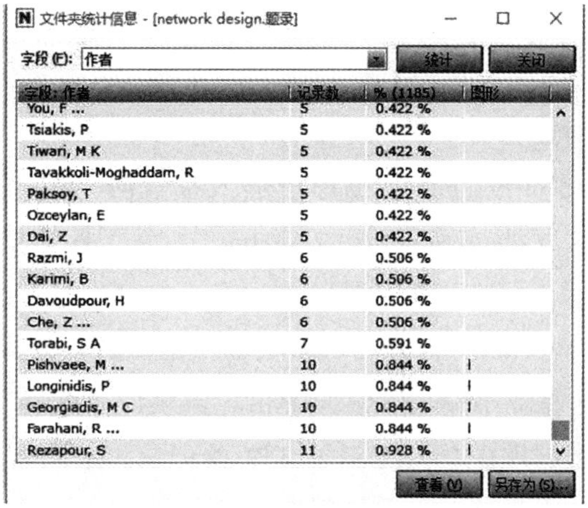

文件夹统计信息 - [network design.题录]

字段 (F): 作者　统计　关闭

字段: 作者	记录数	% (1185)	图形
You, F ...	5	0.422 %	
Tsiakis, P	5	0.422 %	
Tiwari, M K	5	0.422 %	
Tavakkoli-Moghaddam, R	5	0.422 %	
Paksoy, T	5	0.422 %	
Ozceylan, E	5	0.422 %	
Dai, Z	5	0.422 %	
Razmi, J	6	0.506 %	
Karimi, B	6	0.506 %	
Davoudpour, H	6	0.506 %	
Che, Z ...	6	0.506 %	
Torabi, S A	7	0.591 %	
Pishvaee, M ...	10	0.844 %	
Longinidis, P	10	0.844 %	
Georgiadis, M C	10	0.844 %	
Farahani, R ...	10	0.844 %	
Rezapour, S	11	0.928 %	

查看 (V)　另存为 (S)...

图 1.19　供应链网络设计研究作者分布

Transportation Research Part E-Logistics and Transportation Review、*International Journal of Production Economics*、*Computers & Industrial Engineering* 和《物流技术》是供应链网络设计研究领域的重要杂志。在研究学者方面，Rezapour、Farahani、Georgiadis、Longinidis、Pishvaee 等在供应链网络设计领域做出了巨大的贡献。

表1.3　　　　　　　　供应链网络设计文献总体统计结果

项目	结果
时间	1998—2010年：128篇（30.476%） 2011年：23篇（5.476%） 2012年：30篇（7.143%） 2013年：38篇（9.048%） 2014年：63篇（15.000%） 2015年：65篇（15.476%） 2016年：64篇（15.238%） 2017年：9篇（2.143%）
期刊	*International Journal of Production Research*：17篇（4.048%） *Transportation Research Part E-Logistics and Transportation Review*：15篇（3.571%） *International Journal of Production Economics*：12篇（2.857%） *Computers & Industrial Engineering*：12篇（2.857%） 《物流技术》：11篇（2.619%）
作者	Rezapour, S.：11篇（0.928%）；Farahani, R.Z.：10篇（0.844%）；Georgiadis, M.C.：10篇（0.844%）；Longinidis, P.：10篇（0.844%）；Pishvaee, M.S.：10篇（0.844%）

4. 供应商评估选择

我们在Web of Science数据库中输入检索词"supply chain supplier selection""supply chain supplier evaluation"，为了保证较高的相关性和避免过多的文献，只选取检索词在"title"中出现"supply chain supplier selection""supply chain supplier evaluation"的文献，总共得到209条记录。在CNKI数据库中输入检索词"供应链供应商选择"，得到130条记录。从两个数据库中总共得到了339条记录，采用NoteExpress软件导入题录，查找重复题录，重复判定字段设置为"题录类型""期刊""年份""标题""关键字"和"作者"等。删掉其中的重复题录36条，得到记录数为303的供应链供应商数据库（见图1.20）。然后选择"文件夹统计信息"，分别对"年份""期刊""作者"进行统计，如图1.21、图1.22和图1.23所示。文献总体统计结果如表1.4所示。从图1.21可以看出，关于供应商选择的研究文献数量呈递增的趋势。从表1.4可以看出，*International Journal of Production Economics*、《物流技术》、《物流科技》、*International Journal of Production Research*、*Journal of*

Clear Production 是供应商选择领域的重要杂志。在研究学者方面，可以看出，Ghodsypour、O'Brien、Reuter、Amid、Foerstl 等在供应商选择领域做出了巨大的贡献。

对供应商的选择研究最早、影响也最大的是 Dickson，早在 1966 年他通过分析 170 份对采购经理和采购代理人的调查结果，整理出 23 条

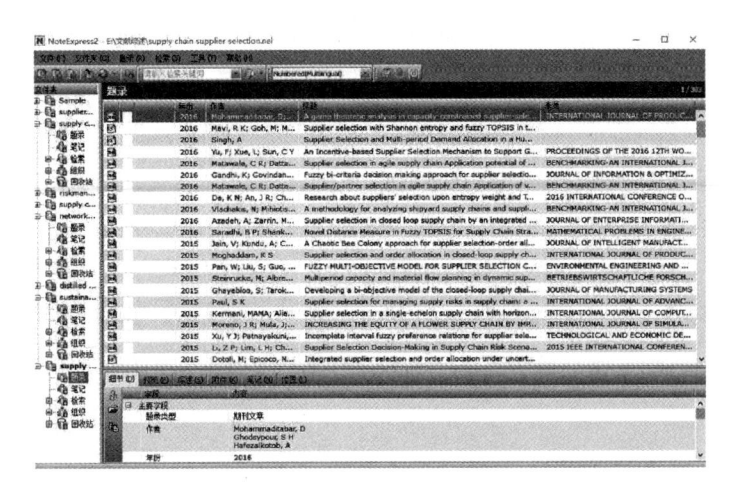

图 1.20　供应链供应商选择研究文献在 NoteExpress 软件中的汇总

图 1.21　供应链供应商选择研究文献年份分布

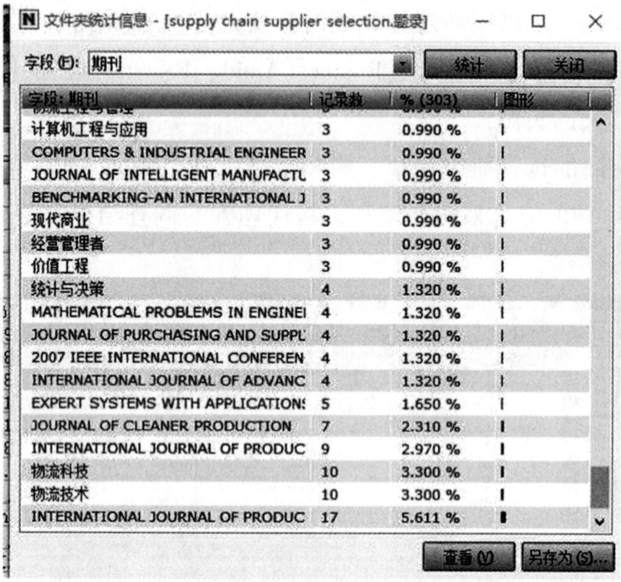

文件夹统计信息 - [supply chain supplier selection.题录]

字段(F): 期刊 统计 关闭

字段: 期刊	记录数	% (303)	图形
计算机工程与应用	3	0.990 %	
COMPUTERS & INDUSTRIAL ENGINEER	3	0.990 %	
JOURNAL OF INTELLIGENT MANUFACTU	3	0.990 %	
BENCHMARKING-AN INTERNATIONAL J	3	0.990 %	
现代商业	3	0.990 %	
经营管理者	3	0.990 %	
价值工程	3	0.990 %	
统计与决策	4	1.320 %	
MATHEMATICAL PROBLEMS IN ENGINEI	4	1.320 %	
JOURNAL OF PURCHASING AND SUPPL	4	1.320 %	
2007 IEEE INTERNATIONAL CONFEREN	4	1.320 %	
INTERNATIONAL JOURNAL OF ADVANC	4	1.320 %	
EXPERT SYSTEMS WITH APPLICATION!	5	1.650 %	
JOURNAL OF CLEANER PRODUCTION	7	2.310 %	
INTERNATIONAL JOURNAL OF PRODUC	9	2.970 %	
物流科技	10	3.300 %	
物流技术	10	3.300 %	
INTERNATIONAL JOURNAL OF PRODUC	17	5.611 %	

查看(V) 另存为(S)...

图 1.22 供应链供应商选择研究文献期刊分布

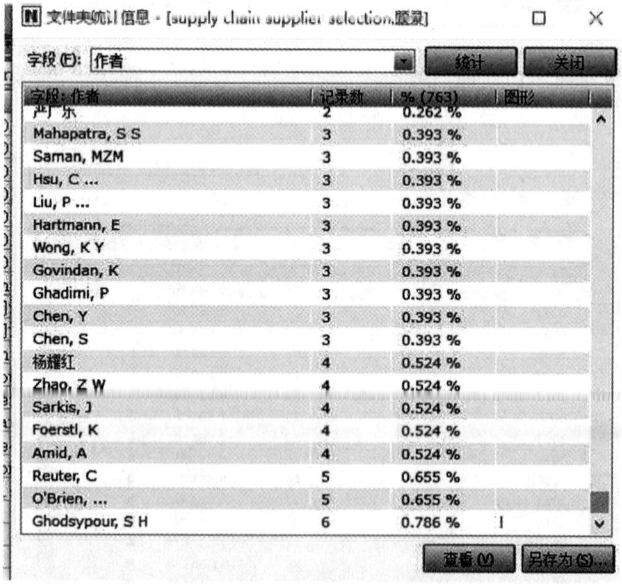

文件夹统计信息 - [supply chain supplier selection.题录]

字段(F): 作者 统计 关闭

字段: 作者	记录数	% (763)	图形
Mahapatra, S S	3	0.393 %	
Saman, MZM	3	0.393 %	
Hsu, C ...	3	0.393 %	
Liu, P ...	3	0.393 %	
Hartmann, E	3	0.393 %	
Wong, K Y	3	0.393 %	
Govindan, K	3	0.393 %	
Ghadimi, P	3	0.393 %	
Chen, Y	3	0.393 %	
Chen, S	3	0.393 %	
杨耀红	4	0.524 %	
Zhao, Z W	4	0.524 %	
Sarkis, J	4	0.524 %	
Foerstl, K	4	0.524 %	
Amid, A	4	0.524 %	
Reuter, C	5	0.655 %	
O'Brien, ...	5	0.655 %	
Ghodsypour, S H	6	0.786 %	

查看(V) 另存为(S)...

图 1.23 供应链供应商选择研究作者分布

表1.4　　　　　　　　供应链供应商选择文献总体统计结果

项目	结果
时间	1998—2010 年：116 篇（38.284%） 2011 年：30 篇（9.901%） 2012 年：25 篇（8.251%） 2013 年：27 篇（8.911%） 2014 年：35 篇（11.551%） 2015 年：43 篇（14.191%） 2016 年：26 篇（8.581%） 2017 年：1 篇（0.330%）
期刊	*International Journal of Production Economics*：17 篇（5.611%） 《物流技术》：10 篇（3.300%） 《物流科技》：10 篇（3.300%） *International Journal of Production Research*：9 篇（2.970%） *Journal of Clear Production*：7 篇（2.310%）
作者	Ghodsypour, S. H.：6 篇（0.786%）；O'Brien, C.：5 篇（0.655%）；Reuter, C.：5 篇（0.655%）；Amid, A.：4 篇（0.524%）；Foerstl, K.：4 篇（0.524%）

供应商选择准则，Dickson 认为，有很多因素会影响供应商的绩效[1]。Weber 等综述了 1967—1990 年关于供应商选择的 74 篇文献后，统计出提及 Dickson 的 23 项供应商选择标准的次数[2]。他们发现价格是讨论最多的一项标准，接下来依次是交货、质量、生产能力/生产设施、地理位置、技术能力、管理和组织等，而其他的因素则很少提及。这一问题被后来的很多学者加以改进和完善，出现了分层次的评价准则体系。不同企业在选择合作伙伴时，可以根据自己的需要设计不同的评价准则。Ho 等回顾了 2000—2008 年国际期刊发表的关于多准则供应商评价和选择方法[3]。Govindan 等回顾了 1996—2011 年在国际科学期刊上发表的

---

[1] Dickson, G. W., "An Analysis of Vendor Selection Systems and Decisions", *Journal of Purchasing*, 2 (1), 1966: 5-17.

[2] Weber, C. A., Current, J. R., & Benton, W. C., "Vendor Selection Criteria and Methods", *European Journal of Operational Research*, 50 (1), 1991: 2-18.

[3] Ho, W., Xu, X., & Dey, P. K., "Multi-criteria Decision Making Approaches for Supplier Evaluation and Selection: A Literature Review", *European Journal of Operational Research*, 202 (1), 2010: 16-24.

绿色供应商选择文献[1]。Wu 和 Barnes 回顾了 2001—2011 年发表的供应合作伙伴决策的文章[2]。Chai 等提供了一个 2008—2012 年决策者做供应商选择的系统的文献综述[3]。Igarashi 研究了绿色供应商选择问题。回顾了 1991—2011 年 21 年间的 60 篇文章[4]。Wetzstein 等研究了 1990—2015 年主要期刊的 221 篇关于供应商选择的文章,得出数学方法成为供应商选择的主流。关于绿色和可持续战略方法的供应商选择正处于研究的早期阶段,代表着未来研究的主流方向。随着外包的广泛流行,选择合适的供应商越来越重要[5]。可见可持续供应商的选择已逐渐成为企业发展的重要关注点。可持续供应商选择是一个包括定性与定量因素的多准则决策问题,因此有必要采用多准则决策方法来研究[6]。

5. 供应链风险管理

我们在 Web of Science 数据库中输入检索词"supply chain risk management""supply chain risk evaluation",总共得到 338 条记录。在 CNKI 数据库中输入检索词"供应链风险管理""供应链风险评估",得到 153 条记录。从两个数据库中总共得到了 491 条记录,采用 NoteExpress 软件导入题录,查找重复题录,重复判定字段设置为"题录类型""期刊""年份""标题""关键字"和"作者"等。删掉其中的重复题录

---

[1] Govindan, K., Rajendran, S., Sarkis, J., & Murugesan, P., "Multi—criteria Decision Making Approaches for Green Supplier Evaluation and Selection: A Literature Review", *Journal of Cleaner Production*, 98, 2015: 66 – 83.

[2] Wu, C., & Barnes, D., "A Literature Review of Decision-making Models and Approaches for Partner Selection in Agile Supply Chains", *Journal of Purchasing and Supply Management*, 17 (4), 2011: 256 – 274.

[3] Chai, J., Liu, J. N., & Ngai, E. W., "Application of Decision-making Techniques in Supplier Selection: A Systematic Review of Literature", *Expert Systems with Applications*, 40 (10), 2013: 3872 – 3885.

[4] Igarashi, M., de Boer, L., & Fet, A. M., "What is Required for Greener Supplier Selection? A Literature Review and Conceptual Model Development", *Journal of Purchasing and Supply Management*, 19 (4), 2013: 247 – 263.

[5] Wetzstein, A., Hartmann, E., Benton Jr, W. C., & Hohenstein, N. O., "A Systematic Assessment of Supplier Selection Literature-state-of-the-art and Future Scope", *International Journal of Production Economics*, 182, 2016: 304 – 323.

[6] Xia, W., & Wu, Z., "Supplier Selection with Multiple Criteria in Volume Discount Environments", *Omega*, 35 (5), 2007: 494 – 504.

29 条，得到记录数为 462 的可持续供应链的数据库（见图 1.24），然后选择"文件夹统计信息"，分别对"年份""期刊""作者"进行统计，如图 1.25、图 1.26 和图 1.27 所示。文献总体统计结果如表 1.5 所示。从图 1.25 可以看出，关于供应链风险管理的研究从 2006 年开

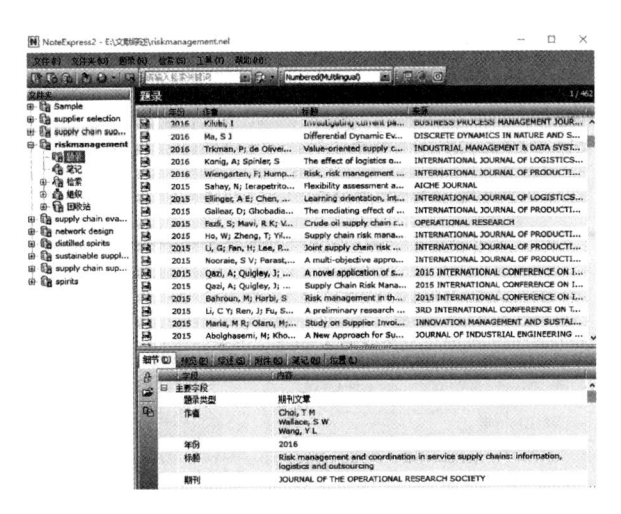

图 1.24　供应链风险管理研究文献在 NoteExpress 软件中的汇总

图 1.25　供应链风险管理研究文献年份分布

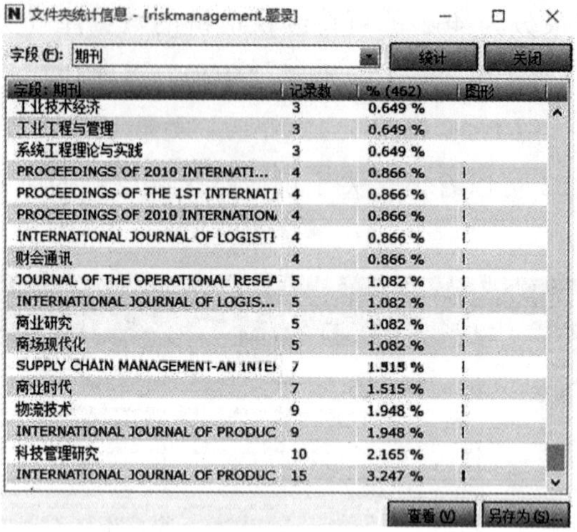

字段: 期刊	记录数	% (462)	图形
工业技术经济	3	0.649 %	
工业工程与管理	3	0.649 %	
系统工程理论与实践	3	0.649 %	
PROCEEDINGS OF 2010 INTERNATI...	4	0.866 %	ǀ
PROCEEDINGS OF THE 1ST INTERNATI	4	0.866 %	ǀ
PROCEEDINGS OF 2010 INTERNATION	4	0.866 %	ǀ
INTERNATIONAL JOURNAL OF LOGISTI	4	0.866 %	ǀ
财会通讯	4	0.866 %	ǀ
JOURNAL OF THE OPERATIONAL RESEA	5	1.082 %	ǀ
INTERNATIONAL JOURNAL OF LOGIS...	5	1.082 %	ǀ
商业研究	5	1.082 %	ǀ
商场现代化	5	1.082 %	ǀ
SUPPLY CHAIN MANAGEMENT-AN INTE	7	1.515 %	ǀ
商业时代	7	1.515 %	ǀ
物流技术	9	1.948 %	ǀ
INTERNATIONAL JOURNAL OF PRODUC	9	1.948 %	ǀ
科技管理研究	10	2.165 %	ǀ
INTERNATIONAL JOURNAL OF PRODUC	15	3.247 %	ǀ

图 1.26　供应链风险管理研究文献期刊分布

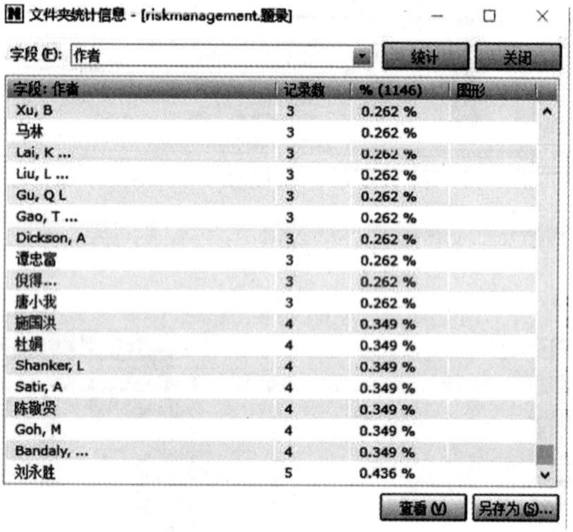

字段: 作者	记录数	% (1146)	图形
Xu, B	3	0.262 %	
马林	3	0.262 %	
Lai, K ...	3	0.262 %	
Liu, L ...	3	0.262 %	
Gu, Q L	3	0.262 %	
Gao, T ...	3	0.262 %	
Dickson, A	3	0.262 %	
谭忠富	3	0.262 %	
倪得...	3	0.262 %	
唐小我	3	0.262 %	
施国洪	4	0.349 %	
杜娟	4	0.349 %	
Shanker, L	4	0.349 %	
Satir, A	4	0.349 %	
陈敬贤	4	0.349 %	
Goh, M	4	0.349 %	
Bandaly, ...	4	0.349 %	
刘永胜	5	0.436 %	

图 1.27　供应链风险管理研究文献作者分布

始越来越得到学者的重视。从表 1.5 可以看出，*International Journal of Production Economics*、《科技管理研究》、*International Journal of Production Research*、《物流技术》、《商业时代》是供应链风险管理领域的重要杂志。在研究学者方面，刘永胜、Bandaly、Goh、陈敬贤、Satir 在供应链风险管理领域做出了巨大的贡献。

表1.5　　　　　　　供应链风险管理文献总体统计结果

项目	结果
时间	1995—2010 年：213 篇（46.105%） 2011 年：37 篇（8.009%） 2012 年：34 篇（7.359%） 2013 年：45 篇（9.740%） 2014 年：49 篇（10.606%） 2015 年：42 篇（9.091%） 2016 年：41 篇（8.874%） 2017 年：1 篇（0.216%）
期刊	*International Journal of Production Economics*：15 篇（3.247%） 《科技管理研究》：10 篇（2.165%） *International Journal of Production Research*：9 篇（1.948%） 《物流技术》：9 篇（1.948%） 《商业时代》：7 篇（1.515%）
作者	刘永胜：5 篇（0.436%）；Bandaly, D.：4 篇（0.349%）；Goh, M.：4 篇（0.349%）；陈敬贤：4 篇（0.349%）；Satir, A.：4 篇（0.349%）

企业的每一个过程和决策都容易产生不确定性。由于错误的评估和判断失误可能导致不可预见的风险，当发现得太晚时可能产生重要的影响，因此不确定性需要持续的监测和管理。随着不确定性的增加，风险管理变得越来越重要。近几十年来，风险管理这个术语被广泛应用于决策理论、金融、精算科学、医疗、营销、管理、应急计划和心理学等领域。

（1）风险含义

尽管有很长的历史了，但是"风险"这个概念还是模糊的，经常是不明确的。"风险"的起源不能清楚地界定，因为这个词似乎起源于不同的文化[①]。一种说法是"风险"的欧洲概念的词源分析表示其来源于

---

① Heckmann, I., Comes, T., & Nickel, S., "A Critical Review on Supply Chain Risk-Definition, Measure and Modeling", *Omega*, 52, 2015: 119–132.

希腊的导航术语"rhizikon",描述需要避免"海上的困境"①。从这个意义上说,"风险"的最佳定义就是恐惧或冒险。前者指商业活动和身体、精神上的困扰,后者意味着将金钱冒险作为一项战略。另一种说法是"风险"最早源于意大利语"Risicar",意思是"胆敢"(大胆、无畏),"胆敢"是对人类有冒险性的一种描述②。冒险意味有获利的机会。在英文中,"Risk"强调不利事件发生的可能性。Claypool 等将"风险"定义为测量不良反应的概率和严重程度③。因此,"风险"的本质应当是指损失的不确定性④。

(2) 供应链风险

供应链风险在过去几十年已经进行了广泛的研究⑤。典型的供应链风险包括由供应风险引起的中断和延迟,比如供应能力限制、质量问题、供应商流动性问题,以及供应商依赖性、产品设计变更、交货延迟⑥,而采购相关的风险则有汇率变化、存货、缺货⑦。物流运输风险方面,供应链相关风险有套牢的风险和道德风险,需求风险有由牛鞭效应引起的需求变动和不准确的预测、信息失真和存货堆积,基础设施

---

① Morgan, M. G., & Small, M., "Uncertainty: A Guide to Dealing with Uncertainty in Quantitative Risk and Policy Analysis", *International Journal of Forecasting*, 8 (1), 1990: 119 – 120.

② Khan, O., & Burnes, B., "Risk and Supply Chain Management: Creating a Research Agenda", *The International Journal of Logistics Management*, 18 (2), 2007: 197 – 216.

③ Claypool, E., Norman, B. A., & Needy, K. L., "Modeling Risk in a Design for Supply Chain problem", *Computers & Industrial Engineering*, 78, 2014: 44 – 54.

④ 周南洋:《供应链的风险识别、评估研究》,博士学位论文,中南大学,2008 年。

⑤ Zsidisin, G. A., Ellram, L. M., Carter, J. R., & Cavinato, J. L., "An Analysis of Supply Risk Assessment Techniques", *International Journal of Physical Distribution & Logistics Management*, 34 (5), 2004: 397 – 413; Jüttner, U., "Supply Chain Risk Management: Understanding the Business Requirements from a Practitioner Perspective", *The International Journal of Logistics Management*, 16 (1), 2005: 120 – 141; Tang, O., & Musa, S. N., "Identifying Risk Issues and Research Advancements in Supply Chain Risk Management", *International Journal of Production Economics*, 133 (1), 2011: 25 – 34.

⑥ Chopra, S., & Sodhi, M. S., "Supply-chain Breakdown", *MIT Sloan Management Review*, 46 (1), 2004: 53 – 61.

⑦ Hallikas, J., Virolainen, V. M., & Tuominen, M., "Risk Analysis and Assessment in Network Environments: A Dyadic Case Study", *International Journal of Production Economics*, 78 (1), 2002: 45 – 55.

和系统风险有中断、设备失灵。风险可以分为内部风险和外部风险[1]，也可以分为操作风险和中断风险[2]。供应链风险是组织、网络或环境中的不可预测变量。由于未来的不确定性，这些风险可以在供应链中的任何时间点出现[3]。减少供应链脆弱性水平已被确定为供应链管理领域的一个关键研究问题[4]。Wagner 等将供应链风险定义为物流、信息流和资金流里的负面后果[5]。Christopher 将供应链风险定义为"从最初的供应商到最终产品之间的物流、信息流和产品流的任何风险"[6]。应通过供应链合作伙伴之间的协调或合作来管理供应链风险，以确保盈利能力和连续性。风险不仅会影响企业的盈利能力，也与公司的声誉利害攸关[7]。供应链风险作为风险的一种，既具有风险的普遍特征，也具有自身的特点。总体来说，供应链风险具有客观性、传递性、多元性、复杂性、动态性、整体性和系统性等特点[8]。其中风险传递生命周期如图1.28 所示。

---

[1] Goh, M., Lim, J. Y., & Meng, F., "A Stochastic Model for Risk Management in Global Supply Chain Networks", *European Journal of Operational Research*, 182 (1), 2007: 164 – 173.

[2] Tang, C. S., "Perspectives in Supply Chain Risk management", *International Journal of Production Economics*, 103 (2), 2006: 451 – 488.

[3] Aqlan, F., & Lam, S. S., "Supply Chain Optimization under Risk and Uncertainty: A Case Study for High-end Server Manufacturing", *Computers & Industrial Engineering*, 93, 2016: 78 – 87.

[4] Neiger, D., Rotaru, K., & Churilov, L., "Supply Chain Risk Identification with Value-focused Process engineering", *Journal of Operations Management*, 27 (2), 2009: 154 – 168.

[5] Wagner, S. M., & Bode, C., "An Empirical Examination of Supply Chain Performance along Several Dimensions of Risk", *Journal of business logistics*, 29 (1), 2008: 307 – 325.

[6] Christopher, M., Peck, H., Rutherford, C., & Jüttner, U., "Understanding Supply Chain Risk: A Self-assessment Workbook". Cranfield University, School of Management, Department for Transport, 2003.

[7] Venkatesh, V. G., Rathi, S., & Patwa, S., "Analysis on Supply Chain Risks in Indian Apparel Retail Chains and Proposal of Risk Prioritization Model using Interpretive Structural Modeling", *Journal of Retailing and Consumer Services*, 26, 2015: 153 – 167.

[8] 周南洋：《供应链的风险识别、评估研究》，博士学位论文，中南大学，2008 年；马林：《基于 SCOR 模型的供应链风险识别、评估与一体化管理研究》，博士学位论文，浙江大学，2005 年；易海燕：《供应链风险的管理与控制研究》，博士学位论文，西南交通大学，2007 年；邱映贵：《供应链风险传递及其控制研究》，博士学位论文，武汉理工大学，2010 年。

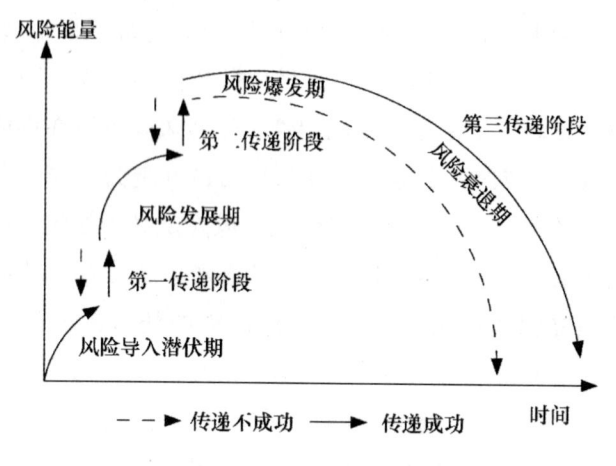

图1.28　风险传递生命周期

（3）供应链风险管控

由于全球化的发展，从业人员和研究人员更加注重供应链风险管理[1]。因为更短的产品生命周期和不确定性的增加，供应链风险管理已经成为现代社会面临的挑战[2]。不同的趋势加重了风险的暴露度[3]。Neiger 等人认为供应链风险目标为最小化供应商缺少遵守要求的能力的风险、最小化糟糕供应商的合作的风险、最小化供应商财务不稳定的风险、最小化与供应商交流之间不标准的工作流的风险、最小化供应商依赖的风险和最小化供应商成为竞争者的风险[4]。

---

[1] Neiger, D., Rotaru, K., & Churilov, L., "Supply Chain Risk Identification with Value-focused Process Engineering", *Journal of Operations Management*, 27 (2), 2009: 154 - 168; Ghadge, A., Dani, S., & Kalawsky, R., "Supply Chain Risk Management: Present and Future Scope", *The International Journal of Logistics Management*, 23 (3), 2012: 313 - 339.

[2] Christopher, M., & Lee, H., "Mitigating Supply Chain Risk through Improved Confidence", *International Journal of Physical Distribution & Logistics Management*, 34 (5), 2004: 388 - 396.

[3] Norrman, A., & Jansson, U., "Ericsson's Proactive Supply Chain Risk Management Approach after a Serious Sub-supplier Accident", *International Journal of Physical Distribution & Logistics Management*, 34 (5), 2004: 434 - 456; Bakshi, N., & Kleindorfer, P., "Co-opetition and Investment for Supply-chain Resilience", *Production and Operations Management*, 18 (6), 2009: 583 - 603; Christopher, M., & Towill, D. R., "Developing Market Specific Supply Chain Strategies", *The International Journal of Logistics Management*, 13 (1), 2002: 1 - 14.

[4] Neiger, D., Rotaru, K., & Churilov, L., "Supply Chain Risk Identification with Value-focused Process Engineering", *Journal of Operations Management*, 27 (2), 2009: 154 - 168.

（4）供应链风险管理过程

风险管理是人们对各种风险的认识、控制和处理的主动行为，它包括识别风险来源，分析风险发生的可能性和后果的严重程度（评估风险级别），并决定如何处置风险的全过程[①]。风险管理中往往存在风险与效率的冲突，怎样在较低风险情况下取得较高的效率是风险管理的目标。一般而言，风险管理大致可以分为风险识别（Risk Identification）、风险衡量（Risk Measurement）、风险评估（Risk Assessment）、风险控制（Risk Control）四个阶段[②]，其过程图如图 1.29 所示。

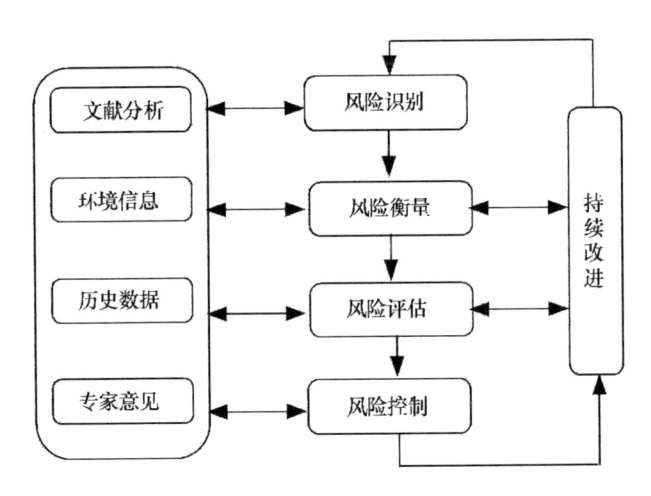

图 1.29　风险管理过程

风险识别是风险管理的第一步，是有效进行供应链风险管理的基础，借助工具识别出所有与供应链相关的风险[③]。风险衡量确定风险事

[①] 杨康：《基于复杂网络理论的供应链网络风险管理研究》，博士学位论文，北京交通大学，2014 年。

[②] 周南洋：《供应链的风险识别、评估研究》，博士学位论文，中南大学，2008 年；Giannakis, M., & Paladopoados, T., "Supply Chain Sustainability: A Risk Management Approach", *International Journal of Production Economics*, 171, 2016: 455 – 470; Hallikas, J., Karvonen, I., Pulkkinen, U., Virolainen, V. M., & Tuominen, M., "Risk Management Processes in Supplier Networks", *International Journal of Production Economics*, 90 (1), 2004: 47 – 58.

[③] Robert J. Chapman, *Simple Tools and Techniques for Enterprise Risk Management*, John Wiley & Sons, 2011.

件发生的概率以及对供应链的影响程度。通过主客观估计结合的方法对供应链上的风险进行估计和量化。风险评估是对已识别出的风险进行相对重要性排序，分析风险的潜在原因和后果等，为风险应对策略提供依据[1]。风险控制是提出风险应对策略并监控其影响，识别由于供应链动态性引起的或政策法规的改变引起的任意变动，然后提出新的解决办法[2]。采用基于全球供应链环境的有效风险管理策略越来越具挑战性[3]。许多学者已经发展了各种不同的策略去管理供应链风险[4]。风险缓解和控制策略分为主动和被动两类方法[5]。一般来说，风险应对策略主要有规避、控制（减少）、转移和接受（自留）四种策略。现将这四种常用的供应链风险应对措施介绍如下。

规避（avoid）可以避免导致风险出现的行为[6]。控制（control）是努力降低风险实践发生的可能性。分担（share）是和供应商合作实现风险分担，这可能包括通过保险进行风险转移[7]。自留/接受（retain/accept）是接受潜在发生损害，以免其他策略的实际损失（成本）比潜在损失的最大成本还要高[8]。

---

[1] Giannakis, M., & Paladopados, T., "Supply Chain Sustainability: A Risk Management Approach", *International Journal of Production Economics*, 121, 2016: 455–470.

[2] Teresa Wu, Jennifer Blackhurst, Managing Supply Chain Risk and Vulnerability: Tools and Methods for Supply Chain Decision Makers, Springer Science & Business Media, 2009.

[3] Christopher, M., & Towill, D., "An Integrated Model for the Design of Agile Supply Chains", *International Journal of Physical Distribution & Logistics Management*, 31 (4), 2001: 235–246.

[4] Tang, C. S., "Perspectives in Supply Chain Risk Management", *International Journal of Production Economics*, 103 (2), 2006: 451–488.

[5] Ghadge, A., Dani, S., Chester, M., & Kalawsky, R., "A Systems Approach for Modelling Supply Chain Risks", *Supply Chain Management: An International Journal*, 18 (5), 2013: 523–538.

[6] Miller, K. D., "A Framework for Integrated Risk Management in International Business", *Journal of International Business Studies*, 23 (2), 1992: 311–331.

[7] David Vose, *Risk Analysis: A Quantitative Guide*, John Wiley & Sons, 2008.

[8] Ibid..

6. 供应链绩效评价

通过在 Web of Science 数据库中输入检索词"supply chain evaluation""supply chain assessment",共得到 759 条记录。在 CNKI 数据库中输入检索词"供应链评价",得到 80 条记录。从两个数据库中总共得到了 839 条记录,采用 NoteExpress 软件导入题录,查找重复题录,重复判定字段设置为"题录类型""期刊""年份""标题""关键字"和"作者"等。删掉其中的重复题录 7 条,得到记录数为 832 的可持续供应链的数据库(如图 1.30 所示)。然后选择"文件夹统计信息",分别对"年份""期刊""作者"进行统计,如图 1.31、图 1.32 和图 1.33 所示。文献总体统计结果如表 1.6 所示。从年份分布图可以看出,关于供应链绩效评价的研究从 2004 年开始进入突飞猛进的发展阶段。对文献年份、作者、期刊等信息统计如表 1.6 所示。可以看出,*International Journal of Production Economics*、*Journal of Clear Production*、*International Journal of Production Research*、*Production Planning & Control*、*Computers & Industrial Engineering* 等是供应链绩效评价领域的重要杂志。而在研究学者方面,Ji、Wang、Govindan、Li 等在供应链绩效评价领域做出了巨大的贡献。

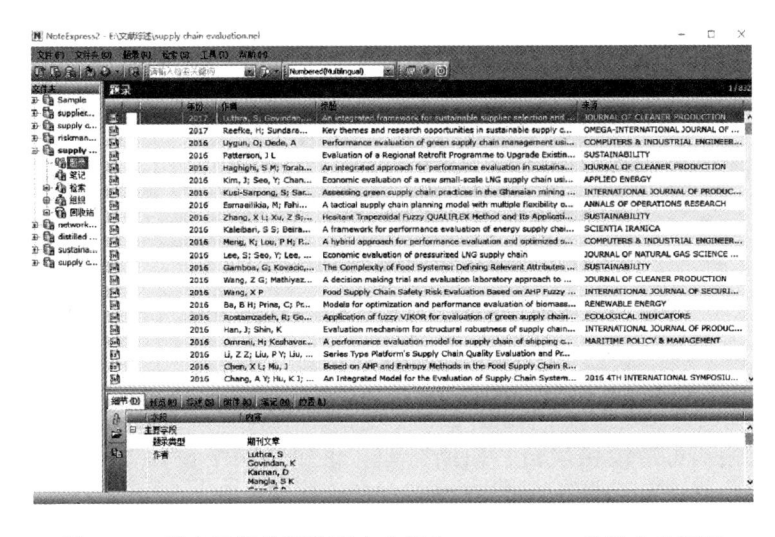

图 1.30 供应链绩效评价研究文献在 NoteExpress 软件中的汇总

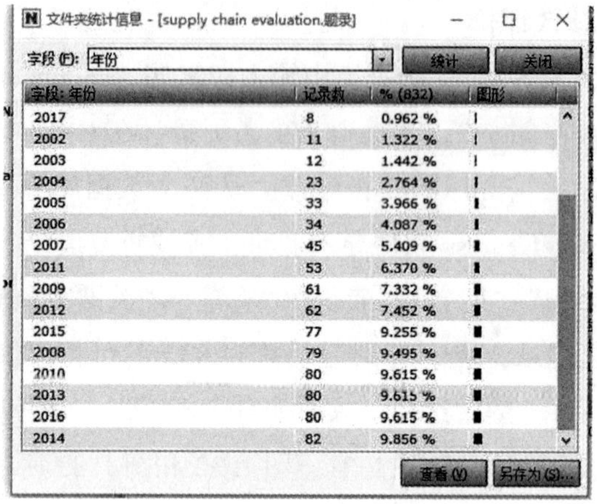

文件夹统计信息 - [supply chain evaluation.题录]

字段 (F): 年份

字段：年份	记录数	% (832)	图形
2017	8	0.962 %	
2002	11	1.322 %	
2003	12	1.442 %	
2004	23	2.764 %	
2005	33	3.966 %	
2006	34	4.087 %	
2007	45	5.409 %	
2011	53	6.370 %	
2009	61	7.332 %	
2012	62	7.452 %	
2015	77	9.255 %	
2008	79	9.495 %	
2010	80	9.615 %	
2013	80	9.615 %	
2016	80	9.615 %	
2014	82	9.856 %	

图 1.31　供应链评价研究文献年份分布

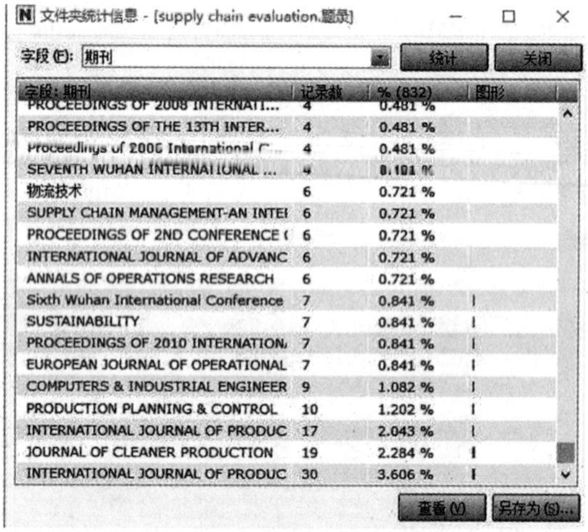

文件夹统计信息 - [supply chain evaluation.题录]

字段 (F): 期刊

字段：期刊	记录数	% (832)	图形
PROCEEDINGS OF 2008 INTERNATI...	4	0.481 %	
PROCEEDINGS OF THE 13TH INTER...	4	0.481 %	
Proceedings of 2006 International C...	4	0.481 %	
SEVENTH WUHAN INTERNATIONAL ...	4	0.481 %	
物流技术	6	0.721 %	
SUPPLY CHAIN MANAGEMENT-AN INTEI	6	0.721 %	
PROCEEDINGS OF 2ND CONFERENCE (	6	0.721 %	
INTERNATIONAL JOURNAL OF ADVANC	6	0.721 %	
ANNALS OF OPERATIONS RESEARCH	6	0.721 %	
Sixth Wuhan International Conference	7	0.841 %	
SUSTAINABILITY	7	0.841 %	
PROCEEDINGS OF 2010 INTERNATION	7	0.841 %	
EUROPEAN JOURNAL OF OPERATIONAL	7	0.841 %	
COMPUTERS & INDUSTRIAL ENGINEER	9	1.082 %	
PRODUCTION PLANNING & CONTROL	10	1.202 %	
INTERNATIONAL JOURNAL OF PRODUC	17	2.043 %	
JOURNAL OF CLEANER PRODUCTION	19	2.284 %	
INTERNATIONAL JOURNAL OF PRODUC	30	3.606 %	

图 1.32　供应链评价研究文献期刊分布

（二）综合分析

我们从可持续供应链、白酒行业、供应链网络设计、供应商选择、供应链风险管理和供应链绩效评价六个方面对文献进行汇总分析。通过阅读标题与摘要来确定相关性，对所有文献进行初步删选整理，得到文献数目分布如表 1.7 所示。

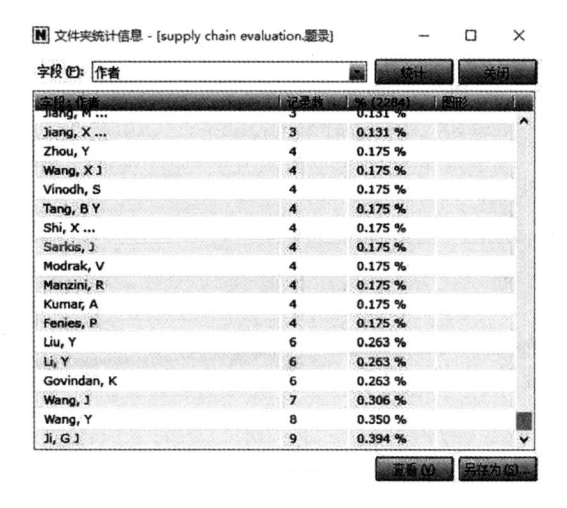

图1.33 供应链评价研究文献作者分布

表1.6 供应链评价文献总体统计结果

项目	结果
时间	1995—2010年：390篇（46.875%） 2011年：53篇（6.370%） 2012年：62篇（7.452%） 2013年：80篇（9.615%） 2014年：82篇（9.856%） 2015年：77篇（9.255%） 2016年：80篇（9.615%） 2017年：8篇（0.962%）
期刊	*International Journal of Production Economics*：30篇（3.606%） *Journal of Clear Production*：19篇（2.284%） *International Journal of Production Research*：17篇（2.043%） *Production Planning & Control*：10篇（1.202%） *Computers & Industrial Engineering*：9篇（1.082%）
作者	Ji, G. J.：9篇（0.394%）；Wang, Y.：8篇（0.350%）；Wang, J.：7篇（0.306%）；Govindan, K.：6篇（0.263%）；Li, Y.：6篇（0.263%）

表1.7 可持续供应链文献总体统计

	可持续供应链	白酒行业	供应链网络设计	供应商选择	供应链评价	风险管理
SCI	664	375	336	186	752	322
CNKI	70	387	84	117	80	140
总计	734	762	420	303	832	462

选择题录中最新的 314 篇可持续供应链和白酒的相关文献的关键词输入 NodeXL，将出现同一篇文章的关键词添加连线，并将属于同一个子图的关键词进行分组，得到图 1.34。可见，文献关键词表现得比较集中，说明关于可持续供应链的研究主题比较集中。在 NodeXL 中添加网络图中的顶点标签，并计算各关键词顶点的连线数，以顶点的大小区别显示连线从多到少的关键词，过滤连线少于 20 的关键词，得到图 1.35。可以看出，可持续主题在研究中排第一，排第二的是方法类主题。可以看到最显著的关键词"Sustainability"，说明可持续供应链的研

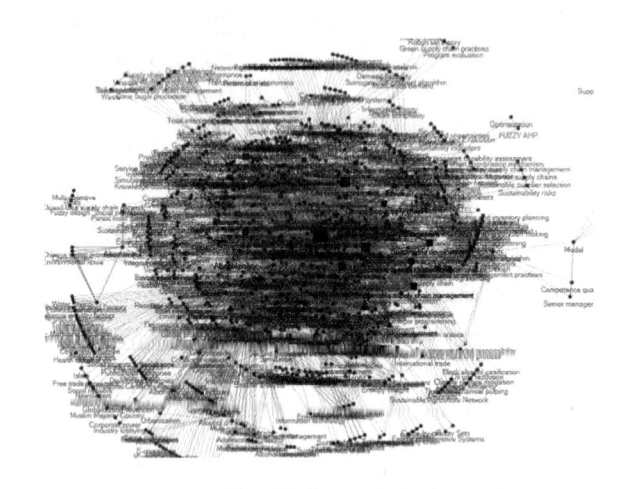

图 1.34 可持续供应链研究关键词网络图

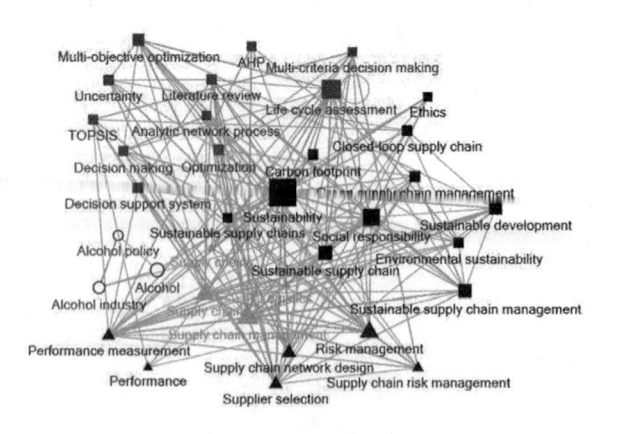

图 1.35 过滤后可持续供应链研究关键词

究重点在于可持续性，其次是生命周期评价（Life Cycle Assessment）和社会责任（Social Responsibility），说明可持续供应链研究的热点集中在可持续性、生命周期评价方法和社会责任上。

三　研究框架

随着经济全球化的发展，各利益相关者对工作条件和环境保护的要求越来越高，可持续供应链的发展在近年来得到了广大学者专家的重视。对于白酒行业来说，如何将可持续发展理论应用于白酒供应链，以评价优化供应链网络，提高供应链盈利能力，具有很重要的理论价值和现实意义。在这一领域虽然有一些研究，但多数局限于单目标研究，缺少将可持续供应链的三个维度集成的方法。因此，本书以可持续供应链为研究背景，主要针对白酒行业中网络优化、评价选择和风险管理系统问题进行研究，构建优化模型，设计相应的算法进行求解，同时通过实际应用案例分析证明求解方法的科学性、有效性和实用性，从而构建适合白酒行业的可持续供应链系统优化决策方法。以下是本书的研究思路、技术路线和研究内容。

（一）研究思路

我们遵循问题导向的研究思路，通过深入研究发现问题，抽象提炼分析问题，理论推演构建模型，改进创新设计算法，实际应用剖析案例，从白酒行业可持续供应链问题入手，对白酒可持续供应链的研究背景和研究现状进行梳理后，形成以下研究思路，如图1.36所示。

研究目的是解决白酒行业可持续供应链中的优化评价问题。因此，首先应该仔细理解研究对象和明确研究方向，研究的前提是对白酒行业可持续供应链进行广泛研究分析，深入挖掘白酒可持续供应链中网络设计、供应商选择、风险管理、供应链评价中存在的问题。在这些研究基础上，归纳提炼出可持续供应链中的关键问题，对相关问题进行深入研究，建立白酒行业可持续供应链的数学模型。

对发现的关键问题，从理论的角度进行深入的分析，结合可持续供

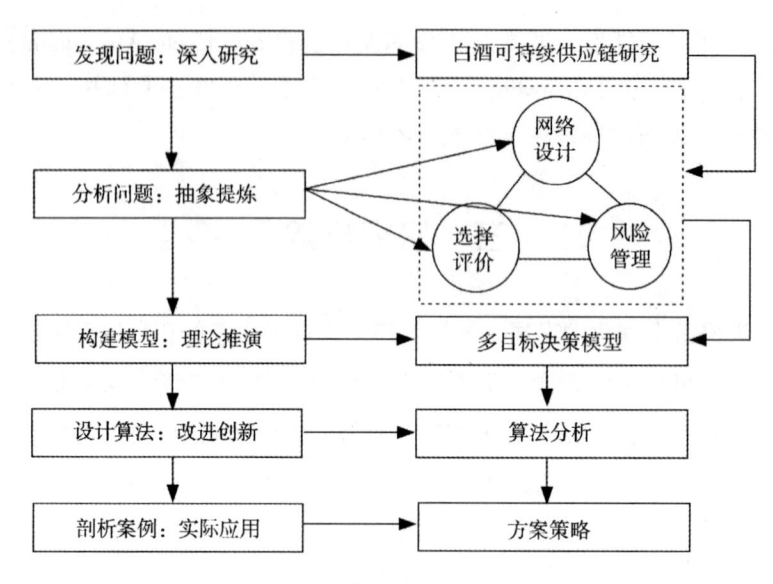

图1.36 研究思路

应链研究的成果，重点考虑了白酒行业中网络设计、供应商选择、风险管理、供应链评价等问题。根据问题的具体情况，阐述问题的关键因素，探索其内在的规律，提出这些问题的数学模型。建立数学模型定量化分析以上问题，进一步探索可持续供应链的内涵。

在对问题进行深层分析的基础上，针对相关问题的多目标决策特点，构建多目标决策模型。从经济、环境、社会三个维度对白酒行业可持续供应链进行分析研究。同时，进一步分析数学模型的相关性质。针对具体情况，设计求解算法。运用决策理论相关算法进行求解。

为了检验本书所建立的模型的科学性、有效性、实用性和合理性，将模型应用到实际问题中。通过对案例的剖析，对模型的结果进行深层次的分析，发现结果的规律性，同时案例的实际数据提供了许多有价值的信息，得到更多有意义的结论。

（二）技术路线

根据研究思路，以可持续供应链研究理论为指导，以多目标优化理论、模糊随机不确定理论、决策理论为主要理论工具，运用文献调查法、专家访谈法、数学建模法、统计分析法、案例分析法等研究方法展开研究。具体技术路线如图 1.37 所示。

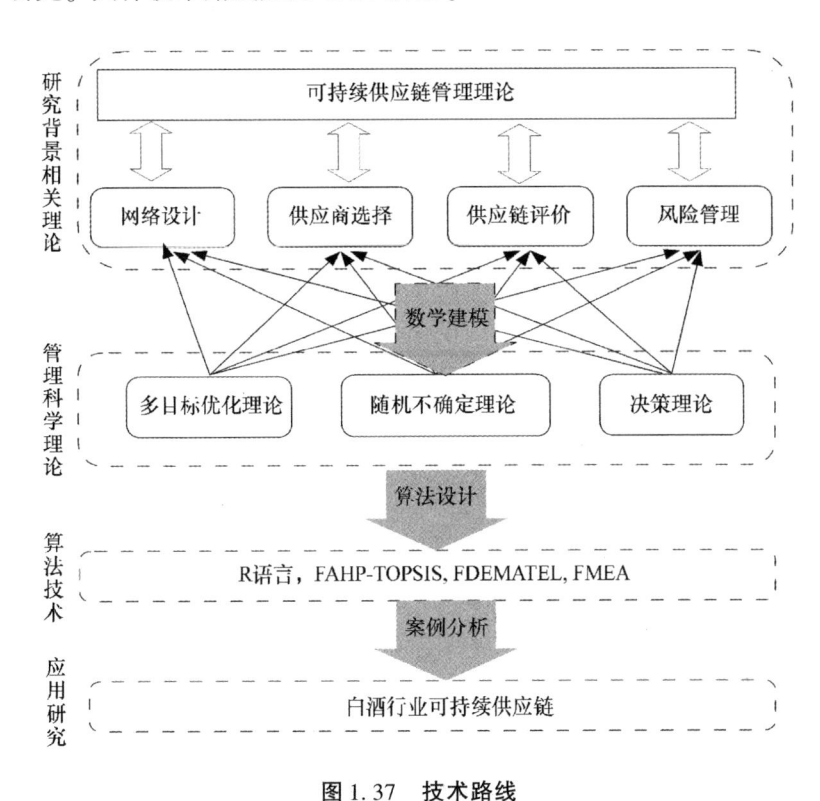

图 1.37　技术路线

研究对象的特点决定了必须以可持续供应链管理理论、随机不确定理论、多目标优化理论、模糊理论和管理决策理论为指导，才能保证研究具有实际意义。我们研究了在模糊随机环境下的白酒行业可持续供应链网络设计问题、供应商选择问题、风险管理问题以及供应链评价问题。对模糊随机变量的处理必须用到不确定决策理论的相关知识。白酒可持续供应链管理问题需要用到多目标规划理论，而考虑多目标管理问题时，需要用到 R 语言、模糊 AHP – TOPSIS、模糊 DEMATEL 等方法来求解。

（三）研究内容

本书的主要研究内容包括引言、理论基础、白酒可持续供应链网络设计模型及应用、白酒可持续供应链供应商选择模型及应用、白酒可持续供应链风险管控模型及应用、白酒可持续供应链绩效评价模型及应用、结语，共七章。研究框架如图 1.38 所示。

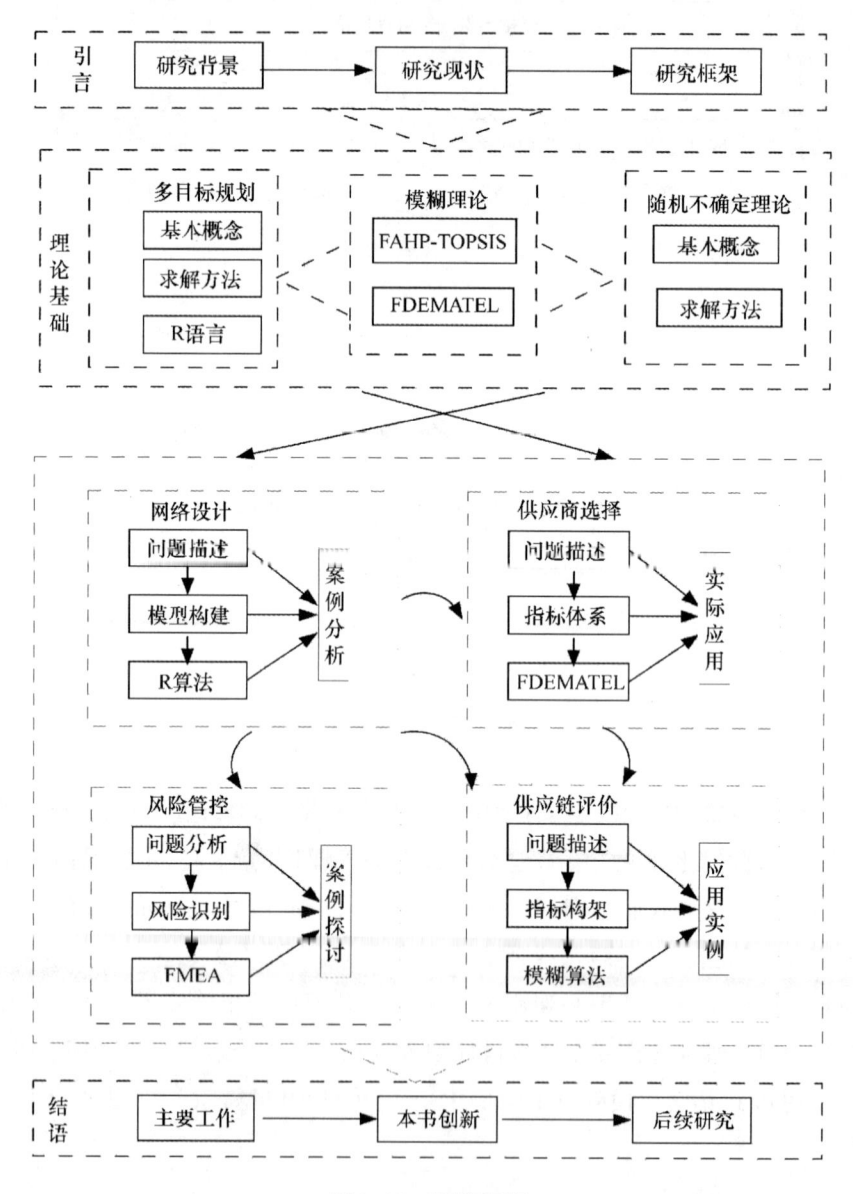

图 1.38 研究框架

引言部分从研究背景、研究现状、研究框架三个方面进行了阐述，介绍了本书的理论和现实背景，阐明研究目的和意义。运用文献综述方法，系统梳理以可持续供应链、网络设计、供应商选择、风险管理和供应链评价为主题的关键研究文献，为本书提供启示。研究背景部分主要是通过实际白酒行业供应链研究发现问题、明确研究目的和研究意义，指出了研究的重要性。研究现状部分通过对国内外相关问题及方法研究进行总结分析。研究框架从研究思路、技术路线、研究内容三个方面对全书进行归类概括说明，其中包含研究的方法和途径。

理论基础部分根据研究问题的需要，在概述核心理论的基础上，分析了多目标理论、模糊理论、随机不确定理论和可持续供应链。

网络设计部分针对白酒供应链的多目标优化问题，分析了白酒行业供应链网络设计中的经济、环境和社会问题。构建了考虑经济成本最低、环境影响最小、社会福利最大的多目标优化模型。并通过实际案例分析证实了算法的有效性。

供应商选择部分构建了白酒可持续供应链评价指标体系，经济、环境和社会三个维度共计 15 个指标，利用模糊 DEMATEL 方法对四川某白酒企业的供应商进行可持续评价选择，得出了有价值的结论。

风险管控部分根据可持续的三个维度将风险划分为经济风险、环境风险和社会风险，其中经济风险 14 个、环境风险 8 个、社会风险 8 个，并运用 FMEA 方法对风险进行了分析。

供应链评价部分构建了一个包含 5 个经济指标、5 个环境指标、5 个社会指标的供应链评价体系，给出了 5 个选择方案。运用模糊 AHP-TOPSIS 方法对供应链做了评价，根据排序结果得到选择方案。

最后对白酒可持续供应链的主要工作和研究结论进行归纳，总结本书创新，并对后续研究工作进行展望。

第二章 理论基础

为了研究白酒行业可持续供应链管理决策问题，首先需要对书中出现的多目标规划理论、模糊决策理论、随机不确定理论和可持续供应链管理理论这四方面的基础知识进行回顾。

一 模糊理论

实际的白酒供应链环境中存在许多不确定因素。有些不确定是由于因素自身难以按照精确的标准进行界定和区分；有些掺杂了人为的主观判断，导致对其描述含混不清；有些则是由于缺少统计数据而难以准确估计。为了研究白酒可持续供应链这种不确定的环境影响，需要对模糊的基础知识进行回顾。

（一）基本概念

下面主要介绍模糊数及模糊变量等基本概念和性质。

1. 模糊集和模糊数

"模糊"的概念是用于描述行为活动和观察现象的集合没有确切的边界的情形。在实际生活中广泛存在模糊的描述，如"时间长或短""可爱""美丽""满意度高或低"等，所有这些描述都没有确切的值或者边界，很难用经典的集合论或者概率论处理。"模糊集"在这种背景下被提了出来。Zadeh 在 1965 年提出了模糊集的概念，用来描述主观的不确定性①。模糊集的核心内涵是隶属度函数，模糊集的隶属度函数可以描述对象属于该集合的程度。隶属度往往在 [0, 1] 的范围，0 表示对象完全不属于这个集合，1 表示对象完全属于这个集合。

【定义2.1】（模糊集）假设 U 为论域，令 $\tilde{A}$ 为论域 U 的一个子集。$\forall x \in U$，函数 $u_{\tilde{A}} : U \to [0,1]$ 都指定了一个值 $u_{\tilde{A}} \in [0,1]$ 与之对应。$u_{\tilde{A}}(x)$ 在元素 x 的值反映了元素 x 隶属于 $\tilde{A}$ 的程度，称集合 $\tilde{A}$ 为模糊子集，$u_{\tilde{A}}(x)$ 称为 $\tilde{A}$ 的隶属函数。

若 $u_{\tilde{A}}(x)$ 的值越接近1，则 x 越属于 $\tilde{A}$；若 $u_{\tilde{A}}(x)$ 的值越接近0，则 x 越不属于 $\tilde{A}$。模糊集常用序对的形式表示为：

$$\tilde{A} = \{(x, u_{\tilde{A}}(x)) \mid x \in X\}$$

【定义2.2】（置信水平）②若 $\alpha \in [0,1]$，$A_\alpha = \{x \in X \mid u_{\tilde{A}}(x) \geq \alpha\}$，则 A_α 称为模糊集 $\tilde{A}$ 的 α - 截集。表示为隶属度函数大于等于 α - 的元素所组成的集合，其中 α 称为置信水平值。

【定义2.3】（模糊数）③假设 $\tilde{A}$ 为一个模糊集，它的隶属函数设为 $u_{\tilde{A}} : R \to [0,1]$。若：

(1) $\forall 0 \leq \alpha \leq 1$，$\tilde{A}$ 是上半连续的，即 α - 截集 $A_\alpha = \{x \in X \mid u_{\tilde{A}}(x) \geq \alpha\}$ 是一个闭集；

(2) $\tilde{A}$ 是正规的，则 $A_1 \neq \theta$；

(3) $\tilde{A}$ 是凸的，则 A_α 是 R 的一个凸子集，对 $\forall 0 \leq \alpha \leq 1$；

(4) $\tilde{A}$ 支撑的闭凸包 $A_0 = cl[co\{x \in R \mid u_{\tilde{A}}(x) > 0\}]$ 是紧的，则 $\tilde{A}$ 被称为模糊数。

由定义2.3可知，模糊数 $\tilde{A}$ 的 α - 截集实际上是实数域 R 上的闭区间，即

$$A_\alpha = \{x \in R \mid u_{\tilde{A}}(x) \geq \alpha\} = [A_\alpha^L, A_\alpha^R], \alpha \in [0,1]$$

---

① Zadeh, L. A., "Fuzzy Sets", *Information and Control*, 8 (3), 1965：338 - 353.
② Dubois, D., Prade, H., "Operations on Fuzzy Numbers", *International Journal of Systems Science*, 9 (6), 1978：613 - 626.
③ Ibid..

其中，A_α^L 和 A_α^R 分别表示闭区间 A_α 的左端点和右端点。

2. 模糊隶属度函数

模糊隶属度函数在不同的系统中可能以不同的形式表现。在实际应用中，常见的模糊隶属度函数有三角隶属度函数、梯形隶属度函数。其中三角模糊数 $\tilde{A}$ 表示为 (l,m,u)。参数 l、m 和 u 分别表示模糊事件的最小可能值、最有期望值和最大可能值。三角模糊隶属度函数图形如图2.1所示。其表达式如下：

$$u_A(x) = \begin{cases} 0, & x < l \\ \dfrac{x-l}{m-l}, & l \leqslant x \leqslant m \\ \dfrac{u-x}{u-m}, & m \leqslant x \leqslant u \\ 0, & x > u \end{cases} \quad (2.1)$$

其中，l、m 和 u 是实数，且满足 $l \leqslant m \leqslant u$。如图2.1所示，其左右边的三角模糊隶属度函数可表示为：

$$\tilde{A} = (A^{L(y)}, A^{R(y)}) = [l + (m-l)y, u + (u-m)y], y \in [0,1]$$

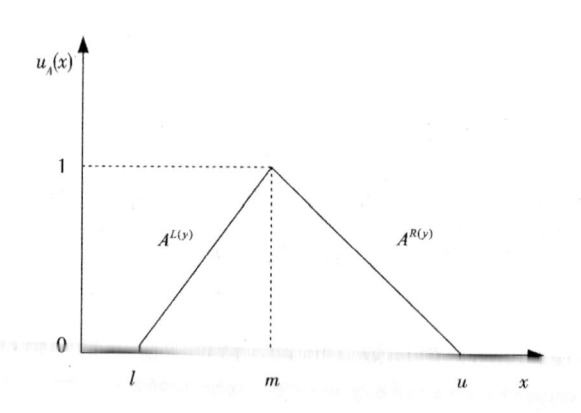

图2.1 三角模糊隶属度函数

在有的情况下，如参数的取值范围为 $[a,b]$，最可能的范围是 $[c,d]$，这种模糊参数需要用梯形模糊数表示。梯形模糊隶属度函数实质上可以看作是三角模糊隶属度函数的一种扩展形式，其表达式如下：

$$u_A(x) = \begin{cases} 0, & x < a \\ \dfrac{x-a}{c-a}, & a \leq x \leq c \\ 1, & c \leq x \leq d \\ \dfrac{x-b}{d-b}, & d \leq x \leq b \\ 0, & x \geq b \end{cases}$$

$\tilde{A} = (a,c,d,b)$，$\tilde{A}$ 则称为梯形模糊数，如图 2.2 所示。

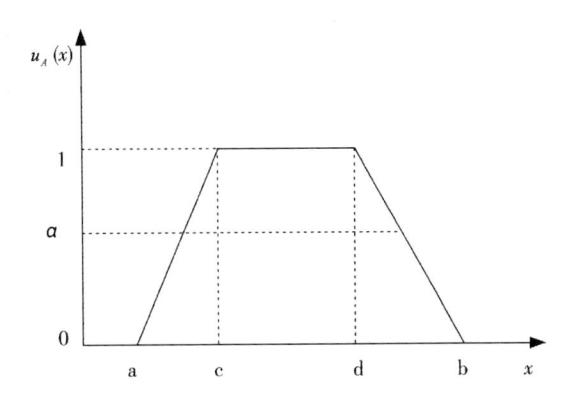

图 2.2　梯形模糊隶属度函数

如果 $\tilde{A}_1 = (l_1,m_1,u_1)$ 和 $\tilde{A}_2 = (l_2,m_2,u_2)$ 是两个三角模糊数（见图 2.3），则其加法、乘法、减法、除法和倒数的运算规则表达如下：

$$\tilde{A}_1 + \tilde{A}_2 = (l_1,m_1,u_1) + (l_2,m_2,u_2) = (l_1+l_2,m_1+m_2,u_1+u_2) \tag{2.2}$$

$$\tilde{A}_1 \times \tilde{A}_2 = (l_1,m_1,u_1) \times (l_2,m_2,u_2) = (l_1l_2,m_1m_2,u_1u_2) \tag{2.3}$$

$$\lambda \times \tilde{A}_1 = (\lambda,\lambda,\lambda) \times (l_1,m_1,u_1) = (\lambda l_1,\lambda m_1,\lambda u_1),\lambda > 0 \tag{2.4}$$

$$\tilde{A}_1 - \tilde{A}_2 = (l_1,m_1,u_1) - (l_2,m_2,u_2) = (l_1-l_2,m_1-m_2,u_1-u_2) \tag{2.5}$$

$$\tilde{A}_1 \div \tilde{A}_2 = (l_1,m_1,u_1) \div (l_2,m_2,u_2) = (l_1 \div l_2,m_1 \div m_2,u_1 \div u_2) \tag{2.6}$$

$$\tilde{A}_1^{-1} = (l_1, m_1, u_1)^{-1} = \left(\frac{1}{l_1}, \frac{1}{m_1}, \frac{1}{u_1}\right) \quad (2.7)$$

$\tilde{A}_1 = (l_1, m_1, u_1)$ 和 $\tilde{A}_2 = (l_2, m_2, u_2)$ 的距离公式表示如下：

$$d(\tilde{A}_1, \tilde{A}_2) = \sqrt{\frac{1}{3}[(l_1 - l_2)^2 + (m_1 - m_2)^2 + (u_1 - u_2)^2]} \quad (2.8)$$

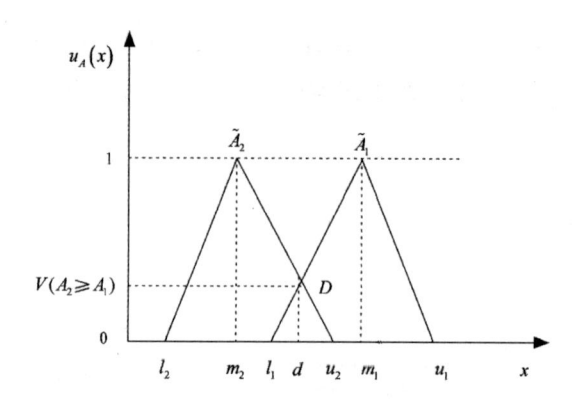

图 2.3 三角模糊隶属度函数交集

3. 模糊变量

Kaufmann 首先引入了模糊变量的概念[1]，Zadeh 等学者在其基础上对模糊变量理论进行了进一步发展[2]。Zadeh 在 1978 年提出的可能性理论，是模糊领域研究发展的一个重要的里程碑。随后，众多专家学者对其进行了深入的研究，Dubois 和 Prade[3]，以及 Nahmias[4] 的研究使得这一理论框架得到了进一步完善。在概率论里，随机变量用概率分布函数来表示，而在可能性理论里模糊变量则可用可能性分布函数表示。由可能性理论，一个模糊变量被定义为一个凸的正规模糊集，而一个模糊变量的可能性分布函数则被定义为相应模糊集的隶属函数。从数学角度来

---

[1] Kaufmann, A., *Introduction to the Theory of Fuzzy Subsets*, Academic Press, 1975.

[2] Zadeh, L. A., "Fuzzy Sets as a Basis for a Theory of Possibility", *Fuzzy Sets and Systems*, 1 (1), 1978: 3-28.

[3] Dubois, D., Prade, H., "Operations on Fuzzy Numbers", *International Journal of Systems Science*, 9 (6), 1978: 613-626.

[4] Nahmias, S., "Fuzzy Variables", *Fuzzy Sets and Systems*, 1 (2), 1978: 97-110.

理解，模糊变量是定义在模糊空间中可以描述事物模糊特征的可变化的模糊数。下面给出模糊变量的定义。

【定义2.4】[1] 从可能性空间 $(\Theta, P(\Theta), Pos)$ 到实直线 R 的一个函数 ξ，ξ 的隶属度函数为 μ，对任一的 $A \in P(\Theta)$，$Pos\{A\} = \sup\{u(\xi(\theta)) \mid \theta \in A\}$，则 ξ 为模糊变量。其模糊隶属度函数如下[2]：

$$u(x) = Pos\{\theta \in \Theta \mid \xi(\theta) = x\}$$

为了测量某一模糊事件发生的可能性，有很多种度量方法。首先，如果决策者的偏好是乐观型，则适合用可能性测度。

【定义2.5】令 Θ 为非空集合，且 $P(\Theta)$ 为集合 Θ 的幂集。对任一 $A \in P(\Theta)$ 都存在一个非负数 $Pos(\Theta)$，需满足三个基本条件：

(1) $Pos(\theta) = 0$；

(2) $Pos(\Theta) = 1$；

(3) $Pos\{\cup_i A_i\} = \sup Pos\{A_i\}$，对于 Pos 是可测的，称为可能性测度，三元总体 $(\Theta, P(\Theta), Pos)$ 可称为可能性空间，函数 Pos 为可能性测度。

【定义2.6】ξ 是可能性空间 $(\Theta, P(\Theta), Pos)$ 上的一个模糊变量，则其隶属函数 $u: R \to [0,1]$ 可由可能性测度 Pos 表示。

$$u(x) = Pos\{\theta \in \Theta \mid \xi(\theta) = x\}$$

【定义2.7】如果一个定义在 $Pos(\Theta)$ 上的集函数 Nec 满足两个基本条件：(1) $Nec\{\varphi\} = 0$，且 $Nec\{\Theta\} = 1$；(2) 对 $P(\Theta)$ 的任何子集簇 $\{A_i \mid i \in I\}$，其中 I 是指标集，$Nec\{\bigcap_{i \in I} A_i\} = \inf_{i \in I}\{A_i\}$ 均成立，那么函数 Nec 可称为必然性测度。A 的必然性测度是其补集 A^c 的不可能性。

假设 $(\Theta, P(\Theta), Pos)$ 为一个可能性空间，A 是 $P(\Theta)$ 上的一个集合，则 A 的必然性测度 Nec 是：

$$Nec\{A\} = 1 - Pos\{A^c\}$$

因此，必然性测度是可能性测度的对偶，以及对任意的 $A \in P(\Theta)$，

---

[1] Nahmias, S., "Fuzzy Variables", *Fuzzy Sets and Systems*, 1 (2), 1978: 97-110.

[2] Dubois, D., Prade, H., "Operations on Fuzzy Numbers", *International Journal of Systems Science*, 9 (6), 1978: 613-626.

均有 $Pos\{A\} + Nec\{A^c\} = 1$。

4. 模糊随机变量

模糊随机变量最早由 Kwakernaak 提出[1]，后来许多学者从不同的角度对模糊随机变量进行了定义。这里引用 Puri 和 Ralescu 对模糊随机变量在实数集合上的定义[2]。R 为所有实数的集合，$F_c(R)$ 为所有模糊变量的集合，$K_c(R)$ 为所有非空有界闭区间。

【定义 2.8】(Ω, F, P) 是概率空间，如果 $\forall 0 < \alpha \leq 1$，集值函数 $\xi_\alpha : \Omega \to K_c(R)$，$\xi_\alpha(\omega) = (\xi(\omega))\alpha = \{x \mid x \in R, u_{\xi(\omega)} \geq \alpha\}$，$\forall \omega \in \Omega$ 是可测的，则称映射 $\xi : \Omega \to F_c(R)$ 为 (Ω, F, P) 上的模糊随机变量。简单地说，模糊随机变量是一个数值为模糊值的随机变量。

如果 $\forall (\omega) \in \Omega, \xi(\omega)$ 是三角模糊变量，则 ξ 是三角模糊随机变量，用 $\xi(\omega) = (a(\omega) - l(\omega), a(\omega), a(\omega) + r(\omega))$，$\omega \in \Omega$。在这种情况下，如果 $l(\omega)$ 和 $r(\omega)$ 为常量，则模糊随机变量 ξ 可以表示为 $\xi(\omega) = (a(\omega) - l, a(\omega), a(\omega) + r)$。

（二）期望算子

为了处理不确定变量，需要将模糊变量和模糊随机变量转化为清晰值，模糊变量和模糊随机变量都可以用期望值算子将其转化为确定值。先介绍一种处理模糊变量的方法。一个模糊集 $\tilde{A}$ 的期望值等价于：

$$E(\tilde{A}) = \frac{\int_{-\infty}^{+\infty} x u_{\tilde{A}}(x) dx}{\int_{-\infty}^{+\infty} u_{\tilde{A}}(x) dx}$$

另外，带模糊测度 Cr 的期望值算子也是常用的方法[3]。设 λ 表示决策者态度的乐观—悲观指标，则以三角模糊变量 $\xi = (a, b, c)$ 为例，其

---

[1] Kwakernaak, H., "Fuzzy Random Variables—Definitions and Theorems", *Information Sciences*, 15 (1), 1978: 1 - 29.

[2] Puri M. L., Ralescu D. A., "Fuzzy Random Variables", *Journal of Mathematical Analysis and Applications*, 114 (2), 1986: 409 - 422.

[3] Xu, J., Zeng, Z., *Fuzzy-like Multiple Objective Multistage Decision Making*, Springer International Publishing, 2014.

期望值的表达式如下：

$$E^{Cr}(\xi) = \begin{cases} \dfrac{\lambda}{2}a + \dfrac{b}{2} + \dfrac{(1-\lambda)}{2}c, & c \leq 0 \\ \dfrac{\lambda}{2}(a+b) + \dfrac{\lambda c^2 - (1-\lambda)b^2}{2(c-b)}, & b \leq 0 \leq c \\ \dfrac{\lambda}{2}(c+b) + \dfrac{(1-\lambda)b^2 - \lambda a^2}{2(b-a)}, & a \leq 0 \leq b \\ \dfrac{(1-\lambda)a + b + \lambda c}{2}, & 0 \leq c \end{cases}$$

同样地，对于梯形模糊变量 $\xi = (a,b,c,d)$，经过带模糊测度 Cr 的期望值算子处理后，其期望值为：

$$E^{Cr}(\xi) = \begin{cases} \dfrac{\lambda}{2}(a+c) + \dfrac{1-\lambda}{2}(d+b), & b \leq 0 \\ \dfrac{\lambda}{2}(a+c) + \dfrac{\lambda b^2 - (1-\lambda)d^2}{2(b-d)}, & d \leq 0 \leq b \\ \dfrac{\lambda}{2}(a+c+d+b), & c < 0 \leq d \\ \dfrac{\lambda}{2}(d+b) + \dfrac{(1-\lambda)c^2 - \lambda a^2}{2(c-a)}, & a < 0 \leq c \\ \dfrac{(1-\lambda)(a+c) + \lambda(d+b)}{2}, & 0 \leq a \end{cases}$$

对于模糊随机变量的期望值，定义如下：

【定义2.9】[①] 设 $\tilde{\xi}$ 是概率空间 (Ω,F,P) 的模糊随机变量，若 $\tilde{\xi}$ 的期望值 $E(\tilde{\xi})$ 是实数空间的唯一集合，$\forall \alpha \in (0,1]$，则 $E(\tilde{\xi})$ 满足：

$$E(\tilde{\xi})_\alpha = \int_\Omega \xi_\alpha dP = \{\int_\Omega f(\omega)dP(\omega) : f \in L^1(P), f(\omega) \in \xi_\alpha(\omega) a.s. [P]\}。$$

其中，$\int_\Omega \xi_\alpha dP$ 是关于 P 的 Aumann 积分，$L^1(P)$ 表示 P 上的所有可积函数 $f:\Omega \to R$。

[①] Puri M. L., Ralescu D. A., "Fuzzy Random Variables", *Journal of Mathematical Analysis and Applications*, 114 (2), 1986: 409–422.

【引理 2.1】[①] 设 (Ω, F, P) 为完整的概率空间，$\xi:\Omega \to F_c(R)$ 是双重模糊随机变量。则 $\forall \alpha \in (0,1]$，$E(\xi)$ 的 α - 水平截集取值范围可以表示为：

$$(E(\xi))_\alpha = [(E_\alpha^-(\xi)),(E_\alpha^+(\xi))] = [\int_\Omega (\xi(\omega))_\alpha^- dP(\omega),$$

$$\int_\Omega (\xi(\omega))_\alpha^+ dP(\omega)]$$

计算模糊随机变量的期望值，可以结合决策者的偏好，利用混合式清晰化方法[②]。首先将模糊随机变量转化为 (γ,α) - 水平的梯形模糊数。$\sigma \in [0,\sup p_\varphi(x)]$ 为随机变量给定的概率水平，$\gamma \in \left[\dfrac{|\xi|_R - |\xi|_L}{|\xi|_R - |\xi|_L + \varphi_\sigma^R - \varphi_\sigma^L}, 1\right]$ 为可能性水平，都反映了决策者的偏好与态度。

设模糊随机变量为 $\tilde{\xi} = ([\xi]_L, \varphi(\omega), [\xi]_R)$。其中 $\varphi(\omega)$ 为随机变量，并服从正态分布 $N(\mu, \eta^2)$。将模糊随机变量转化为 (γ, α) - 水平梯形模糊数的步骤如下。

（1）通过统计或专家访谈等方式收集数据预测 $[\xi]_L$、$[\xi]_R$、μ 和 η^2 的数值。

（2）采用群决策的方法[③]估计决策者的态度，继而计算出概率水平 γ 和 σ 的值。

（3）设 φ_σ 是随机变量 $\varphi(\omega)$ 的 σ - 切平集，即

$$\varphi_\sigma = [\varphi_\sigma^L, \varphi_\sigma^R] = \{x \in R \mid f_\varphi(x) \geqslant \sigma\}$$

其中，上下边界：

[①] Puri M. L., Ralescu D. A., "Fuzzy Random Variables", *Journal of Mathematical Analysis and Applications*, 114 (2), 1986: 409 - 422.

[②] Xu, J., Zeng Z., *Fuzzy-like Multiple Objective Multistage Decision Making*, Springer International Publishing, 2014.

[③] Herrera, F., Herrera-Viedma, E., "A Model of Consensus in Group Decision Making Under Linguistic Assessments", *Fuzzy Sets and Systems*, 78 (1), 1996: 73 - 87; Wu, Z., & Xu, J., "A Consistency and Consensus based Decision Support Model for Group Decision Making with Multiplicative Preference Relations", *Decision Support Systems*, 52 (3), 2012: 757 - 767.

$$\varphi_\sigma^L = \inf\{x \in L \mid f_\varphi(x) \geq \sigma\} = \mu - \sqrt{-2\eta^2 \ln(\sqrt{2\pi}\sigma\eta)}$$

$$\varphi_\sigma^R = \inf\{x \in R \mid f_\varphi(x) \geq \sigma\} = \mu + \sqrt{-2\eta^2 \ln(\sqrt{2\pi}\sigma\eta)}$$

(4) 将模糊随机变量 $\tilde{\xi} = ([\xi]_L, \varphi(\omega), [\xi]_R)$ 转化为 (γ, α)-水平的梯形模糊变量 $\tilde{\xi}_{(\gamma,\sigma)}$：

$$\tilde{\tilde{\xi}} \to \tilde{\xi}_{(\gamma,\sigma)} = ([\xi]_L, \tilde{\xi}, [\xi]_R)$$

其中，$\underline{\xi} = [\xi]_R - (\gamma[\xi]_R - \varphi_\sigma^L)$，$\bar{\xi} = [\xi]_L + \gamma(\varphi_\sigma^R - [\xi]_L)$。隶属度函数 $\tilde{\xi}_{(\gamma,\sigma)}(x)$ 表示为：

$$\mu_{(\gamma,\sigma)}(x) = \tilde{\xi} \begin{cases} 0, & x < [\xi]_L \ or \ x > [\xi]_R \\ \dfrac{x - [\xi]_L}{\bar{\xi} - [\xi]_L}, & [\xi]_L \leq x < \underline{\xi} \\ 1, & \underline{\xi} \leq x \leq \bar{\xi} \\ \dfrac{[\xi]_R - x}{[\xi]_R - \bar{\xi}}, & \bar{\xi} < x \leq [\xi]_R \end{cases}$$

将模糊随机变量 $\tilde{\xi}$ 转化为模糊变量 $\tilde{\xi}_{(\gamma,\sigma)}$ 后，再利用上述梯形模糊变量的期望值算法可以推算出模糊变量 $\tilde{\xi}_{(\gamma,\sigma)}$ 的期望值 $E^{Cr}[\tilde{\xi}_{(\gamma,\sigma)}]$。例如，通常实际应用中的模糊数的下边界大于 0，即 $a > 0$，这时梯形模糊变量 $\tilde{\xi}_{(\gamma,\sigma)}$ 的期望值可以表示为：$E^{Cr}[\tilde{\xi}_{(\gamma,\sigma)}] = \dfrac{1-\lambda}{2}([\xi]_L + \underline{\xi}) + \dfrac{\lambda}{2}(\bar{\xi} + [\xi]_R)$。模糊变量的期望值对于模糊理论和实践都有着重要意义，文中采用如下定义[①]：

$$E|\xi| = \int_{-\infty}^{0} Cr\{\xi \geq \gamma\} dr - Cr\{\xi \leq \gamma\} dr$$

其中，ξ 为定义在可能性空间 $[\Theta, P(\Theta), Pos]$ 上的一个模糊变量。

---

① Liu, B., *Theory and Practice of Uncertain Programming*, Springer, 2009.

显然，对于三角模糊数 $\xi = (a,b,c)$，其期望值可表示为 $E|\xi| = \frac{1}{3}(a+b+c)$；对于梯形模糊数 $\xi = (a,b,c,d)$，其期望值可表示为 $E|\xi| = \frac{1}{4}(a+b+c+d)$。

二 随机不确定理论

在经济生活中，决策无处不在，决策环境复杂多变，受到来自经济、自然、政治、技术等多方面的影响。因此，在实际生活中不确定性是不可避免的。在研究实际问题的推动下，随机性不确定现象下的决策问题研究已成为近年来研究的重点。对于白酒企业的供应链网络设计来说，配送中心的布局及成本、运营费用、运输模式、碳排放量和社会影响力等都是很难确定的信息。随机理论具备完善的理论体系，可以描述决策环境中的这种客观不确定性[1]。

设有非空集合 Ω，Ω 是可列的，例如，$\Omega = [0, 1]$，Λ 是一个在 Ω 的 Borel 代数。A 中的每一个元素是一个事件。为给出一个关于概率的公理化定义，有必要为每一个事件 A 分配一个数字 $\Pr\{A\}$ 用于表示事件 A 可能发生的概率。为保证 $\Pr\{A\}$ 具备一些特定的概率所应该具有的性质，必须满足如下公理[2]：

公理 1. （归一性）$\Pr\{\Omega\} = 1$。

公理 2. （非负性）对任一的 $A \in \Omega$ 有 $\Pr\{A\} \geqslant 0$。

公理 3. （可列可加性）对每一个可数序列的互不相交的事件 $\{A_i\}$，有：

$$\Pr\{\bigcup_{i=1}^{\infty} A_i\} = \sum_{i=1}^{\infty} \Pr\{A_i\} \qquad (2.9)$$

【定义 2.10】（概率空间）集函数 Pr 称为概率，如果它满足上面的

---

[1] 李宗敏：《建筑施工场地设施布局与安保随机模型及其应用》，博士学位论文，四川大学，2014 年。

[2] Billingsley, P., *Probability and Measure*, John Wiley & Sons, 2008.

三条公理，相应的 (Ω,A,Pr) 称为概率空间。

【定义 2.11】(随机变量)[1] 设 (Ω,A,Pr) 是一个概率空间。一个定义在 Ω 上的实值函数 ξ 称为随机变量，如有：

$$\xi^{-1}(B) = \{\omega \in \Omega : \xi(\omega) \in B\} \in A, \forall B \in B \quad (2.10)$$

其中，B 是在 $R = (-\infty, +\infty)$ 上的 Borel 集的 σ 代数，也就是说，一个随机变量 ξ 是从 (Ω,A,Pr) 到 (R,B) 的可测转换。注：对所有在 R 上的区间 I，要求 $\xi^{-1}(I) \in A$。定义在 (R,B) 上的随机变量 ξ 包含了在 R 上的测度 $\mathrm{Pr}\xi$，可将其定义如下：

$$P_{r\xi}B = P_r\{\xi^{-1}(B)\}, B \in B \quad (2.11)$$

可见，$P_{r\xi}$ 为 SS 上的概率测度，称其为 ξ 的概率分布。

【例 2.1】若概率空间 (Ω,A,P_r) 是 $(\omega_1,\omega_2,\omega_3)$，且 $P_r\{\omega_1\} = 0.3$，$P_r\{\omega_2\} = 0.5$，$P_r\{\omega_3\} = 0.2$。函数 ξ 表示为：

$$\xi(\omega)\begin{cases} -1, \omega = \omega_1 \\ 0, \omega = \omega_1 \\ 1, \omega = \omega_1 \end{cases} \quad (2.12)$$

则 ξ 为一个随机变量。

【定义 2.12】[2] (1) 如果 $P_r\{\xi < 0\} = 0$，则该随机变量是非负的；(2) 如果 $P_r\{\xi \leq 0\} = 0$，则该随机变量是正的；(3) 如果存在一个有限序列 $\{x_1, x_2, \cdots, x_m\}$ 满足：

$$P_r\{\xi \neq x_1, \xi \neq x_2, \cdots, \xi \neq x_m\} = 0 \quad (2.13)$$

则该随机变量是简单的；(4) 如果存在一个可数序列 $\{x_1, x_2, \cdots\}$ 满足：

$$P_r\{\xi \neq x_1, \xi \neq x_2, \cdots\} = 0 \quad (2.14)$$

则该随机变量是离散的。

【定义 2.13】[3] 有定义在概率空间 (Ω,A,P_r) 上的随机变量 ξ_1 和 ξ_2，若 $\forall \omega \in \Omega$，有 $\xi_1(\omega) = \xi_2(\omega)$，则 $\xi_1 = \xi_2$。

---

[1] Feller, W., *An Introduction to Probability Theory and Its Applications*, Vol. 2, John Wiley & Sons, 2008.

[2] Ibid..

[3] Klaus, K., *Probability Theory*, Addison-Wesley Publishing Company, 1965.

【定义 2.14】① 如果 $\forall x \in R$ 有：
$$F(x) = P_r\{-\infty \leq \xi \leq x\} = P_r\{\omega \in \Omega \mid \xi(w \leq x)\}$$
则 $F(x)$ 可称为随机变量 ξ 取值小于等于 x 的分布函数。

三 多目标规划理论

多目标规划问题的各个子目标有时并不协调，甚至是相互冲突的，而且多目标规划问题的求解不能不顾及其他目标而只追求一个目标的最优化。一个目标的改善可能会导致另一个或多个目标的降低，也就是说，所有目标都同时达到最优解的情况是不存在的。所以，多目标规划的目的是使用合理的求解方法实现各子目标之间的协调和折中，使得总体上各子目标都尽可能达到最优化。

多目标规划的数学形式可以描述为：
$$miny = f(x) = \{f(x_1), f(x_2), \cdots, f(x_m)\}$$
$$s.t.\ g(x) = \{x \mid g_i(x) \leq 0, i = 1, 2, \cdots, p\}$$
$$x = (x_1, x_2, \cdots, x_n) \in X, y = (y_1, y_2, \cdots, y_n) \in Y$$

其中，x 为决策向量，X 为决策向量组成的决策空间，y 为目标向量，Y 为目标向量组成的目标空间。$g_i(x) \leq 0$ 表示第 i 个约束。

（一）基本概念

最近几十年来，多目标规划的研究越来越受到人们的重视，并且得到了广泛的应用。在现实生活中，例如在经济、管理和工程等领域，一个方案好坏的衡量需要用多个指标来判断，与单目标优化问题不同的是多目标优化问题的解并非唯一，而是一组最优解集。从而引出了在多目标规划理论中最重要的一个基本概念，就是 Pareto 解集。Pareto 解集的概念是由经济学家 Vilfredo Pareto 首次提出，即一个解在某个目标上是最好的，但在其他目标上可能是较差的，但是 Pareto 最优解集内部的

---

① Durrett, R., *Probability: Theory and Examples*, Cambridge University Press, 2010.

元素之间是不可比较的①。

【定义 2.15】(非劣解)② 有多目标规划问题的可行域表示为 X，如果 $x \in X$，且不存在另一个可行点 x'，有 $x' \in X$ 满足 $f_i(x) \leqslant f_i(x')$，$i = 1,\cdots,m$，其中至少有一个严格不等式成立，则称 x 为该多目标规划中的一个非劣解。

【定义 2.16】(Pareto 解集)③ Pareto 解集为所有非劣解的集合。

如何判定 Pareto 解集的优劣是理论研究和实际应用中的重要问题。一般来说，理想的 Pareto 解集应满足三个条件：(1) 通过求解方法得到的 Pareto 解集应尽可能地与理论上的 Pareto 解集接近；(2) Pareto 解集的分布应尽可能均匀；(3) Pareto 解集的扩展性应该尽可能好。进一步地，Zitzler 等提出了评价 Pareto 解集在上述条件中的表现的 3 种指标④。

1. 平均距离指标

$$M_1 = \frac{1}{|N|} \sum_{a' \in X'} \min\{\|a' - \bar{a}\|; \bar{A} \in \bar{Y}\}$$

其中，X' 为求得的 Pareto 解集，N 是该解集中的非劣解个数，$\bar{Y}$ 是理论 Pareto 解集。用 M_1 值的大小来评判求得的 Pareto 解集与理论 Pareto 解集的趋紧程度，M_1 值越小，Pareto 解集就越趋近理论 Pareto 解集。

2. 分布指标

$$M_2 = \frac{1}{|N-1|} \sum_{a' \in X'} |\{b' \in X'; \|a' - b'\| < \sigma\}|$$

其中，σ 是一个给定的临近参数，用 M_2 值的大小来评判分布的均匀度，M_2 值越小，说明 Pareto 解集分布越满意。

---

① 王小平、曹立明：《遗传算法——理论、应用与软件实现》，西安交通大学出版社 2002 年版。
② Gaspar-Cunha, A., Covas, J. A., "Robustness in Multi-objective Optimization Using Evolutionary Algorithms", *Computational Optimization and Applications*, 39 (1), 2008: 75-96.
③ Ibid..
④ Zitzler, E., Deb, K., & Thiele, L., "Comparison of Multiobjective Evolutionary Algorithms: Empirical Results", *Evolutionary Computation*, 8 (2), 2000: 173-195.

3. 扩展性指标

$$M_3 = \sqrt{\sum_{i=1}^{m} \max\{||a'-b'||; a',b' \in X'\}}$$

若 M_3 越大，则求得的 Pareto 解集的扩展性就越好。

（二）求解方法

根据多目标规划问题的优化和决策顺序，多目标优化方法被 David 等归纳成了三类，即先验优先权、交互式以及后验优先权方法[1]。其中，先验优先权方法指的是事先制定各个目标的优先权重，将多目标规划转化为单目标规划，进而求得该单目标的最优解，从而确定各目标值。在交互式方法中，优先权的设置是与非劣解的搜索过程交替进行的，可以认为是后验优先权方法和先验优先权方法的结合。而后验优先权方法是指先找出多目标规划的所有非劣解，再根据决策者的偏好选取相应的决策。

根据上述分类方法，Bäck 等总结出了以下相对应的三种多目标处理方法[2]。

1. 聚合法

聚合法就是利用优先权的方法把多个目标转为单目标规划再进行求解，包括字典序法、目标向量法、分层序列法和 ε 约束法等[3]。聚合法由于解决多目标优化非常简捷方便，因此在实践研究中得到了最广泛的应用。然而，聚合法实际上忽略了多目标的本质，而且在转化过程中加入了主观的权重，可见主观臆断对结果的影响比较大，而当决策者对问题认识不清或经验不足时，会导致权重赋值不合理，难以得到满意的结果。

2. 准则选择法

准则选择法不是直接对多目标进行相关赋值处理，而是结合具体的

---

[1] David A., Van Veldhuizen, Gary B. Lamont, *Evolutionary Computation and Convergence to a Pareto Front*, Stanford University California, 1999, 221-228.

[2] Bäck, Thomas, David B. Fogel, and Zbigniew Michalewicz, *Handbook of Evolutionary Computation*, CRC Press, 1997.

[3] 安伟刚：《多目标优化方法研究及其工程应用》，博士学位论文，西北工业大学，2005 年。

求解算法,以选取的准则进行进化操作。经研究发现,这种方法实际上是将算法中的适应值进行线性求和。聚合法的权重由决策者主观赋值,而准则选择法中的权重是由算法中当前的种群决定,由此可见这种方法客观上降低了主观臆断对结果的影响,但是这种方法难以处理非凸集问题[1]。

3. Pareto 集方法

基于提出的 Pareto 解集概念,Pareto 集方法的基本思想是在进化算法中将多目标值映射到一种基于秩的适应度函数中。因此,Pareto 集方法与前两种方法相比更加贴近多目标的本质,更容易得到客观的解集。在目前的研究中,已经有很多算法被嵌入 Pareto 集方法来处理多目标算法,例如最常见的就是多目标遗传算法,多目标粒子群算法等。

四 可持续供应链

近年来,随着各界对环境保护、社会责任和经济效益的广泛关注,可持续供应链的概念引起了学者和实践者极大的兴趣。同时,由于来自众多利益相关者的巨大压力,尤其是来自顾客、政府和非政府组织的压力及越来越激烈的竞争,可持续发展已经成为当今企业发展的重要任务。随着全球化的发展,负面事件将会对企业的发展造成越来越大的影响,尤其是生态环境方面和社会责任方面的事件更是如此。传统的研究主要关注的是经济绩效,忽略了环境和社会的影响。因此,对综合考虑经济效益、环境保护和社会责任的可持续供应链管理的研究就显得尤为重要[2]。

在过去几十年,决策者越来越关注可持续性。而可持续发展定义为"既能满足当代人的需要,又不对后代人满足其需要的能力构成危害的

---

[1] Schaffer, J. David. "Multiple Objective Optimization with Vector Evaluated Genetic algorithms", *Proceedings of the First International Conference on Genetic Algorithms and Their Applications*, Lawrence Erlbaum Associate Inc., Publishers, 1985.

[2] Seuring, S., Müller, M., "From a Literature Review to a Conceptual Framework for Sustainable Supply Chain Management", *Journal of Cleaner Production*, 16 (15), 2008: 1699 – 1710.

发展"①。考虑到这个定义的模糊性，很多不同的解释被用来描述可持续性。尽管对可持续性有很多不同的理解，但是在商业领域，大家普遍接受的概念是 Elkington 提出的三重底线（triple bottom line，TBL）理论，即将经济、环境和社会维度综合考虑②。这个概念从早期主要关注局部环境优化转移到综合全面考虑供应链的三个维度，这对供应链发展起着重要的作用，并引领供应链走向了一个新时期。

随着经济全球化的发展，越来越多的企业和组织对经济效益、环境保护和社会责任进行整体协调，实现组织的可持续性目标。Cooper 等将供应链管理（SCM）定义为从物料采购到终端客户产品交付的过程中对物流、资金流和信息流的管理③。Linton 等将可持续性和供应链联系起来，认为可持续性必须整合超越供应链管理核心的问题和流程④。Seuring 和 Müller 将可持续供应链管理定义为物质、信息和资本流动的管理，以及供应链各公司之间的合作，同时从经济、环境和社会三个方面来考虑客户和利益相关者的要求。可持续供应链中的成员需要实现环境和社会标准以保持在供应链中，同时通过满足客户预期需求来维持竞争力⑤。Carter 和 Rogers 将可持续供应链管理定义为实现组织的社会、环境和经济目标并协调系统关键的业务流程，以提高公司的长期经济绩效⑥。由此可见，可持续供应链管理是通过对供应链运营、资源、信息和资金的管理，最大限度地提高供应链的盈利能力，同时最大限度地减

---

① Brundtland, G. H., Khalid, M., Agnelli, S., Al-Athel, S. Chidzero, B., *Our Common Future*, New York, 1987: 8.

② Elkington, J., "Parterships from Cannibals with Forks: The Triple Bottom Line of 21st Century Business", *Environmental Quality Management*, 8 (1), 1998: 37 – 51.

③ Cooper, M. C., Lambert, D. M., & Pagh, J. D., "Supply Chain Management: More than a new Name for Logistics", *The International Journal of Logistics Management*, 8 (1), 1997: 1 – 14.

④ Linton, J. D., Klassen, R., Jayaraman, V., "Sustainable Supply Chains: An introduction", *Journal of Operations Management*, 25 (6), 2007: 1075 – 1082.

⑤ Seuring, S., Müller, M., "From a Literature Review to a Conceptual Framework for Sustainable Supply Chain Management", *Journal of Cleaner Production*, 16 (15), 2008: 1699 – 1710.

⑥ Carter, C. R., Rogers, D. S., "A Framework of Sustainable Supply Chain Management Toward New Theory", *International Journal of Physical Distribution & Logistics Management*, 38 (5), 2008: 360 – 387.

少环境影响,并使社会福利最大化。基于三重底线的可持续供应链管理表明,在社会、环境和经济绩效的交叉点,组织参与的活动不仅对自然环境和社会有积极影响,而且会给企业带来长期的经济效益和竞争优势[1](见图2.4)。

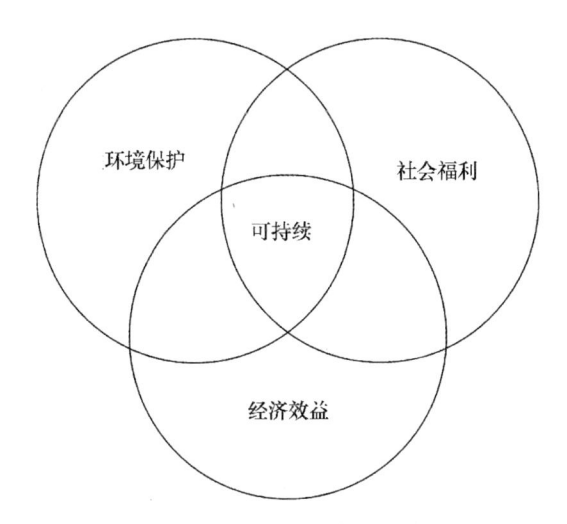

图2.4 基于三重底线的可持续供应链

---

[1] Elkington, J., "Partnerships from Cannibals with Forks: The Triple Bottom Line of 21st-Century Business", *Environmental Quality Management*, 8 (1), 1998: 37–51; Carter, C. R., Rogers, D. S., "A Framework of Sustainable Supply Chain Management: Moving Toward New Theory", *International Journal of Physical Distribution & Logistics Management*, 38 (5), 2008: 360–387.

第三章　白酒可持续供应链网络设计模型及应用

近年来，可持续供应链网络设计（Sustainable Supply Chain Network Design，SSCND）引起了学术界和企业界的广泛关注[1]。企业范围的优化和可持续发展为未来供应链设计研究提供了明确的机会[2]。可持续的供应链网络设计试图确定最佳的供应链配置，使组织能够最大化其长期的经济利益、社会福利和环境绩效，它包括战略、战术和运营三个层次的决策[3]。供应链网络设计通常涉及关于设施的数量、位置和容量，配送中心，市场

---

[1] Bairamzadeh, S., Pishvaee, M. S., & Saidi-Mehrabad, M., "Multiobjective Robust Possibilistic Programming Approach to Sustainable Bioethanol Supply Chain Design under Multiple uncertainties", *Industrial & Engineering Chemistry Research*, 55 (1), 2015: 237 – 256; Zaimes, G., Vora, N., Chopra, S., Landis, A., & Khanna, V., "Design of Sustainable Biofuel Processes and Supply Chains: Challenges and Opportunities", *Processes*, 3 (3), 2015: 634 – 663; Corsano, G., Vecchietti, A. R., & Montagna, J. M., "Optimal Design for Sustainable Bioethanol Supply Chain Considering Detailed Plant Performance Model", *Computers & Chemical Engineering*, 35 (8), 2011: 1384 – 1398.

[2] Garcia, D. J., & You, F., "Supply Chain Design and Optimization: Challenges and Opportunities", *Computers & Chemical Engineering*, 81, 2015: 153 – 170.

[3] Eskandarpour, M., Dejax, P., Miemczyk, J., & Péton, O., "Sustainable Supply Chain Network Design: An Optimization-oriented Review", *Omega*, 54, 2015: 11 – 32; Chaabane, A., Ramudhin, A., & Paquet, M., "Design of Sustainable Supply Chains under the Emission Trading Scheme", *International Journal of Production Economics*, 135 (1), 2012: 37 – 49; Govindan, K., Jafarian, A., & Nourbakhsh, V., "Bi-objective Integrating Sustainable Order Allocation and Sustainable Supply Chain Network Strategic Design with Stochastic Demand Using a Novel Robust Hybrid Multi-objective Metaheuristic", *Computers & Operations Research*, 62, 2015: 112 – 130.

需求，供应商选择等决策[1]。来自不同行业的企业越来越重视这种管理产品从原产地到消费地的流动的决策[2]。供应链的有效设计对于研究学者来说即使单从经济绩效（如总成本）考虑都是一项具有挑战性的技术任务，更何况加入了环境和社会等多个维度的可持续性要求，更是增加了建模和优化的难度[3]。可持续挑战和全球性问题，如气候变化、社会发展需要同时考虑多指标、多目标、多衡量度、多方参与的问题，并优化供应链网络[4]。为了使企业发展同时达到经济、环境和社会层面的可持续性，诸如采购、生产、运输、销售等所有相关的活动都必须在供应链优化模型中进行逻辑有效的组织[5]。据统计，通过降低包装费用和优化了上亿公里的卡车配送路线，沃尔玛的碳排放量下降了，同时节省了2亿美元的成本；通过投资员工健康计划，强生公司节省了2.5亿美元的医疗费用[6]。优化设计对于企业供应链来说具有重要的经济效益、环境效益和社会效益。

一 问题描述

供应链设计和规划涉及主要的商业和工业活动，比如材料获得、制造、包装、运输和回收，如果不能适当管理，所有这些活动都可能造成

---

[1] Varsei, M., & Polyakovskiy, S., "Sustainable Supply Chain Network Design: A Case of the Wine Industry in Australia, *Omega*, 66, 2017: 236 – 247; Eskandarpour, M., Dejax, P., Miemczyk, J., & Péton, O., "Sustainable Supply Chain Network Design: An Optimization-oriented Review", *Omega*, 54, 2015: 11 – 32.

[2] Sunil, C., & Peter, M., "Supply Chain Management: Strategy, Planning and Operation", *Pearson Education International*, 2010, 34（2）: 221 – 222.

[3] Tang, C. S., & Zhou, S., "Research Advances in Environmentally and Socially Sustainable Operations", *European Journal of Operational Research*, 223（3）, 2012: 585 – 594; Garcia, D. J., & You, F., "Supply Chain Design and Optimization: Challenges and Opportunities", *Computers & Chemical Engineering*, 81, 2015: 153 – 170.

[4] Garcia, D. J., & You, F., "Supply Chain Design and Optimization: Challenges and Opportunities", *Computers & Chemical Engineering*, 81, 2015: 153 – 170.

[5] Corsano, G., Vecchietti, A. R., & Montagna, J. M., "Optimal Design for Sustainable Bioethanol Supply Chain Considering Detailed Plant Performance Model", *Computers & Chemical Engineering*, 35（8）, 2011: 1384 – 1398.

[6] Kramer, M. R., & Porter, M., "Creating Shared Value", *Harvard Business Review*, 89（1/2）, 2011: 62 – 77.

负面的环境和社会影响①。传统上，网络设计优化模型主要考虑供应链的经济层面。近年来，人们对环境和社会问题越来越关注②。然而，大多数研究主要涉及一个或两个维度，很少有研究同时考虑到所有三个层面③。社会可持续性是最不明确的可持续性的组成部分，也被称为"缺失支柱"。与经济和环境可持续性相比，它受到的关注仍然较小④；然而，近年来，如何解决社会支柱并将其整合到可持续发展框架中已经取得了重大进展⑤。因此，迫切需要综合和平衡经济目标、环境目标和社会目标的决策研究。下面分别陈述可持续供应链网络设计中的网络维度和关键问题。

（一）网络维度

在过去几十年中，工业操作对最小化环境影响的过程设计和开发给予了相当多的关注，环保的产品设计涉及从概念设计到最终产品交付和处置的环境保护意识。d'Amore 和 Bezzo 在混合整数线性规划（MILP）中同时考虑了经济目标和环境目标。其中经济指标用净现值表示，环境指标用的温室气体排放量来表示⑥。Guillén-Gosálbez 和 Grossmann 论述了考虑经济和环境问题的可持续化学过程的最佳设计和规划。他们用

---

① Fahimnia, B., Reisi, M., Paksoy, T., & Özceylan, E., "The Implications of Carbon Pricing in Australia: An Industrial Logistics Planning Case Study", *Transportation Research Part D: Transport and Environment*, 18, 2013: 78 - 85.

② Chaabane, A., Ramudhin, A., & Paquet, M., "Design of Sustainable Supply Chains under the Emission Trading Scheme", *International Journal of Production Economics*, 135 (1), 2012: 37 - 49.

③ Seuring, S., "A Review of Modeling Approaches for Sustainable Supply Chain Management", *Decision Support Systems*, 54 (4), 2013: 1513 - 1520.

④ Carter, C. R., & Liane Easton, P., "Sustainable Supply Chain Management: Evolution and Future Directions", *International Journal of Physical Distribution & Logistics Management*, 41 (1), 2011: 46 - 62.

⑤ Zore, Ž., Čuček, L., & Kravanja, Z., "Syntheses of Sustainable Supply Networks with a New Composite Criterion—Sustainability Profit", *Computers & Chemical Engineering*, 102, 2017: 139 - 155.

⑥ D'Amore, F., & Bezzo, F., "Strategic Optimisation of Biomass—Based Energy Supply Chains for Sustainable Mobility", *Computers & Chemical Engineering*, 87, 2016: 68 - 81.

Eco-indicator 99 评估环境影响，运用的是生命周期评估（LCA）方法[1]。他们用双准则随机混合整数非线性规划（MINIP）方法，考虑了净现值最大化和给定概率水平下的环境影响最小化模型[2]。Zhang 等提出了优化可持续供应链的多目标优化框架。三个可持续性目标是总成本、温室气体排放量和交货时间，通过案例分析得出，通常仅通过相对较小的成本增加就可以实现温室气体排放量或交货时间的显著减少[3]。Govindan 等提出了一个双目标模型：最小化成本和环境影响，并将模型应用于汽车工业[4]。Chaabane 等制定了一个框架，以评估在铝行业各种成本和运营策略下的经济和环境目标（GHG 排放）之间的权衡。该模型表明，高效的碳管理战略将帮助决策者以成本效益的方式实现可持续发展目标[5]。Neto 等用 DEA 和 MOP - 多目标计划方法为可持续物流网络的设计和评价制定了一个框架，认为利润和环境影响是平衡的，并应用于欧洲纸浆和造纸工业来验证框架的有效性[6]。

除了环境问题，供应链还面临越来越大的绩效压力和商业声誉风险。社会问题不仅会威胁到公司的品牌形象，而且会影响整个供应链的

---

[1] Guillén-Gosálbez, G., & Grossmann, I., "A Global Optimization Strategy for the Environmentally Conscious Design of Chemical Supply Chains under Uncertainty in the Damage Assessment Model", *Computers & Chemical Engineering*, 34（1），2010：42 – 58.

[2] Guillén-Gosálbez, G., & Grossmann, I. E., "Optimal Design and Planning of Sustainable Chemical Supply Chains under Uncertainty", *AIChE Journal*, 55（1），2009：99 – 121.

[3] Zhang, Q., Shah, N., Wassick, J., Helling, R., & Van Egerschot, P., "Sustainable Supply Chain Optimisation: An Industrial Case Study", *Computers & Industrial Engineering*, 74，2014：68 – 83.

[4] Govindan, K., Jafarian, A., & Nourbakhsh, V., "Bi-Objective Integrating Sustainable Order Allocation and Sustainable Supply Chain Network Strategic Design with Stochastic Demand Using a Novel Robust Hybrid Multi-objective Metaheuristic", *Computers & Operations Research*, 62，2015：112 – 130.

[5] Chaabane, A., Ramudhin, A., & Paquet, M., "Design of Sustainable Supply Chains under the Emission Trading Scheme", *International Journal of Production Economics*, 135（1），2012：37 – 49.

[6] Neto, J. Q. F., Bloemhof-Ruwaard, J. M., van Nunen, J. A., & van Heck, E., "Designing and Evaluating Sustainable Logistics Networks", *International Journal of Production Economics*, 111（2），2008：195 – 208.

经济可行性[1]。经常听到危及大型跨国公司声誉的报道,如 Nike、Walmart、GAP、Adidas 或 C&A 近年来由于运营期间发生的问题而被指责[2]。不健康的工作条件或环境污染(局部)是经常被提及的问题。Pishvaee 等解决了在不确定条件下基于社会责任的供应链网络设计的问题,开发了一个双目标数学规划模型(robust possibilistic programming),其目标函数是最小化总成本和最大化供应链社会责任,具体指标包括创造就业机会的数量,最大限度地提高就业机会,最大限度地减少生产的废弃物总量、工作损失造成的损失天数和潜在危险产品的数量[3]。Zore 等研究的由经济、环境和社会指标组成的多属性评价都用货币形式表示,因此可以合并,将多目标优化问题转化为单目标[4]。Seay 认为生产过程对社会、环境和经济的影响已经成为公众、公司和监管机构的一个重要关注点,并运用这样的思想解决了生物质供应链的最优设计问题[5]。Miret 等也重点研究了可持续发展维度的多目标优化问题,涉及经济、环境和社会三个维度[6]。外部压力促使公司采用可持续的供应链网络设计战略[7]。组织的可持续发展举措及其企业战略必须密切相关。客户

---

[1] Seuring, S., Müller, M., "From a Literature Review to a Conceptual Framework for Sustainable Supply Chain Management", *Journal of Cleaner Production*, 16 (15), 2008: 1699 – 1710; Schaltegger, S., Burritt, R., Varsei, M., Soosay, C., Fahimnia, B., & Sarkis, J., "Framing Sustainability Performance of Supply Chains with Multidimensional Indicators", *Supply Chain Management:: An International Journal*, 19 (3), 2014: 242 – 257.

[2] Frost, S., & Burnett, M., "Case Study: The Apple iPod in China", *Corporate Social Responsibility and Environmental Management*, 14 (2), 2007: 103 – 113.

[3] Pishvaee, M. S., Razmi, J., & Torabi, S. A., "Robust Possibilistic Programming for Socially Responsible Supply Chain Network Design: A New Approach", *Fuzzy Sets and Systems*, 206, 2012: 1 – 20.

[4] Zore, Ž., Čuček, L., & Kravanja, Z., "Syntheses of Sustainable Supply Networks with a New Composite Criterion—Sustainability Profit", *Computers & Chemical Engineering*, 102, 2017: 139 – 155.

[5] Seay, J. R., "Education for Sustainability: Developing a Taxonomy of the Key Principles for Sustainable Process and Product Design", *Computers & Chemical Engineering*, 81, 2015: 147 – 152.

[6] Miret, C., Chazara, P., Montastruc, L., Negny, S., & Domenech, S., "Design of Bioethanol Green Supply Chain: Comparison between First and Second Generation Biomass Concerning Economic, Environmental and Social Criteria", *Computers & Chemical Engineering*, 85, 2016: 16 – 35.

[7] Ageron, B., Gunasekaran, A., & Spalanzani, A., "Sustainable Supply Management: An Empirical Study", *International Journal of Production Economics*, 140 (1), 2012: 168 – 182.

有可能对那些不了解其影响的公司产生消极的态度。因此与可持续性有关的声誉问题已成为企业关注的重点。公司需要将环境和社会绩效指标纳入决策，以减轻风险并获得经济利益[1]。尽管有这样的需求，也只有少数学者努力将供应链网络设计的社会层面纳入模型中，考虑到了所有三个维度[2]。Mota 等整合了可持续发展的三个维度，重点讨论了可持续性的经济支柱[3]。Schaltegger 等提出了一个识别和评估各种经济、环境和社会绩效指标的工具，并应用 AHP 方法来评价社会因素[4]。随后 Varsei 和 Polyakovskiy 提出了包括经济、环境和社会目标的可持续葡萄酒供应链网络设计的通用模型。模型从三个维度考虑，最大限度地减少整个供应链的固定成本和可变成本，最大限度地减少供应商、酿酒厂、装瓶厂、配送中心和需求点之间的运输活动所排放的温室气体总量，最大限度地提高供应链网络的社会可持续性，如就业或对地区 GDP 的影响[5]。Pérez-Fortes 等考虑了沿着预定的计划范围优化经济（最大 NPV）、环境影响（最小）和社会指标（最大值），并将其应用于生物供应链[6]。You 等阐述了在经济、环境和社会目标下纤维素乙醇供应链的最优设计和规划。经济目标由年度成本总额衡量，环境目标由生命周期温室气体排放

---

[1] Schaltegger, S., Burritt, R., Varsei, M., Soosay, C., Fahimnia, B., & Sarkis, J., "Framing Sustainability Performance of Supply Chains with Multidimensional Indicators", *Supply Chain Management: An International Journal*, 19 (3), 2014: 242–257.

[2] Eskandarpour, M., Dejax, P., Miemczyk, J., & Péton, O., "Sustainable Supply Chain Network Design: An Optimization-oriented Review", *Omega*, 54, 2015: 11–32.

[3] Mota, B., Gomes, M. I., Carvalho, A., & Barbosa-Povoa, A. P., "Towards Supply Chain Sustainability: Economic, Environmental and Social Design and Planning", *Journal of Cleaner Production*, 105, 2015: 14–27.

[4] Schaltegger, S., Burritt, R., Varsei, M., Soosay, C., Fahimnia, B., & Sarkis, J., "Framing Sustainability Performance of Supply Chains with Multidimensional Indicators", *Supply Chain Management: An International Journal*, 19 (3), 2014: 242–257.

[5] Varsei, M., & Polyakovskiy, S., "Sustainable Supply Chain Network Design: A Case of the Wine Industry in Australia", *Omega*, 66, 2017: 236–247.

[6] Pérez-Fortes, M., Laínez-Aguirre, J. M., Arranz-Piera, P., Velo, E., & Puigjaner, L., "Design of Regional and Sustainable Bio-based Networks for Electricity Generation Using a Multi-Objective MILP Approach", *Energy*, 44 (1), 2012: 79–95.

量衡量,社会目标由累积的当地就业数量衡量[1]。

Xu 等以泸州老窖集团责任有限公司的供应链为例设计了一种随机模糊多目标混合整数非线性规划模型,以最小化供应链总成本和最大化顾客服务为目标,用基于生成树的遗传树算法进行求解,数值实验结果验证了该方法的有效性[2]。苗利等介绍了传统生物接触氧化法处理大型白酒企业废水的有关工程设计和运行情况[3]。在此分析的白酒企业供应链包括四个主要环节:原材料供应商、生产商、配送中心和零售商(如专卖店、超市和餐饮业),如图 3.1 所示。从图中看出白酒物流模式更趋向于销售物流,物流是由酒厂向经销商配送产品。

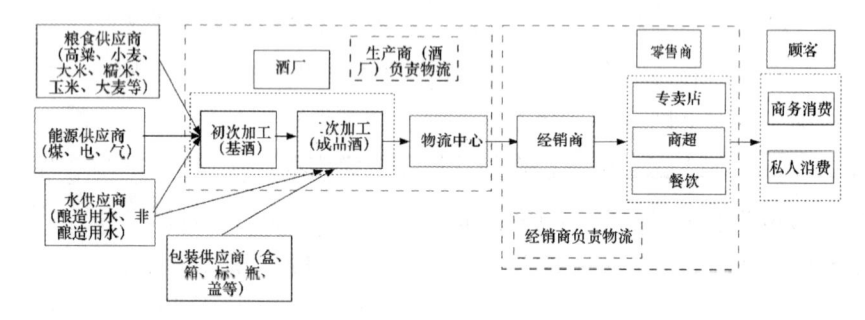

图 3.1　中国白酒供应链

(二) 关键问题

白酒企业的供应链是从三重底线角度研究可持续性的沃土。2015年,中国白酒行业生产总量为 131.28 亿升,同比增长 4.43%。据统计,中国是世界上生产和消费烈性酒最多的国家。中国的白酒消费处于世界领先水平,约占全球总消费量的1/3。2015 年,中国白酒行业的总经济价值为 5559 亿元,比 2014 年的 5283 亿元增长 5.22%。该行业涉

---

[1] You, F., Tao, L., Graziano, D.J., & Snyder, S.W., "Optimal Design of Sustainable Cellulosic Biofuel Supply Chains: Multiobjective Optimization Coupled with Life Cycle Assessment and Input-output Analysis", *AIChE Journal*, 58 (4), 2012: 1157–1180.

[2] Xu, J., Liu, Q., & Wang, R., "A Class of Multi-objective Supply Chain Networks Optimal Model under Random Fuzzy Environment and Its Application to the Industry of Chinese Liquor", *Information Sciences*, 178 (8), 2008: 2022–2043.

[3] 苗利、吴少杰、寇刘秀:《大型白酒企业废水处理工程的设计与运行》,《环境科学与技术》2004 年第 2 期。

及1263家规模以上白酒企业和约40.2万名工作人员。白酒行业的物流费用占其总费用的比例约为20%。因此，白酒供应链对中国经济和社会的贡献是显著的。此外，白酒生产与环境问题密切相关，包括从白酒生产和分配中排放的大量温室气体。白酒企业生产过程会产生被称为酒糟的非蒸馏剩余物。由于污染问题，酒糟处理是蒸馏酒生产过程中最重要和最具挑战性的问题之一。通常，丢弃的酒糟会造成相当大的环境问题。酒糟具有快速降解的特性，因此，它不适合存储[①]。酒糟可以再利用为动物的饲料、土地肥料和沼气生产等。由于白酒的大规模生产、配送以及相关的经济、环境和社会影响，考虑到其特定的生产过程，分析和优化白酒供应链设计至关重要。应用运营研究和管理科学理论，在实践中，优化白酒企业供应链网络可能会为白酒业务带来创新的商业模式。

应促进可持续供应链发展的需要，针对白酒行业可持续供应链中的网络设计优化管理进行深入的研究。经济、环境和社会是可持续供应链考虑的三个维度。目前，尽管有大量有重要价值的针对网络设计的研究，但是大都从经济角度来考虑，很少从可持续供应链的三个维度，即经济、环境、社会去优化。关于白酒行业的研究也比较多，但是将白酒放在供应链的高度进行研究的文献依然较少，而关于白酒供应链可持续性方面的研究就更少了。

关于白酒可持续供应链的研究存在以下几个方面的问题。（1）有很多文献是关于白酒行业的研究，关于白酒供应链研究的文献存在不全面、不足的问题。现有的研究可以分为以下几类：一是蒸馏酒酿造技术研究；二是专门针对某一家或某一类白酒的研究；三是对白酒行业的营销模式、品牌、行业现状和发展趋势的研究。（2）现有文献大多数集中于研究一个维度——经济维度，也有一部分文献关注环境问题或同时考虑两个维度（如环境、经济等），很少有文献同时考虑可持续性的三

---

① Corsano, G., Vecchietti, A. R., & Montagna, J. M., "Optimal Design for Sustainable Bioethanol Supply Chain Considering Detailed Plant Performance Model", *Computers & Chemical Engineering*, 35 (8), 2011: 1384-1398.

个维度，即经济、环境和社会层面，因此同时考虑三个维度的白酒可持续供应链的研究还很不成熟。（3）现有研究集中关注配送过程中的碳排放问题，很少考虑生产过程中的碳排放问题；然而，白酒的生产过程比较特殊，生产过程中的碳排放对环境的影响较大，需要综合考虑。（4）社会可持续性是可持续性中最不明确的组成部分，被称为"缺失支柱"，与经济和环境可持续性相比，它受到的关注仍然较小；供应链网络设计中的社会维度如何度量，现有研究还不完善。

迄今为止，在白酒领域很少有研究同时考虑经济、环境和社会三个可持续性维度[①]。对白酒企业而言，关于可持续性和供应链管理之间的联系的研究仍处于起步阶段，特别是在供应链建模和优化方面。就我们所知，由于白酒企业供应链有其独特的具体操作流程，至今还没有将经济、环境和社会三个维度的可持续性与白酒供应链网络设计联系起来的研究文献。提出一个白酒企业的供应链网络设计模型，同时包含经济、环境和社会三个维度，并在寻找平衡决策中分析可能的情景，具有重要的理论和实践意义。

二 模型构建

白酒供应链包括供应商、生产商、配送中心和需求点。原材料被购买并运输到每个酿酒厂，在这里将它们转换成产品。酿酒厂的生产过程可以由不同阶段组成。一组供应商 S 可以向一组白酒厂 D 供应原料。白酒产品可以通过配送中心 C 分配。最终产品从配送中心运输到不同的需求点 P，其中 N 表示整个供应链。优化白酒企业供应链网络设计需考虑多个可持续发展目标。该模型旨在为白酒供应链的设计提供一个综合的

[①] Seuring, S., Müller, M., "From a Literature Review to a Conceptual Framework for Sustainable Supply Chain Management", *Journal of Cleaner Production*, 16 (15), 2008: 1699 – 1710; Seuring, S., "A Review of Modeling Approaches for Sustainable Supply Chain Management", *Decision Support Systems*, 54 (4), 2013: 1513 – 1520; Eskandarpour, M., Dejax, P., Miemczyk, J., & Péton, O., "Sustainable Supply Chain Network Design: An Optimization-oriented Review", *Omega*, 54, 2015: 11 – 32.

决策支持系统，整合经济、环境和社会因素，最大限度地减少供应链总成本和温室气体排放量，并最大限度地提高供应链网络的社会影响。为了构建白酒行业可持续供应链中网络设计的多目标决策优化问题，首先给出了模型构建所需的数学符号，其次给出经济目标、环境目标、社会目标、约束条件，最后构建了白酒供应链网络设计整体的优化决策模型。

（一）模型符号

经济目标是最小化供应链固定成本和可变成本的总和，包括采购、生产、运输、储存、建立设施的资本投资、废弃物处理、副产品收益等。环境目标是最小化白酒企业生产、供应链节点企业和生产过程之间的运输活动所排放的温室气体总量。社会目标是最大化供应链网络的社会可持续性（如就业、收入或区域人均 GDP 等）。为了配送产品，考虑几种运输模式，并且 T 表示公路、铁路和水路运输的一组模式。多式联运在许多情况下是具有成本效益的。下面介绍作为多目标 MIP 的可持续供应链网络设计的通用模型所需要的符号。建议模型的问题集有 S 供应商集合 $s \in S$，D 白酒厂集合 $d \in D$，C 分销中心集合 $c \in C$，P 需求点集合 $p \in P$，N 整个供应链集合 $n \in N$，T 运输模式集合 $t \in T$。

参数包括：c_λ^d 表示第 λ 个酒厂的建设成本；c_i 表示第 i 个配送中心的建设成本；c_d^m 表示从供应商 S 到酒厂 D 的原材料采购成本；y_d^m 表示从供应商 S 到酒厂 D 的原材料采购量；c_d^p 表示在酒厂 D 白酒的单位生产成本；y_d^p 表示在酒厂 D 白酒的生产量；$c_{\theta t}^{sd}$ 表示从 S 到 D 以 T 种模式运输的运输费用单位成本；$y_{\theta t}^{sd}$ 表示从 S 到 D 以 T 种模式运输的白酒数量；$c_{\theta t}^{dc}$ 表示从 D 到 C 以 T 种模式运输的运输费用单位成本；$y_{\theta t}^{dc}$ 表示从 D 到 C 以 T 种模式运输的白酒数量；$c_{\theta t}^{cp}$ 表示从 C 到 P 以 T 种模式运输的运输费用单位成本；$y_{\theta t}^{cp}$ 表示从 C 到 P 以 T 种模式运输的白酒数量；c_i^s 表示在配送点 C 的单位平均仓储成本；y_i^s 表示在配送点 C 的白酒仓储量；c_d^w 表示在酒厂 D 的单位平均废弃物处理成本；y_d^w 表示在酒厂 D

的废弃物总量；c_d^b 表示在酒厂 D 的单位副产品得益；y_d^b 表示在酒厂 D 的副产品量；e_p^d 表示酒厂 D 生产单位白酒产生的碳排放量；$e_{\theta t}^{sd}$ 表示从供应商 S 到酒厂 D 以运输模式 T 运输的单位原材料的碳排放量（CO_2 排放量）；$e_{\theta t}^{dc}$ 表示从酿酒厂 D 到配送中心 C 以运输模式 T 运输的单位产品的碳排放量；$e_{\theta t}^{cp}$ 表示从配送中心 C 到消费点 P 以运输模式 T 运输的单位产品的碳排放量；e_d^w 表示酿酒厂 D 产生的单位废弃物碳排放量；j_n 表示整个供应链创造的工作机会；φ_n 表示整个供应链创造的工作机会对应的影响权重；g_n 表示整个供应链对 GDP 的贡献；η_n 表示整个供应链 GDP 贡献对应的影响权重。

决策变量包括：u_λ^d 表示第 λ 个酒厂建 1，不建 0，$u_\lambda^d \in [0,1]$；x_i 表示第 i 个配送中心建 1，不建 0，$x_i \in [0,1]$。

（二）经济模型

经济目标是最小化经济成本。最小总成本＝总固定成本（酒厂和配送中心建设费用）＋总采购成本＋总制造成本＋总运输成本＋总存储成本＋总废弃物处理成本－总副产品得益。总固定成本包括网络中所有涉及设施的建筑物和设备的年度固定成本（TFC），在这里指酒厂和配送中心的建设费用。第二项表示由供应商供应到酿酒厂的材料的总购买成本。第三项计算酿酒厂的总制造成本。第四项是总运输成本。第五项是配送中心白酒的总存储成本。第六项是酿酒厂的总废弃物处理成本。第七项是总副产品（酒糟）的得益。

1. 总固定成本（TFC）

供应链网络中相关设施设备的年度固定成本总额包括酿酒厂的建设成本和配送中心的建设成本。

$$TFC = \sum_{d \in D} c_\lambda^d u_\lambda^d + \sum_{c \in C} c_i x_i \tag{3.1}$$

2. 原材料总采购成本（TMC）

原材料总采购成本表示从供应链 S 到酒厂 D 的总的采购成本。

$$TMC = \sum_{s \in S} \sum_{d \in D} c_d^m y_d^m \tag{3.2}$$

3. 白酒总制造成本（TPC）

$$TPC = \sum_{d \in D} c_d^p y_d^p \tag{3.3}$$

4. 总运输成本（TTC）

供应商总运输成本是从供应商 S 到酒厂 D，酒厂 D 到配送中心 C，从配送中心 C 到消费点 P 的成本之和。

$$TTC = \sum_{t \in T}(\sum_{s \in S}\sum_{d \in D} c_{\theta t}^{sd} y_{\theta t}^{sd} + \sum_{d \in D}\sum_{c \in C} c_{\theta t}^{dc} y_{\theta t}^{dc} + \sum_{c \in C}\sum_{p \in P} c_{\theta t}^{cp} y_{\theta t}^{cp}) \tag{3.4}$$

5. 总存储成本（TSC）

TSC 表示在配送中心 C 的总的仓储成本。

$$TSC = \sum_{c \in C} c_i^s y_i^s \tag{3.5}$$

6. 总废弃物处理成本（TWC）

白酒生产过程中的废弃物主要是指生产过程中产生的锅底水、废液等。

$$TWC = \sum_{d \in D} c_d^w y_d^w \tag{3.6}$$

7. 总副产品得益（TBC）

白酒企业生产过程产生称为酒糟的非蒸馏剩余物。酒糟可以再利用为动物的饲料、土地肥料和沼气生产等，可以通过销售获得收入。因此，这里总的副产品得益是指销售酒糟的收入。

$$TBC = \sum_{d \in D} c_d^b y_d^b \tag{3.7}$$

8. 供应链总成本（TC）

这里供应链总成本就是上述成本之和，即供应链总成本 = 总固定成本 + 总采购成本 + 总制造成本 + 总运输成本 + 总存储成本 + 总废弃物处理成本 – 总副产品得益，$TC = TFC + TMC + TPC + TTC + TSC + TWC - TBC$。

$$TC = (\sum_{d \in D} c_\lambda^d u_\lambda^d + \sum_{c \in C} c_i x_i) + \sum_{s \in S}\sum_{d \in D} c_d^m y_d^m + \sum_{d \in D} c_d^p y_d^p + \sum_{t \in T}(\sum_{s \in S}\sum_{d \in D} c_{\theta t}^{sd} y_{\theta t}^{sd} + \sum_{d \in D}\sum_{c \in C} c_{\theta t}^{dc} y_{\theta t}^{dc} + \sum_{c \in C}\sum_{p \in P} c_{\theta t}^{cp} y_{\theta t}^{cp}) + \sum_{c \in C} c_i^s y_i^s + \sum_{d \in D} c_d^w y_d^w - \sum_{d \in D} c_d^b y_d^b \tag{3.8}$$

(三) 环境模型

白酒可持续供应链中的环境目标是最小化白酒供应链运营所产生的年二氧化碳当量，即温室气体排放量（TE）。它计算整个供应链中所有运输活动产生的碳排放量，从供应商 S 到酿酒厂 D 和配送中心 C，然后到需求点 P。

1. 生产过程中的碳排放量（TPE）

白酒生产过程中需要消耗水电气等能源，这个过程中会产生一定的碳排放。

$$TPE = \sum_{d \in D} e_p^d y_p^d \quad (3.9)$$

2. 运输过程中的碳排放量（TTE）

产品在配送过程中需要消耗汽油、柴油等燃料，产生一定碳排放。运输过程包括三个阶段，采购原材料时从供应商 S 配送到酿酒厂 D，从酿酒厂 D 到配送中心 C，从配送中心 C 到消费点 P。

$$TTE = \sum_{t \in T} \left(\sum_{s \in S} \sum_{d \in D} e_{\theta t}^{sd} y_{\theta t}^{sd} + \sum_{d \in D} \sum_{c \in C} e_{\theta t}^{dc} y_{\theta t}^{dc} + \sum_{c \in C} \sum_{p \in P} e_{\theta t}^{cp} y_{\theta t}^{cp} \right) \quad (3.10)$$

3. 废弃物处理过程中的碳排放量（TWE）

$$TWE = \sum_{d \in D} e_d^w y_d^w \quad (3.11)$$

4. 总的碳排放量（TE）

白酒供应链产生的碳排放总量包括生产过程中的碳排放量、运输过程中的碳排放量和废弃物处理过程中的碳排放量。即碳排放量 = 生产过程中的碳排放量 + 运输过程中的碳排放量 + 废弃物处理过程中的碳排放量。

$$TE = \sum_{d \in D} e_p^d y_p^d + \sum_{t \in T} \left(\sum_{s \in S} \sum_{d \in D} e_{\theta t}^{sd} y_{\theta t}^{sd} + \sum_{d \in D} \sum_{c \in C} e_{\theta t}^{dc} y_{\theta t}^{dc} + \sum_{c \in C} \sum_{p \in P} e_{\theta t}^{cp} y_{\theta t}^{cp} \right) + \sum_{d \in D} e_d^w y_d^w$$

$$(3.12)$$

(四) 社会模型

社会影响评估指数有很多，在这里，白酒供应链的总体社会影响是供应链创造的工作机会和相应影响系数的乘积加上供应链的 GDP 乘以相应的影响系数。

$$SW = \sum_{n \in N}(j_n \varphi_n + g_n \eta_n) \quad (3.13)$$

（五）总体模型

总体目标是建立经济、环境和社会影响之间的权衡方案，这是一个多目标模型。模型考虑的是最小化总成本、最小化环境影响和最大化社会福利。因此，总体模型如下：

$$\min(TC, TE, -SW) \quad (3.14)$$

$$s.t. \begin{cases} y_d^p \leq P_\lambda \\ \sum_{d \in D} c_\lambda^d u_\lambda^d + \sum_{c \in C} c_i x_i \leq B \\ \sum_{c \in C} \sum_{p \in P} y_{\theta t}^{cp} \leq \sum_{d \in D} \sum_{c \in C} y_{\theta t}^{dc} \leq \sum_{d \in D} y_d^p \\ \sum_{c \in C} y_i^s \leq \sum_{c \in C} \sum_{d \in D} y_{\theta t}^{dc} \\ s \in S \\ d \in D \\ c \in C \\ p \in P \\ t \in T \\ q \in Q \\ u_\lambda^d \in [0,1], \lambda = 1,2,\cdots,h \\ x_i \in [0,1], i = 1,2,\cdots,n \end{cases} \quad (3.15)$$

1. 假设条件

提出的模型基于以下常见假设：客户的需求必须得到满足；生产能力能够满足市场需求；考虑单一类型的产品；每个需求点的需求量已知。

2. 约束条件

为了保证模型有可行解，模型必须有一定的逻辑约束。

（1）生产能力约束。每个酒厂都有自己的生产能力限制，白酒生产量不能超过其最大生产量，这里用 P_λ 表示第 λ 个酒厂生产白酒的最大量。

$$y_d^p \leq P_\lambda \tag{3.16}$$

（2）建设成本约束。企业对于修建固定设施的费用每年都有一个预算，不能超过其预算，这里用 B 表示年度预算最大值。

$$\sum_{d \in D} c_\lambda^d u_\lambda^d + \sum_{c \in C} c_i x_i \leq B \tag{3.17}$$

（3）产品配送量约束。每年的产品配送量小或等于其生产的产品量，二级配送量小或等于一级配送量。

$$\sum_{c \in C} \sum_{p \in P} y_{\theta t}^{cp} \leq \sum_{d \in D} \sum_{c \in C} y_{\theta t}^{dc} \leq \sum_{d \in D} y_d^p \tag{3.18}$$

（4）仓储约束。配送中心的仓储量要少或等于配送到仓储中心产品量。

$$\sum_{c \in C} y_i^s \leq \sum_{c \in C} \sum_{d \in D} y_{\theta t}^{dc} \tag{3.19}$$

三　案例分析

基于上面提到的通用模型，在此提出一个具体模型，用于优化主要核心公司的供应链网络设计。以四川地区一家白酒企业的供应链为例，命名为企业 A。它的市场份额和产量较大，是中国十大白酒企业之一。由于中国酒类生产和销售具有较强的区域性，在这种情况下，作为国家知名品牌的白酒企业 A，其主要销售地区是成都和重庆。

（一）现实背景

为了模拟案例企业的供应链，酿酒厂的位置在模型中固定在四川地区。生产优质白酒的最重要因素是拥有很好的窖池，良好的窖池需要适当的水分、土壤、气候、微生物和生态环境。案例中的白酒企业 A 位于四川省 B 市，当地非常适合生产酿造白酒。企业 A 是一家规模很大的白酒酿造厂。白酒物流具有自己独特的特点。从供应商到酒厂的物资运输是由供应商负责，而从酒厂到经销商的物流是由酒厂负责的。目前的分销网络由遍布全国的 12 个租赁仓库组成。这些租赁仓库分别位于成都、重庆、广州、长沙、上海、郑州、北京、厦门、济南、西安、南京和呼和浩特。考虑到白酒的价值较高，为满足消费者的需求，白酒厂现在的配送模式是用货车从公路配送白酒产品到这12个配送中心。由于企业面临越来越激烈的竞争，租金日渐高涨，物流配送成本居高不下，货运车辆碳排放量也比较高，对环境有一定的负面影响，为更好地控制供应链成本，减少环境影响、最大化社会影响力，企业A打算对配送模式进行多样化选择，因铁路安全可靠，成本较低，碳排放量也较低，水路成本低廉，碳排放量最低，企业A决定综合运用公路、铁路和水路运输。考虑到成本的高昂和租金的上涨，企业A打算在这12个城市中选择3个城市建设配送中心，从酒厂到这3个配送中心可以选用公路、铁路或水路运输。然后另外的9个城市作为配送点，用汽车直接配送，这样可以及时响应顾客的需求。为了实现这一目标，企业A决定将配送中心内部化。因为这家白酒企业追求可持续的形象，故当前物流网络的优化被定义为供应链战略决策，不仅应该考虑物流成本，而且应该分析环境和社会影响。这有助于我们分析现有网络与优化后的网络在经济、环境和社会目标方面的差距。企业A现在面临的问题是：(1) 选择哪3个城市作为配送中心，可以使供应链成本最小、环境影响最小，同时社会影响力最大；(2) 从酒厂到配送中心用什么运输模式可以实现经济、环境和社会的最优目标；(3) 每个配送中心的总体配送量是多少，这是不确定的；(4) 这3个配送中心如何满足其他9个配送点的配送量，做到成本最低、环境影响最小、社会福利最大；(5) 酒厂和3个配送中心、9个配送点的社会影响系数是多少。这些都需要通过模型算法进行求解。由于模型中涉及三种配送模式的选择、配送中心选择、二级配送点路径选择等多个0-1变量，因此选用了现在在大数据研究领域应用很广泛的R语言。R语言是用于统计分析和绘图的编程语言，它与著名的统计编程语言S有着密切的关系[①]。

碳排放（温室气体）是根据中国运输部门统计数据公布的排放因子计算的。这些因素如表3.1所示。

[①] 叶文春：《浅谈r语言在统计学中的应用》，《中共贵州省委党校学报》2008年第4期。

表 3.1　　　　　　　　　　　碳排放

运输模式	排放系数	类型
铁路	0.0165	机车
公路	0.0556	大卡车
水路	0.0133	集装箱船

为了衡量企业 A 供应链网络的社会影响，考虑了与配送中心位置相关的两个同等加权的社会类别：失业、地区人均国内生产总值（地区人均 GDP）。这些类别背后的逻辑是，从社会可持续性的角度来看，企业 A 将通过安排配送中心来改善其供应链的社会影响，即设置在失业率较高（即对就业的影响）和区域人均 GDP 较低（即投资不发达地区）的区域。这两个指标用来确定酒厂和配送中心的社会影响系数。

为了衡量社会影响，提出了模糊层次分析法（模糊 AHP）及其相关的 $\tilde{1}$ — $\tilde{9}$ 成对比较尺度（见表 3.2）。采用这种方法在两个选定的社会类别方面对每个分配中心进行评分，并确定相关的社会系数。

表 3.2　　　　　　　　　　失业率比较值

分值（%）	语言变量	隶属函数
[0-0.5)	没有影响	(1, 1, 1)
[0.5-1)	介于 $\tilde{1}$ 和 $\tilde{3}$ 之间	(1, 2, 3)
[1-1.5)	影响弱	(2, 3, 4)
[1.5-2)	介于 $\tilde{3}$ 和 $\tilde{5}$ 之间	(3, 4, 5)
[2-2.5)	影响强	(4, 5, 6)
[2.5-3)	介于 $\tilde{5}$ 和 $\tilde{7}$ 之间	(5, 6, 7)
[3-3.5)	影响很强	(6, 7, 8)
[3.5-4)	介于 $\tilde{7}$ 和 $\tilde{9}$ 之间	(7, 8, 9)
[4-4.5)	极端影响	(8, 9, 9)

表 3.2 和表 3.3 根据中国国家统计局和中国地方统计局发布的统计数据分别给出了这些城市的失业率和地区人均国内生产总值，还显示了相应的隶属函数以反映当前的失业率和区域人均 GDP 率。应该注意的是，这些分数是基于决策者对这些城市的失业率和区域人均 GDP 率的历史判断得出的。

表3.3　当地人均GDP占全国人均GDP的比较值得分

分值（%）	语言变量	隶属函数
[4-4.5)	没有影响	(1, 1, 1)
[3.5-4)	介于$\tilde{1}$和$\tilde{3}$之间	(1, 2, 3)
[3-3.5)	影响弱	(2, 3, 4)
[2.5-3)	介于$\tilde{3}$和$\tilde{5}$之间	(3, 4, 5)
[2-2.5)	影响强	(4, 5, 6)
[1.5-2)	介于$\tilde{5}$和$\tilde{7}$之间	(5, 6, 7)
[1-1.5)	影响很强	(6, 7, 8)
[0.5-1)	介于$\tilde{7}$和$\tilde{9}$之间	(7, 8, 9)
[0-0.5)	极端影响	(8, 9, 9)

表3.4列出了由失业和人均GDP调整的归一化社会系数。例如，北京的两个选定类别的相关分数为（5，6，7）和（5，6，7），并且给定相应比例，配送中心的标准化系数近似等于0.6667[①]。在这项研究中考虑12个分销中心，并假设归一化社会系数的较高者将对分销中心所在的位置和区域产生更大的社会影响。使用这些系数，我们将社会维度纳入我们提出的网络设计模型。

表3.4　基于失业率和当地人均GDP的归一化社会系数

候选配送中心	失业率（%）	衡量值	当地人均GDP占全国GDP的比重	衡量值	规范值
北京	1.20	(2, 3, 4)	2.20	(4, 5, 6)	0.4444
上海	4.00	(8, 9, 9)	2.15	(4, 5, 6)	0.7593
成都	2.82	(5, 6, 7)	1.51	(5, 6, 7)	0.6667
重庆	3.40	(6, 7, 8)	1.03	(6, 7, 8)	0.7778
郑州	2.20	(4, 5, 6)	1.61	(5, 6, 7)	0.6111
长沙	2.89	(5, 6, 7)	2.38	(4, 5, 6)	0.6111
广州	2.15	(4, 5, 6)	2.88	(3, 4, 5)	0.5000
西安	3.40	(6, 7, 8)	1.36	(6, 7, 8)	0.7778

---

① （5+5，6+6，7+7）/（9+9，9+9，9+9）=36/54=0.6667。

续表

候选配送中心	失业率（%）	衡量值	当地人均 GDP 占全国 GDP 的比重	衡量值	规范值
济南	2.40	(4, 5, 6)	1.80	(5, 6, 7)	0.6111
厦门	3.23	(6, 7, 8)	1.96	(5, 6, 7)	0.7222
南京	2.67	(5, 6, 7)	2.34	(4, 5, 6)	0.6111
呼和浩特	4.05	(8, 9, 9)	1.61	(5, 6, 7)	0.8148

(二) 优化建模

下面具体以企业 A 的供应链为例，对其进行可持续网络优化设计。参数包括：c_i 表示修建配送中心的年化固定费用 (20 年)；c_d^f 表示修建酿酒厂的年化固定费用 (20 年)；c_i^k 表示用第 k 种运输模式从酒厂 D 到配送中心 i 的单位运输成本；c_{ij} 表示用公路从配送中心 i 到配送中心 j 的单位运输成本；y_j 表示配送点 j 的需求量；e_i^k 表示从酒厂 D 到配送中心 i 运用第 k 种运输模式产生的单位碳排放量；e_{ij} 表示从配送中心 i 到配送点 j 用公路运输时运送单位产品产生的碳排放量；δ_d 表示酒厂 D 的平均规范化社会影响系数；δ_i 表示配送中心 i 的平均规范化社会影响系数；y_i 表示配送中心 i 的配送量。

决策变量包括：x_i 表示如果选择配送中心 i 为 1，否则为 0，$x_i \in [0, 1]$，$i = 1, 2, \cdots, n$；z_i^k 表示如果运输到配送中心 i 选择 k 种模式为 1，否则为 0，$z_i^k \in [0, 1]$，$k = 1, 2, \cdots, u$；z_{ij} 表示如果从配送中心 i 到配送点 j 走公路为 1，否则为 0，$z_{ij} \in [0, 1]$，$j \neq i, j = 1, 2, \cdots, m$。

1. 经济目标

经济目标是最小化供应链成本，包括从供应商到酿酒厂的采购成本，酿酒厂的生产成本，配送期间的运输成本，生产中的废弃物处理成本，酿酒厂的副产品得益以及与配送中心相关的固定成本。在模型中，主要考虑配送中心和运输模式的选择和优化。

$$f_1(x,y) = \left(\sum_{i=1}^{n} c_i x_i + c_d^f\right) + c_d^m y_d^m + c_d^p y_d^p + c_d^w y_d^w - c_d^b y_d^b + \sum_{i=1}^{n} x_i \sum_{k=1}^{u} z_i^k c_i^k \left(y_i + \sum_{j \neq i}^{m} z_{ij} y_j\right) + \sum_{i=1}^{n} \sum_{j \neq i}^{m} z_{ij} y_j c_{ij} + \sum_{i=1}^{n} x_i c_i^s \left(y_i + \sum_{j \neq i}^{m} z_{ij} y_j\right) \quad (3.20)$$

2. 环境目标

环境目标是最小化生产过程中和运输过程中的碳排放量。

$$f_2(x,y) = e_d^p y_d^p + \sum_{i=1}^{n} x_i \sum_{k=1}^{u} z_i^k e_i^k \left(y_i + \sum_{j \neq i}^{m} z_{ij} y_j \right) + \sum_{i=1}^{n} \sum_{j \neq i}^{m} z_{ij} y_j e_{ij} + e_d^w y_d^w \tag{3.21}$$

3. 社会目标

社会目标是最大化酒厂和配送中心的社会影响力，社会影响力与当地的就业情况和人均 GDP 密切相关，同时也与产量和配送量有直接关系。

$$f_3(x,y) = \delta_d y_d^p + \sum_{i=1}^{n} x_i \delta_i \left(y_i + \sum_{j \neq i}^{m} z_{ij} y_j \right) + \sum_{i=1}^{n} \sum_{j \neq i}^{m} \delta_j z_{ij} y_j \tag{3.22}$$

4. 总体模型

在白酒企业的可持续供应链网络优化中，要求的是最小化供应链成本、最小化环境影响、最大化社会福利。因此，总体模型如下：

$$\min f(x,y) = (f_1(x,y), f_2(x,y), -f_3(x,y)) \tag{3.23}$$

$$s.t. \begin{cases} y_d^p \leq P \\ \sum_{\lambda=1}^{h} c_\lambda^d u_\lambda^d + \sum_{i=1}^{n} c_i x_i \leq B \\ \sum_{i=1}^{n} y_i + \sum_{j \neq i}^{m} y_j \leq y_d^p \\ \sum_{j \neq i}^{m} y_j \leq \sum_{i=1}^{n} y_i \\ \sum_{i=1}^{n} x_i = 3 \\ \sum_{i=1}^{n} x_i + \sum_{j \neq i}^{m} x_j = 12 \\ u_\lambda^d \in [0,1], \lambda = 1,2,\cdots,h \\ x_i \in [0,1], i = 1,2,\cdots,l \\ z_i^k \in [0,1], k = 1,2,\cdots,u \\ z_{ij} \in [0,1], j \neq i, j = 1,2,\cdots,m \end{cases} \tag{3.24}$$

为了求出案例可行解，有以下约束条件。

（1）生产能力约束。每个酒厂都有自己的生产能力限制，白酒生产量不能超过其最大生产量。

$$y_d^p \leqslant P \tag{3.25}$$

（2）建设成本约束。企业对于修建固定设施的费用每年都有一个预算，不能超过其预算，这里用 B 表示年度预算最大值，按 20 年计算。

$$\sum_{\lambda=1}^{h} c_\lambda^d u_\lambda^d + \sum_{i=1}^{n} c_i x_i \leqslant B \tag{3.26}$$

（3）产品配送量约束。所有配送中心和配送点的配送量小于其生产的产品量。

$$\sum_{i=1}^{n} y_i + \sum_{j \neq i}^{m} y_j \leqslant y_d^p \tag{3.27}$$

（4）在 12 个城市里选取且只选取 3 个城市作为配送中心。

$$\sum_{i=1}^{n} x_i = 3 \tag{3.28}$$

（5）所有 12 个城市的需求都要得到满足。

$$\sum_{i=1}^{n} x_i + \sum_{j \neq i}^{m} x_j = 12 \tag{3.29}$$

（三）结果讨论

用 R 语言对企业 A 的优化模型进行求解，得出相应选择方案。分析企业 A 部署的当前供应链网络，并将其与选择方案进行比较，以寻求最优方案。

1 现有模式（S0）

企业 A 位于四川地区的 B 城，现有 12 个租赁的配送中心，配送模式采取的是直接从企业 A 用汽车作为主要的交通工具配送到 12 个城市。现白酒企业的供应链总成本包括原材料采购成本、白酒生产成本、产品配送成本、酒厂的固定投资（20 年年化投资）、12 个配送中心的租赁费用、配送中心的仓储费用、酒厂废弃物的处理成本、酒糟售卖得到的收益。计算得到其每年的供应链总成本为 3278818369.01 元。现有的碳排放量包括生产过程中的碳排放量、产品运输过程中的碳排放量、废弃物处理过程中的碳排放量，算出的碳排放量是每年 227493.13 吨。现有的社会影响力是企业所在地 B 市的社会影响力和 20 个城市的影响力，算出的社会影响力是 273951.80，如表 3.5 所示。

表 3.5　　　　　　当前模式和三种维度下的最优方案

模式	总成本（元/每年）	碳排放量（吨/每年）	社会影响力	配送中心	运输模式
S0	3278818369.01	227493.13	273951.80	12 个（租赁）	公路
S1	3225352575.28	223443.35	346530.26	3 个（修建）	一级：铁路、水路；二级：公路
S2	3229894225.58	222072.11	346538.26	3 个（修建）	一级：铁路、水路；二级：公路
S3	3383864098.32	237121.71	467487.52	3 个（修建）	一级：铁路、水路；二级：公路

2. 最小化成本时获得的最优解决方案（S1）

运用 R 语言从现有的 12 个租赁的配送点中选出 3 个点来作为配送中心，以总成本最低为目标进行计算，总共得到 220 个方案。选择其中成本最低的方案进行分析即三个配送中心是郑州（铁路）、重庆（水路）、长沙（铁路）。其中郑州负责西安、呼和浩特、北京、济南、南京的配送需求，重庆负责成都的配送需求，长沙负责上海、厦门和广州的配送需求。从配送中心到配送点用公路运输。供应链总成本最低时配送中心是重庆、长沙和郑州。此时从企业 A 到重庆走水路，到长沙和郑州走铁路。为了及时响应顾客的需求，从这 3 个配送中心到其他 9 个配送点都采用的是公路汽车配送模式。采用这种配送方法时，企业 A 的供应链总成本降为 3225352575.28 元，和现有配送模式相比，节省了 53465793.73 元，和现有总供应链成本相比，节约了约 1.63%，节省的成本主要在运输费用上。从碳排放量来看，在此种模式下，每年的碳排放量是 223443.35 吨，和现有模式相比，减少的量达 4049.78 吨，减少了 1.78%。而社会影响力变为 346538.26，比现有模式多了 72586.46，增加了 26.50%。

如果对 220 个选择方案进行分析，在这里主要考虑变动的函数，包括配送中心修建成本、运输成本、仓储费用，称其为变动费用。从这 220 个方案中，可以看出最好的选择方案是重庆、长沙和郑州为配送中心的方案，其变动总成本为 154738733.28 元。最差的方案以北京（铁路）、上海（水路）和厦门（铁路）为配送中心，北京负责长沙、济南、呼和浩特的配送任务，上海负责广州、西安和南京的配送要求，厦门满足成都、重庆和郑州的配送情况，其变动成本是 274104380.20 元。最差的方案和最优的方案比较，两者相差 119365646.92 元。如果对这 220 个方案的整体进行分析，可以得到如图 3.2 所示的变动成本与变动成本频率图。

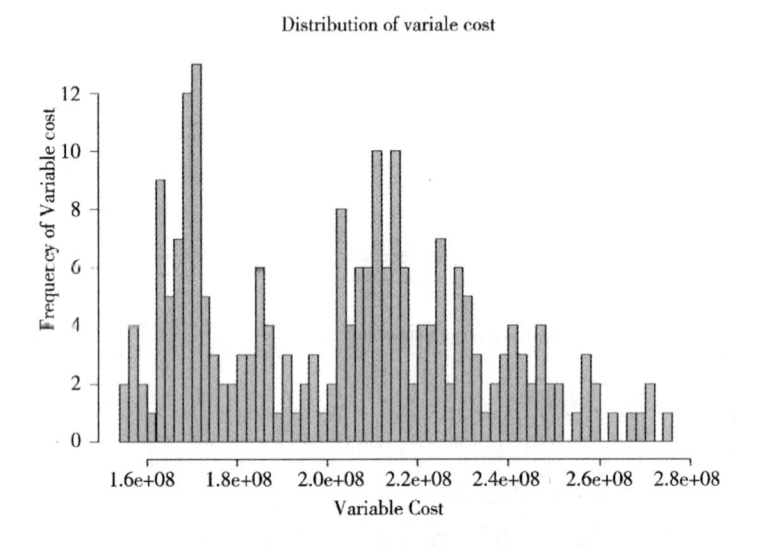

图 3.2　选择方案变动成本与变动成本频率图 S1

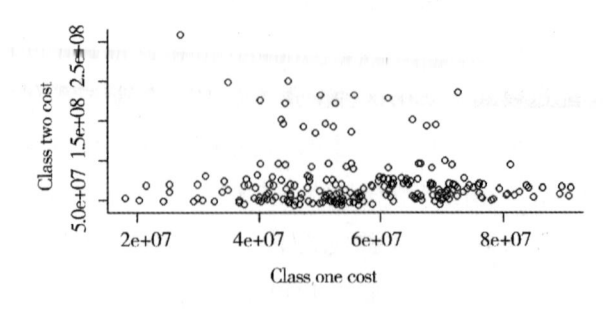

图 3.3　选择方案一级配送成本和二级配送成本散点图 S1

对 220 个方案的一级配送成本和二级配送成本比较，可以得到一级成本和二级成本分布情况的散点图，如图 3.3 所示。也可以得到如图 3.4 所示的 220 个选择方案中配送中心修建成本与仓储成本的散点图。

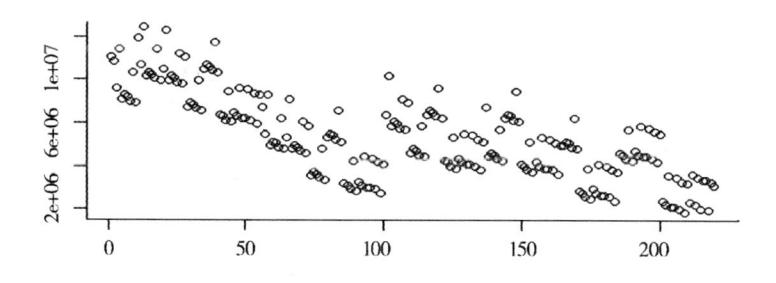

图 3.4　选择方案配送中心修建成本与仓储成本散点图 S1

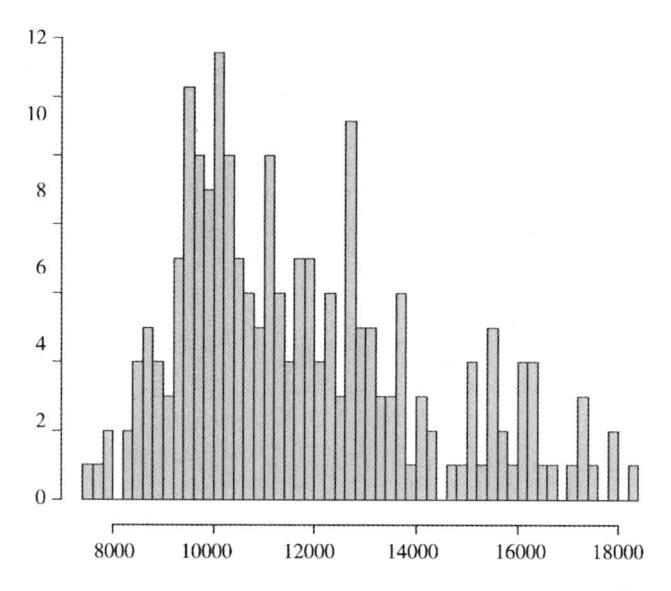

图 3.5　最小化环境影响时选择方案运输阶段的碳排放量和碳排放频率分布图 S2

3. 最小化环境影响时获得的最优解决方案（S2）

在最小化环境影响时运用 R 语言，同样得到 220 个选择方案。其中环境影响最小的方案是选择重庆（水路）、长沙（铁路）和郑州（铁路）为配送中心。其中郑州负责西安、呼和浩特、北京、济南、南京的配送需求，重庆负责成都的配送需求，长沙负责上海、厦门和广州的配送需求。从配送中心到配送点用公路运输。此时供应链的总成本是3229894225.58元，比现有模式节省48924143.43元，节约了1.49%。碳排放量变成222072.11吨，比现有模式少排放5421.02吨，减少了2.38%。社会影响力变为346538.26，和现有模式相比多了72586.46，增加了26.50%。这和S1中的成本最优方案下的社会影响力一致。

如果仅考虑配送过程中的碳排放量，最优方案是选择重庆（水路）、长沙（铁路）和郑州（铁路）为配送中心，此时配送阶段的碳排放量是7576.26吨。而最差的网络路线图是以北京（铁路）、济南（铁路）和呼和浩特（铁路）为配送中心，二级路线分别是济南负责上海、成都、重庆、长沙、广州、西安、厦门、南京和郑州的配送，此时的年碳排放量是18358.75吨，最差和最优的碳排放量相差10782.49吨，最差方案是最优方案碳排放量的2.42倍。220个选择方案的碳排放量和碳排放频率分布如图3.5所示。

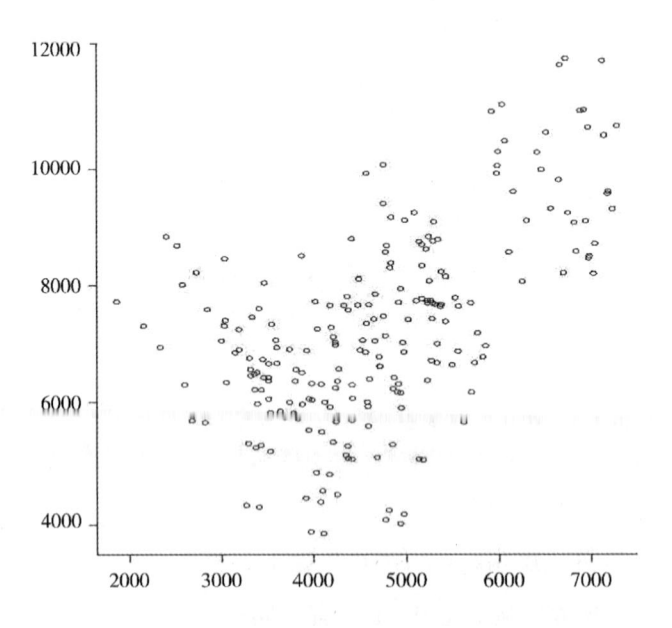

图3.6　最小化环境影响时选择方案的一级碳排放量和二级碳排放量散点图 S2

220个选择方案的一级配送模式下的碳排放量和二级配送模式下的碳排放量散点图如图3.6所示。

4. 最大化社会影响力的最优解决方案（S3）

最大化社会影响力的最优方案是以上海（水路）、厦门（铁路）和南京（水路）修建配送中心，其中南京只负责南京的配送需求，上海负责呼和浩特的配送需求，厦门负责济南、郑州、西安、长沙、重庆、成都和广州的配送需求。从配送中心到配送点用公路运输。此时企业A的供应链总成本变成了3383864098.32，比现有模式增加了105045729.31元的成本，增加了3.20%。碳排放量变成了237121.71吨，比现有模式多了9628.58吨，增加了4.23%。社会影响力变成467487.52，比现有模式多193535.72，增加了70.65%。这个方案说明供应链的社会影响力增加了很多，但同时其经济成本和碳排放量也相应增多。

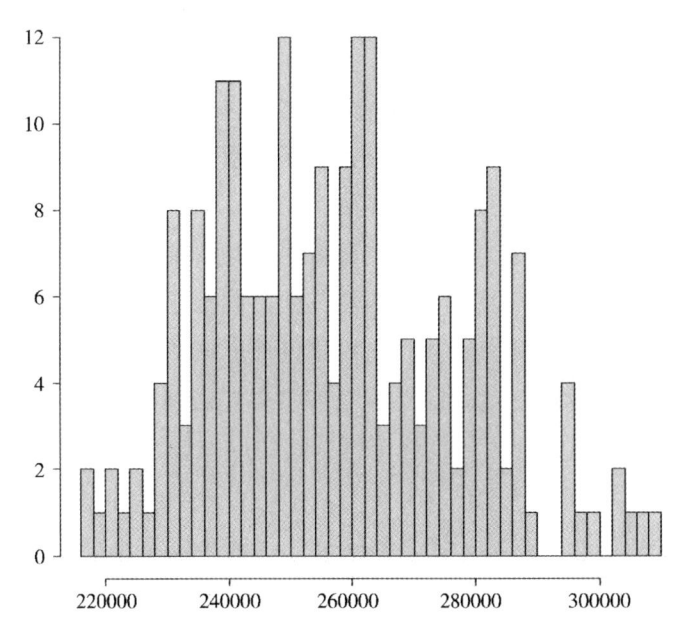

图3.7 选择方案的社会影响力与社会影响力频率分布图 S3

从220个社会影响力方案来看，在只考虑配送中心和配送点的社会影响力的情况下，最优方案的社会影响力是308133.54，最差方案是以北京

(铁路)、西安(铁路)和郑州(铁路)为配送中心,北京负责呼和浩特的配送,西安负责上海、成都、重庆、长沙、广州、厦门、南京和济南的配送,此时的社会影响力是 216526.75。可以看出,最优方案和最差方案的社会影响力值相差 91606.79。220 个社会影响方案的分布图如图 3.7 所示。

四　本章小结

将可持续的三个维度放在一起进行考虑的供应链网络设计分析模型还比较少[1]。构建一个多目标模型,设计白酒企业的可持续供应链网络路线图,可以帮助企业人员和研究人员制定战略布局和决策。我们选用四川一家白酒企业 A 的案例说明模型的适用性和有效性。将可持续性的所有三个维度(即经济、环境和社会)纳入网络设计模式,具体来说,供应链总成本和碳排放分别用作经济和环境目标的衡量标准。关于社会维度,选用模糊 AHP 来衡量社会可持续性,并基于两个选定的指标来确定社会影响系数,即就业情况和当地人均 GDP。应用 R 语言进行求解,结果显示了三个目标之间的权衡关系。该白酒企业案例给设计和管理供应链网络模式提供了新的视角。

研究结果表明企业当前的供应链结构和网络模式在三个可持续目标方面不够高效和具有可持续性。也许其他白酒企业和其他行业中的企业也面临相同的问题,他们的供应链网络设计应该基于可持续发展的三个维度来进行分析和研究。Choi 等认为很多供应链网络的出现不是有目的的设计[2]。但是事实证明不是出于可持续的网络设计可能会产生负面的

---

[1] Eskandarpour, M., Dejax, P., Miemczyk, J., & Péton, O., "Sustainable Supply Chain Network Design: An Optimization-oriented Review", *Omega*, 54, 2015: 11–32; Varsei, M., & Polyakovskiy, S., "Sustainable Supply Chain Network Design: A Case of the Wine Industry in Australia", *Omega*, 66, 2017: 236–247; Tang, C. S., & Zhou, S., "Research Advances in Environmentally and Socially Sustainable Operations", *European Journal of Operational Research*, 223 (3), 2012: 585–594.

[2] Choi, T. Y., Dooley, K. J., & Rungtusanatham, M., "Supply Networks and Complex Adaptive Systems: Control Versus Emergence", *Journal of Operations Management*, 19 (3), 2001: 351–366.

经济、环境和社会影响。世界各地的许多决策者和学者越来越注意这样的问题，即重塑价值链[1]。运营研究和管理科学学者与其他学科学者合作，可以帮助企业将一系列与可持续发展相关的指标纳入供应链分析模型，并帮助他们做出明智的决策。未来的研究可以扩展这项工作，并考虑更多与可持续发展相关的绩效指标。本书也可以为各行各业的决策者提供参考，以可持续发展的要求重塑现有供应链网络。

---

[1] Howard-Grenville, J., Buckle, S. J., Hoskins, B. J., & George, G., "Climate Change and Management", *Academy of Management Journal*, 57 (3), 2014: 615 – 623.

第四章　白酒可持续供应链供应商选择模型及应用

当前，全球经济处于一体化发展中，人们对环境保护和社会责任的可持续要求也越来越高。在可持续发展观和科学发展观的大背景下，传统的企业之争已演变为可持续供应链之争，供应商选择也变成了可持续供应商选择。为了提高企业的竞争优势，供应商选择是可持续供应链合作伙伴关系发展的重要战略任务。可持续的供应商评价和选择对于建立有效的可持续供应链管理机制起着重要作用。为实现可持续的供应链，链中的所有成员必须坚持可持续发展战略[1]。供应商选择方法可以用来选择原材料供应商和终端服务提供商。供应商选择问题可以处理各种有形和无形的问题[2]。"塑化剂"风波给白酒行业带来了严重的负面影响，这可以归为供应商选择不当引起的问题。近年来，白酒企业对于供应商的选择不再只关注经济指标，而是综合考虑各种影响因素，包括经济、环境和

---

[1] Chang, B., Chang, C. W., & Wu, C. H., "Fuzzy DEMATEL Method for Developing Supplier Selection Criteria", *Expert Systems with Applications*, 38 (3), 2011: 1850 – 1858; Orji, I. J., & Wei, S., "An Innovative Integration of Fuzzy-logic and Systems Dynamics in Sustainable Supplier Selection: A Case on Manufacturing Industry", *Computers & Industrial Engineering*, 88, 2015: 1 – 12; Amindoust, A., Ahmed, S., Saghafinia, A., & Bahreininejad, A., "Sustainable Supplier Selection: A Ranking Model Based on Fuzzy Inference System", *Applied Soft Computing*, 12 (6), 2012: 1668 – 1677.

[2] Bai, C., & Sarkis, J., "Integrating Sustainability into Supplier Selection with Grey System and Rough set Methodologies", *International Journal of Production Economics*, 124 (1), 2010: 252 – 264.

社会层面的影响。随着企业可持续发展压力的加大,白酒企业对于供应商的要求也越来越高。在白酒企业越来越关注可持续发展的背景下,如何选择可持续的供应商对于白酒企业来说是一个很有意义和价值的研究议题。

一 维度模型

工业生产对自然环境和人类生活的可持续性有很大的影响和破坏[1]。可持续采购对于企业具有显著的影响,特别是涉及供应商选择的标准[2]。以前,它强调供应商选择指标如质量、成本、交货和服务的战略重要性[3]。随后倡导绿色采购,在供应商选择中加入环境标准,形成了绿色供应商选择的概念[4]。随着全球经济一体化和国际合作的发展,越来越多的企业选择供应商时开始考虑其经济效益、环境保护效应和社会福利,这被称为可持续供应商选择[5]。供应商选择问题一般从选择维度和选择方法来进行研究。

(一) 选择维度

供应商的选择和评价一直是供应链管理的重点,关于供应商选择的

---

[1] Lin, R. J., "Using Fuzzy DEMATEL to Evaluate the Green Supply Chain Management Practices", *Journal of Cleaner Production*, 40, 2013: 32–39.

[2] Igarashi, M., de Boer, L., & Fet, A. M., "What is Required for Greener Supplier Selection? A Literature Review and Conceptual Model Development", *Journal of Purchasing and Supply Management*, 19 (4), 2013: 247–263; Van der Rhee, B., Verma, R., & Plaschka, G., "Understanding Trade-offs in the Supplier Selection Process: The Role of Flexibility, Delivery, and Value-added Services/support", *International Journal of Production Economics*, 120 (1), 2009: 30–41.

[3] Dickson, G. W., "An Analysis of Vendor Selection Systems and Decisions", *Journal of Purchasing*, 2 (1), 1966: 5–17; Weber, C. A., Current, J. R., & Benton, W. C., "Vendor Selection Criteria and Methods", *European Journal of Operational Research*, 50 (1), 1991: 2–18.

[4] Noci, G., "Designing Green'Vendor Rating Systems for the Assessment of a Supplier's Environmental Performance", *European Journal of Purchasing & Supply Management*, 3 (2), 1997: 103–114.

[5] Seuring, S., & Müller, M., "From a Literature Review to a Conceptual Framework for Sustainable Supply Chain Management", *Journal of Cleaner Production*, 16 (15), 2008: 1699–1710; Amindoust, A., Ahmed, S., Saghafinia, A., & Bahreininejad, A., "Sustainable Supplier Selection: A Ranking Model Based on Fuzzy Inference System", *Applied Soft Computing*, 12 (6), 2012: 1668–1677; Elkington, J., "Partnerships from Cannibals with Forks: The Triple Bottom Line of 21st-century Business", *Environmental Quality Management*, 8 (1), 1998: 37–51.

文章比较多。其研究的维度也从以前的单一角度发展到了现在包含经济、环境和社会的可持续多维度。

1. 经济维度为主

Kilincci 和 Onal 从供应商标准、产品绩效标准和服务绩效标准三个方面来评价洗衣机供应商。其中供应商标准选用的指标有财务状况、管理方法、技术能力、质量体系和过程、地理位置、生产设施和能力以及使用看板方法。产品绩效标准包括产品价格、处理（包括运输、仓储、收货、包装等）和产品质量指标。而服务绩效标准包括细节落实、技术支持、提前期和专业化指标[1]。Rezaei 等将航空零售业的供应商选择指标分为产品相关指标、供应商相关指标和战略相关指标。其中产品相关方面又分为 5 个二级指标，分别是成本/价格、产品质量、交货、支持服务以及交货的柔性和响应性。成本/价格指标包括产品价格，上市费（挂牌费）、价格侵蚀、内容相关成本和成本透明度指标。产品质量包括平均故障率、符合规格、产品精细创新、产品包装。交货指标有提前期，符合预订的到期日期，符合预定的订单数量。支持服务指标有售后服务、提供资料、回购能力。交付柔性和响应性指标有数量的柔性和响应性、产品混合的柔性和响应性、提前期柔性、产品上市时间。而在供应商相关方面则分为财务稳定、声誉、社会责任和媒体活动 4 个二级指标。其中声誉用行业中的声誉以及历史表现来描述。社会责任用社会责任及愿意改进社会责任的意愿来表述。战略/关系相关指标又分为 3 个二级指标，分别是分类组合、市场专业知识和组织管理。分类组合从分类深度、分类品种、服务水平/能力来衡量。市场专业知识从市场意识（知名度）、市场经验和资源筹措能力来衡量。而组织管理则从企业经营目标，组织文化，持续改进的承诺、沟通，以及现有关系来衡量[2]。

---

[1] Kilincci, O., & Onal, S. A., "Fuzzy AHP Approach for Supplier Selection in a Washing Machine Company", *Expert Systems with Applications*, 38 (8), 2011: 9656 – 9664.

[2] Rezaei, J., Fahim, P. B., & Tavasszy, L., "Supplier Selection in the Airline Retail Industry Using a Funnel Methodology: Conjunctive Screening Method and Fuzzy AHP", *Expert Systems with Applications*, 41 (18), 2014: 8165 – 8179.

Van der Rhee 等研究了经理们在给定质量情况下如何在成本、价值增值、交货绩效和柔性方面对供应商进行权衡。分析数据来自欧洲（德国、法国、意大利、英国）的生产企业。文章不仅指出了各种属性的重要度，同时也发现了不同文化背景下各种属性重要性排序的不同。比如德国认为价格是最不重要的因素。而其他国家一致认为价格是排在第三重要位置的属性。以前的文献多认为质量、成本和交货是最重要的三个指标，而该文认为排在前三位的是柔性、成本和交货[1]。Amid 等从质量、成本和服务三个方面来评价供应商。其中质量指标用生产能力、瑕疵和全面质量管理来表示。成本用净成本来评价。服务从按时交货、应对变化、产品开发、财务和组织能力来评估[2]。Chen 和 Wu 从成本、质量、交货能力、技术、生产能力和服务六个维度来评估供应商。其中成本指标有产品总成本和成本节省计划。质量指标用投入质量控制、生产能力、可靠性和高收益控制表示。交货能力指标用产品周期、按时交货、交货提前期来衡量。技术指标用设计能力、问题处理能力、持续改进能力来评估。生产能力指标有生产能力柔性、生产量。服务指标则用投诉处理、响应需求、报告生成来衡量[3]。Ho 等总结以前的研究，得出最广泛应用的供应商选择指标是质量，然后是交货、价格/成本、生产能力、服务、管理、科技、研发、金融、柔性、声誉、关系、风险、安全和环境[4]。Chang 等确定的衡量指标有产品质量、产品价格、技术能力、服务、交货绩效、稳定的交货、提前期、及时对需求变化做出反

---

[1] Van der Rhee, B., Verma, R., & Plaschka, G., "Understanding Trade-offs in the Supplier Selection Process: The Role of Flexibility, Delivery, and Value-added Services/Support", *International Journal of Production Economics*, 120 (1), 2009: 30–41.

[2] Amid, A., Ghodsypour, S. H., & O'Brien, C., "A Weighted Maxmin Model for Fuzzy Multi-objective Supplier Selection in a Supply Chain", *International Journal of Production Economics*, 131 (1), 2011: 139–145.

[3] Chen, P. S., & Wu, M. T., "A Modified Failure Mode and Effects Analysis Method for Supplier Selection Problems in the Supply Chain Risk Environment: A Case Study", *Computers & Industrial Engineering*, 66 (4), 2013: 634–642.

[4] Ho, W., Xu, X., & Dey, P. K., "Multi-criteria Decision Making Approaches for Supplier Evaluation and Selection: A Literature Review", *European Journal of Operational Research*, 202 (1), 2010: 16–24.

应、生产能力和财务状况[1]。Ho 等从订单赢得要素方面将指标分为价格、交货可靠性、交货速度、质量一致、需求增大、产品系列、设计、配送、设计领导力、现有供应商、市场销售、商标名称、技术联络和支持、售后服务[2]。Shabanpour 等从输入和输出两个维度来考虑指标。其中输入指标有安全生产和劳动健康成本、生态设计成本、运输费用。输出指标则用产品质量、财务稳定、能源消费效率来表示[3]。Li 等考虑了定性和定量因素,研究了技术能力、产品外观、JIT 能力、价格、交货率和销售服务率 6 个指标和 15 家供应商的数值算例[4]。Chan 和 Kumar 从产品总成本、产品质量、服务绩效、供应商介绍和风险因子五个方面来评估供应商。其中产品总成本考虑了产品价格、运费和关税三个指标。产品质量用产品报废率、交货周期延长、质量评估、质量问题的补救来衡量。服务绩效从交货时间表、技术和研发支持、应对变化、易于交流来考核。供应商介绍指标包括财务状况、客户群、绩效历史、生产设备和能力。而风险因子指标有地理位置、政治稳定、经济、恐怖主义。尽管文中涉及一些社会指标,但是并没有上升到可持续供应商选择的高度[5]。

2. 环境维度为主

随着经济的发展,人们对生态环境愈加关注,开始重视企业的上游供应商对环境的影响。因此,有的文章考虑到了环境保护的问题,从环

---

[1] Chang, B., Chang, C. W., & Wu, C. H., "Fuzzy DEMATEL Method for Developing Supplier Selection Criteria", *Expert systems with Applications*, 38 (3), 2011: 1850 – 1858.

[2] Ho, L. H., Feng, S. Y., Lee, Y. C., & Yen, T. M., "Using Modified IPA to Evaluate Supplier's Performance: Multiple Regression Analysis and DEMATEL Approach", *Expert Systems with Applications*, 39 (8), 2012: 7102 – 7109.

[3] Shabanpour, H., Yousefi, S., & Saen, R. F., "Future Planning for Benchmarking and Ranking Sustainable Suppliers Using Goal Programming and Robust Double Frontiers DEA", *Transportation Research Part D: Transport and Environment*, 50, 2017: 129 – 143.

[4] Li, Y., Liu, X., & Chen, Y., "Supplier Evaluation and Selection Using Axiomatic Fuzzy Set and DEA Methodology in Supply Chain Management", *International Journal of Fuzzy Systems*, 14 (2), 2012: 215 – 225.

[5] Chan, F. T., & Kumar, N., "Global Supplier Development Considering Risk Factors Using Fuzzy Extended AHP-based Approach", *Omega*, 35 (4), 2007: 417 – 431.

境角度，或者从经济和环境两个维度来评估选择供应商。环境角度更多的是关注碳排放。这些文章也对供应商选择的理论研究和实践应用做出了重大的贡献。

Shaw 等考虑到了碳排放问题，选择了成本、质量、提前期、温室气体排放和需求 5 个指标来进行供应商评价[1]。Hsu 等从计划、实施和管理三个维度来评价绿色供应链管理中的供应商。其中计划指标包括碳排放治理、碳排放政策、碳减排目标、碳风险评估、培训相关的碳管理和产品生命周期成本管理。而实施指标包括碳管理措施、参与碳管理的倡议、碳信息管理系统和供应商合作。管理指标包括碳核算与库存、碳核查、碳信息披露和报告[2]。Yu 等探讨了经济和环境两种维度，并认为有三种措施可以迫使代理商提升战略和降低环境危害。首先，根据成员双方能力和绿色因子分配订单。代理商为了获得更多的订单必须完善战略。其次，对于二氧化碳排放设置惩罚函数，代理商为了获得更多的利润必须选择最近的供应商。最后，对于具有高环保因子的代理商进行奖励。通过这个模型市场监管平台可以迫使消费者选择距离最近和绿色因子最高的供应商为其供货[3]。

3. 社会维度为主

随着人们对供应商社会责任的关注，供应商选择也开始考虑社会维度。有的文献单从社会角度来考虑，有的从社会和环境两方面进行思考。Mani 等分析了供应商选择中的社会可持续指标，得出公平、健康、优质教育、住房保障、人口、安全、慈善事业、人权、道德标准、工资、就业、童工、包身工、性别歧视是最重要的社会指标。而对于发展

---

[1] Shaw, K., Shankar, R., Yadav, S. S., & Thakur, L. S., "Supplier Selection Using Fuzzy AHP and Fuzzy Multi-objective Linear Programming for Developing Low Carbon Supply Chain", *Expert Systems with Applications*, 39 (9), 2012: 8182 – 8192.

[2] Hsu, C. W., Kuo, T. C., Chen, S. H., & Hu, A. H., "Using DEMATEL to Develop a Carbon Management Model of Supplier Selection in Green Supply Chain Management", *Journal of Cleaner Production*, 56, 2013: 164 – 172.

[3] Yu, F., Xue, L., Sun, C., & Zhang, C., "Product Transportation Distance Based Supplier Selection in Sustainable Supply Chain Network", *Journal of Cleaner Production*, 137, 2016: 29 – 39.

中国家来说，可以选用性别比例（就业）、生活伙伴、儿童虐待与忽视、医疗保险、经济适用房、收入差距、贫困、高中辍学率、工作时间和结社自由来评价供应商。并将其应用于电子、汽车和水泥产业的社会可持续供应商选择[1]。Goebel 等基于伦理文化的角度进行相关研究，认为公司道德文化的不同要素对于采购经理选择履行社会和环境责任的供应商具有重要的影响[2]。

4. 可持续高度

近年来，考虑环境和社会可持续性的供应商选择研究已经有所增加[3]。Büyüközkan 等构建了如图 4.1 所示的供应商评价结构[4]。Wang 等认为精益生产中的持续改进、社会指标中的健康安全、环保方面有使用具有燃油效率的工具和提高机器利用率，对于中国汽车零配件公司的可持续生产实践具有最大的贡献[5]。Grimm 等在食品行业将供应链分成核心企业、直接供应商、子供应商（sub-supplier）三种角色，并确定了14 个关键成功要素（critical success factors）[6]。

---

[1] Mani, V., Agrawal, R., & Sharma, V., "Supplier Selection Using Social Sustainability: AHP Based Approach in India", *International Strategic Management Review*, 2 (2), 2014: 98 – 112.

[2] Goebel, P., Reuter, C., Pibernik, R., & Sichtmann, C., "The Influence of Ethical Culture on Supplier Selection in the Context of Sustainable Sourcing", *International Journal of Production Economics*, 140 (1), 2012: 7 – 17.

[3] Govindan, K., Rajendran, S., Sarkis, J., & Murugesan, P., "Multi Criteria Decision Making Approaches for Green Supplier Evaluation and Selection: A Literature Review", *Journal of Cleaner Production*, 98, 2015: 66 – 83; Wu, C., & Barnes, D., "A Literature Review of Decision-making Models and Approaches for Partner Selection in Agile Supply Chains", *Journal of Purchasing and Supply Management*, 17 (4), 2011: 256 – 274.

[4] Büyüközkan, G., & Çifçi, G., "A Novel Fuzzy Multi-criteria Decision Framework for Sustainable Supplier Selection with Incomplete Information", *Computers in Industry*, 62 (2), 2011: 164 – 174.

[5] Wang, Z., Subramanian, N., Gunasekaran, A., Abdulrahman, M. D., & Liu, C., "Composite Sustainable Manufacturing Practice and Performance Framework: Chinese Auto-parts Suppliers Perspective", *International Journal of Production Economics*, 170, 2015: 219 – 233.

[6] Grimm, J. H., Hofstetter, J. S., & Sarkis, J., "Critical Factors for Sub-supplier Management: A Sustainable Food Supply Chains Perspective", *International Journal of Production Economics*, 152, 2014: 159 – 173.

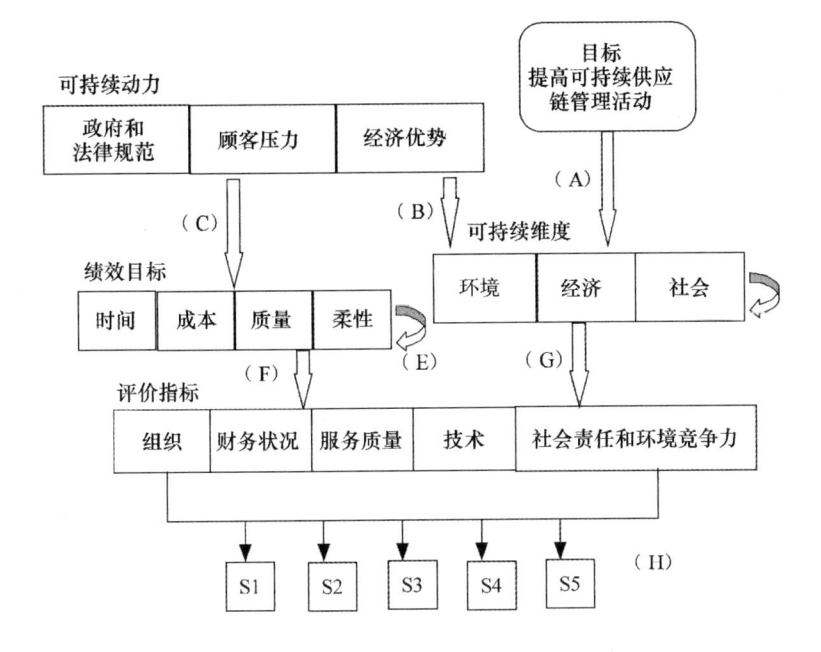

图 4.1 评价结构网络图模型[①]

Luthra 等通过文献分析和专家讨论确定了关于经济、环境和社会三个维度的 22 个可持续供应商指标，并将其应用于印度汽车公司的案例。得出的结论是环境成本、产品质量、产品价格、职业健康和安全体系、环境能力是排列在最前面的 5 个指标，并认为在供应商数量为"3"的时候能得到最高的得分[②]。Govindan 等指出在建筑行业可持续材料的选择具有重要的作用[③]。关于可持续供应商选择指标的部分研究如表 4.1 所示。

[①] Büyüközkan, G., & Çifçi, G., "A Novel Fuzzy Multi-criteria Decision Framework for Sustainable Supplier Selection with in Complete Information", *Computers in Industry*, 62 (2), 2011: 164 – 174.

[②] Luthra, S., Govindan, K., Kannan, D., Mangla, S. K., & Garg, C. P., "An Integrated Framework for Sustainable Supplier Selection and Evaluation in Supply Chains", *Journal of Cleaner Production*, 140, 2017: 1686 – 1698.

[③] Govindan, K., Shankar, K. M., & Kannan, D., "Sustainable Material Selection for Construction Industry—A hybrid Multi-criteria Decision Making Approach", *Renewable and Sustainable Energy Reviews*, 55, 2016: 1274 – 1288.

表 4.1 可持续供应商选择

参考文献	方法	维度	指标
Sarkis 和 Dhavale (2015)[①]	贝叶斯框架	经济	预期方差成本、标准或合同成本；产品或购买服务的质量；准时交货
		环境	供应商能源效率、环境违法行为处罚、使用环境和污染控制技术
		社会	慈善捐款、社区责任、员工流动率
Amindoust 等 (2012)[②]	模糊推理系统	经济	成本/价格、质量、技术能力、生产设施和能力、财政能力、组织管理、交货、服务、关系、柔性
		环境	环境成本、环保设计、环境管理体系、环境能力、环保研发、污染控制、环保产品、资源消耗、能源使用产品的生态设计要求、破坏臭氧层的化学品、废旧电器电子设备、回收利用、绿色供应链、创新
		社会	员工的利益和权利、利益相关者的权利、安全生产和劳动健康、信息披露、尊重政策
Azadi 等 (2015)[③]	模糊 DEA	经济	成本/价格、质量、技术能力、组织管理、生产设施和能力、财政（金融）能力、可靠性、柔性、总出货成本、出货量
		环境	环境费用、环保设计、环境管理体系、环境能力、环保研发、污染控制、环保产品、资源消耗、破坏臭氧层的化学品、回收利用、耗水量、能源消耗、可再生能源、获得 ISO 标准的数量
		社会	员工的利益和权利、利益相关者的权利、安全生产和劳动健康、信息披露、尊重政策
Wang 等 (2015)[④]		经济	运营成本、库存成本、环境成本
		环境	企业浪费、环保形象、二氧化碳排放
		社会	财富创造、技术改进、健康安全

[①] Sarkis, J., & Dhavale, D. G., "Supplier Selection for Sustainable Operations: A Triple-bottom-line Approach Using a Bayesian Framework", *International Journal of Production Economics*, 166, 2015: 177–191.

[②] Amindoust, A., Ahmed, S., Saghafinia, A., & Bahreininejad, A., "Sustainable Supplier Selection: A Ranking Model Based on Fuzzy Inference System", *Applied Soft Computing*, 12 (6), 2012: 1668–1677.

[③] Azadi, M., Jafarian, M., Saen, R. F., & Mirhedayatian, S. M., "A New Fuzzy DEA Model for Evaluation of Efficiency and Effectiveness of Suppliers in Sustainable Supply Chain Management Context", *Computers & Operations Research*, 54, 2015: 274–285.

[④] Wang, Z., Subramanian, N., Gunasekaran, A., Abdulrahman, M. D., & Liu, C., "Composite Sustainable Manufacturing Practice and Performance Framework: Chinese Auto-parts Suppliers' Perspective", *International Journal of Production Economics*, 170, 2015: 219–233.

续表

参考文献	方法	维度	指标
Ghadimi 等（2016）[1]	DANP-TOPSIS（material selection）	经济	初期成本、维修成本、处置成本、生产率、税收、满足顾客要求、税收贡献
		环境	能源减排、回收和再利用的潜力、原料提取、土地征用、水资源利用、废弃物管理、二氧化碳排放、土壤消耗、生产和运输、耗油量
		社会	耐腐蚀、耐火性能、易于施工、使用年限、美学、使用当地材料、健康与安全、劳动力可获得性
Ghadimi 和 Heavey（2014）[2]	Fuzzy Inference System（FIS）	经济	质量：文件控制程序、要求 MDD（模型驱动开发）、医疗器械警戒（不良事件监测）、内部质量审核
			服务/交货：处理和保持产品、产品标识和可追溯性、客户投诉处理、上市后监管
			成本：生产、运输、订货
			技术能力：故障模式影响及危害性分析（FMECA）、技术水平
		环境	环保形象：市场声誉、客户信誉
			污染控制：固体废弃物、危险材料的使用
			绿色竞争力：环保包装、绿色生产
		社会	健康安全：安全审计与评估、职业健康安全管理体系（OHSAS）18001、规范健康和安全条件
			就业实践：培训、纪律和安全实践
Luthra 等（2017）[3]	AHP, VIKOR	经济	产品价格、产品利润、产品质量、柔性、技术和金融能力、生产设施和生产能力、产品交付和服务、提前期要求、运输成本
		环境	环境管理体系、绿色设计与采购、绿色生产、绿色管理、绿色包装与标签、废弃物管理与污染防治、环境成本、环境竞争力、绿色研发与创新

---

[1] Govindan, K., Shankar, K. M., & Kannan, D., "Sustainable Material Selection for Construction Industry—A Hybrid Multi-criteria Decision Making Approach", *Renewable and Sustainable Energy Reviews*, 55, 2016: 1274 – 1288.

[2] Ghadimi, P., & Heavey, C., "Sustainable Supplier Selection in Medical Device Industry: Toward Sustainable Manufacturing", *Procedia Cirp*, 15, 2014: 165 – 170.

[3] Luthra, S., Govindan, K., Kannan, D., Mangla, S. K., & Garg, C. P., "An Integrated Framework for Sustainable Supplier Selection and Evaluation in Supply Chains", *Journal of Cleaner Production*, 140, 2017: 1686 – 1698.

续表

参考文献	方法	维度	指标
Luthra 等（2017）[1]	AHP，VIKOR	社会	职业健康与安全体系、员工利益与权利、利益相关者权利、信息披露
Goebel 等（2012）[2]		社会	在选择新的供应商时，公司的采购专家：确保新供应商持有结社自由和集体谈判权的有效识别；确保新供应商不适用任何形式的强迫或强制劳动；确保新供应商符合童工法；确保新供应商在就业和职业方面没有歧视
		环境	在选择新的供应商时，公司的采购专家：有意识地寻求支持对环境挑战未雨绸缪的方法的供应商；有意识地寻求采取主动，以促进更大的环境责任的供应商；有意识地寻求鼓励发展和推广环保技术的供应商
		道德	公司高层管理者：有规律地显示他们关心道德；指导决策的道德方向；道德行为楷模；代表高的道德标准
		激励	当不道德行为发生时我们组织进行纪律管理；对不道德行为的惩罚在我们组织是严格执行的；组织对不道德行为进行惩罚；组织奖励正直的人；组织奖励道德行为
		行为准则	组织中的采购人员必须承认他们已经阅读并理解行为准则；行为准则广泛分布在组织中；组织中的采购专家要求定期声明他们的行动符合行为准则；组织中的行为规范是正式的
		服从权威	我们组织中的人期待按照他们被告知的去做；在我们组织中老板永远是对的；我们的组织要求服从权威

当然，有的可持续供应商评价标准不仅仅从环境、社会和经济三个维度去考虑。比如 Gold 和 Awasthi 从经济、关系质量、环境、社会和全球风险五个方面来评估可持续供应商。其中经济指标分为成本、质量、柔性、速度、可靠性、创新。关系质量从信任、有效沟通、EDI 来考

---

[1] Luthra, S., Govindan, K., Kannan, D., Mangla, S. K., & Garg, C. P., "An Integrated Framework for Sustainable Supplier Selection and Evaluation in Supply Chains", *Journal of Cleaner Production*, 140, 2017: 1686 – 1698.

[2] Goebel, P., Reuter, C., Pibernik, R., & Sichtmann, C., "The Influence of Ethical Culture on Supplier Selection in the Context of Sustainable Sourcing", *International Journal of Production Economics*, 140 (1), 2012: 7 – 17.

虑。环境指标包括材料、能量、水、生物多样性、排放量、废水废弃物、供应商环境选择流程。社会指标包括劳动实践和得体的工作、人权、社会、产品责任、供应商社会选择流程。风险包括通货风险、政治不稳定导致的中断风险和文化兼容性风险[1]。

（二）模型方法

供应商选择是供应链管理的重要部分，供应商选择方法比较成熟，主要有定性、定量、定性与定量相结合的方法。有的供应商选择用的是单一方法，也有的供应商选择用的是集成混合方法。考虑到评价指标的不确定性，用模糊方法进行的研究相对较多。这里主要从方法的类型上进行分析。

1. 单一研究方法

Roodhooft 和 Konings 提出的基于活动的成本分析法（Activity Based Costing Approach），通过计算供应商的总成本来选择供应商[2]。层次分析法（AHP）是 20 世纪 70 年代由著名运筹学家 Satty 提出的，Weber 等提出利用层次分析法选择合作伙伴[3]。Chan 和 Kumar 应用模糊扩展层次分析法（FEAHP）在考虑风险的情况下对全球供应商发展进行了分析[4]。Azadnia 等提供了一个两阶段模糊 AHP 方法来选择可持续的全球供应商，同时考虑到来自子供应商的可持续风险[5]。Kilincci 和 Onal 将

---

[1] Gold, S., & Awasthi, A., "Sustainable Global Supplier Selection Extended Towards Sustainability Risks from (1 + n) th Tier Suppliers Using Fuzzy AHP Based Approach", *Ifac-Papersonline*, 48 (3), 2015: 966 – 971.

[2] Roodhooft, F., & Konings, J., "Vendor Selection and Evaluation an Activity Based Costing Approach", *European Journal of Operational Research*, 96 (1), 1997: 97 – 102.

[3] Weber, C. A., Current, J. R., & Benton, W. C., "Vendor Selection Criteria and Methods", *European Journal of Operational Research*, 50 (1), 1991: 2 – 18.

[4] Chan, F. T., & Kumar, N., "Global Supplier Development Considering Risk Factors Using Fuzzy Extended AHP-based Approach", *Omega*, 35 (4), 2007: 417 – 431.

[5] Azadnia, A. H., Saman, M. Z. M., Wong, K. Y., Ghadimi, P., & Zakuan, N., "Sustainable Supplier Selection Based on Self-organizing Map Neural Network and Multi Criteria Decision Making Approaches", *Procedia-Social and Behavioral Sciences*, 65 (ICIBSoS), 2012: 879 – 884.

模糊层次分析法用于土耳其的一家洗衣机公司寻找最优的供应商[1]。Gold 和 Awasthi 应用模糊 AHP 方法从经济、关系质量、环境、社会和全球风险五个方面来评估可持续供应商[2]。Amindoust 等运用模糊推理系统来研究可持续供应商选择问题[3]。Ghadimi 和 Heavey 通过模糊推理系统将可持续供应商选择运用在医疗设备行业，认为可持续采购能够带来可持续生产的进步和发展[4]。数据包络分析法（Data Envelopment Analysis，DEA）可以为供应商绩效评估提供很好的定量分析工具[5]。Büyüközkan 等用模糊网络分析法进行可持续供应商选择[6]。Orji 和 Wei 提出了在模糊环境下集成供应商行为信息和系统动力学（System Dynamics）的更可靠的决策支持系统[7]。

DEMATEL（Decision Making Trial and Evaluation Laboratory）模型是一种用于分析复杂系统问题的评价方法，称为决策实验与评价实验室方法。Hsu 等在绿色供应链的碳管理中运用 DEMATEL 方法识别出影响指标，确定了三个维度的 13 个指标。结果表明，在低碳管理供应商选择中，碳信息和培训管理系统是与碳管理相关的最重要的两个影响因素。Hsu 等应用 DEMATEL 方法从计划、实施和管理三个维度来评价绿色供

---

[1] Kilincci, O., & Onal, S. A., "Fuzzy AHP Approach for Supplier Selection in a Washing Machine Company", *Expert Systems with Applications*, 38 (8), 2011: 9656 – 9664.

[2] Gold, S., & Awasthi, A., "Sustainable Global Supplier Selection Extended Towards Sustainability Risks from (1 + n) th Tier Suppliers Using Fuzzy AHP Based Approach", *Ifac-Papersonline*, 48 (3), 2015: 966 – 971.

[3] Amindoust, A., Ahmed, S., Saghafinia, A., & Bahreininejad, A., "Sustainable Supplier Selection: A Ranking Model Based on Fuzzy Inference System", *Applied Soft Computing*, 12 (6), 2012: 1668 – 1677.

[4] Ghadimi, P., & Heavey, C., "Sustainable Supplier Selection in Medical Device industry: Toward Sustainable Manufacturing", *Procedia Cirp*, 15, 2014: 165 – 170.

[5] Li, Y., Liu, X., & Chen, Y., "Supplier Evaluation and Selection Using Axiomatic Fuzzy Set and DEA Methodology in Supply Chain Management", *International Journal of Fuzzy Systems*, 14 (2), 2012: 215 – 225.

[6] Büyüközkan, G., & Çifçi, G., "A Novel Fuzzy Multi-criteria Decision Framework for Sustainable Supplier Selection with Incomplete information", *Computers in industry*, 62 (2), 2011: 164 – 174.

[7] Orji, I. J., & Wei, S., "An Innovative Integration of Fuzzy-logic and Systems Dynamics in Sustainable Supplier Selection: A Case on Manufacturing Industry", *Computers & Industrial Engineering*, 88, 2015: 1 – 12.

应链管理中的供应商选择问题[1]。Chang 等应用模糊 DEMATEL 方法寻找供应链中供应商的影响因子，用模糊 DEMATEL 方法找到关键指标来完善绩效指标方法和提供决策方法[2]。Wu 和 Lee 用模糊 DEMATEL 方法对全球管理者能力进行了评估[3]。Luthra 等用模糊 DEMATEL 方法对太阳能的发展情况进行了评价[4]。

2. 集成研究方法

Rezaei 等应用连接筛选方法和模糊 AHP 方法研究了在航空零售业的供应商选择[5]。Chen 和 Wu 提出了一种改进的故障模式和影响分析（MFMEA）方法，从供应链风险的角度选择新的供应商，并应用层次分析法（AHP）确定每个指标的权重[6]。Shaw 等在考虑碳排放的情况下使用模糊 AHP 和多目标线性规划方法在供应链中选择合适的供应商，并将其方法应用于纺织供应链中[7]。Luthra 等应用混合 AHP 和 VIKOR 方法来评价可持续供应商[8]。Mani 等人用层次分析法和德尔菲

---

[1] Hsu, C. W., Kuo, T. C., Chen, S. H., & Hu, A. H., "Using DEMATEL to Develop a Carbon Management Model of Supplier Selection in Green Supply Chain Management", *Journal of Cleaner Production*, 56, 2013: 164–172.

[2] Chang, B., Chang, C. W., & Wu, C. H., "Fuzzy DEMATEL Method for Developing Supplier Selection Criteria", *Expert Systems with Applications*, 38 (3), 2013: 1850–1858.

[3] Wu, W. W., & Lee, Y. T., "Developing Global Managers' Competencies Using the Fuzzy DEMATEL Method", *Expert Systems with Applications*, 32 (2), 2007: 499–507.

[4] Luthra, S., Govindan, K., Kharb, R. K., & Mangla, S. K., "Evaluating the Enablers in Solar Power Developments in the Current Scenario Using Fuzzy DEMATEL: An Indian Perspective", *Renewable and Sustainable Energy Reviews*, 63, 2016: 379–397.

[5] Rezaei, J., Fahim, P. B., & Tavasszy, L., "Supplier Selection in the Airline Retail Industry Using a Funnel Methodology: Conjunctive Screening Method and Fuzzy AHP", *Expert Systems with Applications*, 41 (18), 2014: 8165–8179.

[6] Chen, P. S., & Wu, M. T., "A Modified Failure Mode and Effects Analysis Method for Supplier Selection Problems in the Supply Chain Risk Environment: A Case Study", *Computers & Industrial Engineering*, 66 (4), 2013: 634–642.

[7] Shaw, K., Shankar, R., Yadav, S. S., & Thakur, L. S., "Supplier Selection Using Fuzzy AHP and Fuzzy Multi-objective Linear Programming for Developing Low Carbon Supply Chain", *Expert Systems with Applications*, 39 (9), 2012: 8182–8192.

[8] Luthra, S., Govindan, K., Kannan, D., Mangla, S. K., & Garg, C. P., "An Integrated Framework for Sustainable Supplier Selection and Evaluation in Supply Chains", *Journal of Cleaner Production*, 140, 2017: 1686–1698.

方法分析了供应商选择中的社会可持续指标[1]。

Li 等用模糊 AHP 方法计算指标的权重，用数据包络分析法（DEA）选择供应商[2]。Shabanpour 等用双层目标法进行可持续供应商选择[3]。Azadnia 运用聚类和多准则决策方法选择可持续供应商[4]。Govindan 等指出在阿拉伯联合酋长国运用混合多准则决策方法去选择最优可持续建筑材料（施工材料）具有很强的现实意义[5]。Zhou 等运用二型模糊集下的多目标 DEA 模型去评价和选择最合适的可持续供应商。用于评价选择供应商的方法有很多[6]。Azadi 等提出在模糊环境下运用集成 DEA 和 Enhanced Russell Measure（ERM）方法来选择最佳可持续供应商，并将其应用到松脂生产公司的可持续供应商选择中去验证其有效性[7]。Sarkis 和 Dhavale 发展了一个基于贝叶斯框架和蒙特卡罗马尔科夫链仿真的新颖的方法论来比较和选择供应商[8]。Uygun 等运用 DEMATEL 和模糊 ANP 技术对电信企业的

---

[1] Mani, V., Agrawal, R., & Sharma, V., "Supplier Selection Using Social Sustainability: AHP Based Approach in India", *International Strategic Management Review*, 2 (2), (2014): 98-112.

[2] Li, Y., Liu, X., & Chen, Y., "Supplier Evaluation and Selection Using Axiomatic Fuzzy Set and DEA Methodology in Supply Chain Management", *International Journal of Fuzzy Systems*, 14 (2), 2012: 215-225.

[3] Shabanpour, H., Yousefi, S., & Saen, R. F., "Future Planning for Benchmarking and Ranking Sustainable Suppliers Using Goal Programming and Robust Double Frontiers DEA", *Transportation Research Part D: Transport and Environment*, 50, 2017: 129-143.

[4] Azadnia, A. H., Saman, M. Z. M., Wong, K. Y., Ghadimi, P., & Zakuan, N., "Sustainable Supplier Selection Based on Self-organizing Map Neural Network and Multi Criteria Decision Making Approaches", *Procedia-Social and Behavioral Sciences*, 65 (ICIBSoS), 2012: 879-884.

[5] Govindan, K., Shankar, K. M., & Kannan, D., "Sustainable Material Selection for Construction Industry——A Hybrid Multi Criteria Decision Making Approach", *Renewable and Sustainable Energy Reviews*, 55, 2016: 1274-1288.

[6] Zhou, X., Pedrycz, W., Kuang, Y., & Zhang, Z., "Type-2 fuzzy Multi-objective DEA Model: An Application to Sustainable Supplier Evaluation", *Applied Soft Computing*, 46, 2016: 424-440.

[7] Azadi, M., Jafarian, M., Saen, R. F., & Mirhedayatian, S. M., "A New Fuzzy DEA Model for Evaluation of Efficiency and Effectiveness of Suppliers in Sustainable Supply Chain Management Context", *Computers & Operations Research*, 54, 2015: 274-285.

[8] Sarkis, J., & Dhavale, D. G., "Supplier Selection for Sustainable Operations: A Triple-bottom-line Approach Using a Bayesian Framework", *International Journal of Production Economics*, 166, 2015: 177-191.

外包供应商进行了评价和选择[1]。Abdullah 和 Zulkifli 提出了一种混合模糊 AHP 方法与一种间隔二型模糊决策试验和评估实验室方法,用于人力资源管理[2]。Ho 等应用 IPA(Importance-Performance Analysis)和 DEMATEL 方法从订单赢得要素方面来评价供应商[3]。

Ho 等总结出在供应商选择中单一方法(58.97%)比集成(综合)方法(41.03%)更受欢迎。在单一方法中,最受欢迎的是 DEA,然后是数学规划、AHP、CBR、ANP、fuzzy set theory、SMART、GA。集成 AHP 方法是更流行的方法。AHP 和很多其他的方法集成过,因为 AHP 简单,易于使用,灵活性大,包括 ANN、bi-negotiation、DEA、fuzzy set theory、GP、grey relational analysis 和多目标规划。其研究证明了多属性决策方法比传统的基于成本的方法更好[4]。

尽管有很多方法用来评价供应商,国内外的专家学者也在不断丰富其理论和算法,使评价结果更加公正、客观;但是,大部分方法需要额外的数据,同时忽略了评价指标间实际存在一种相互影响、制约的关系。DEMATEL 方法被认为是处理评价指标之间重要度和因果关系最好的方法之一[5]。它不需要大量的数据来拟合问题研究,可以直观定量地表示各因素的逻辑关系,将复杂的问题简单化。而决策中的指标具有模糊性,不能用精确的语言进行描述,而模糊理论可以处理这种情况。因

---

[1] Uygun, Ö., Kaçamak, H., & Kahraman, A., "An integrated DEMATEL and Fuzzy ANP Techniques for Evaluation and Selection of Outsourcing Provider for a Telecommunication Company", *Computers & Industrial Engineering*, 86, 2015: 137 – 146.

[2] Abdullah, L., & Zulkifli, N., "Integration of Fuzzy AHP and Interval type – 2 Fuzzy DEMATEL: An Application to Human Resource Management", *Expert Systems with Applications*, 42 (9), 2015: 4397 – 4409.

[3] Ho, L. H., Feng, S. Y., Lee, Y. C., & Yen, T. M., "Using Modified IPA to Evaluate Supplier's Performance: Multiple Regression Analysis and DEMATEL approach", *Expert Systems with Applications*, 39 (8), 2012: 7102 – 7109.

[4] Ho, W., Xu, X., & Dey, P. K., "Multi-criteria Decision Making Approaches for Supplier Evaluation and Selection: A literature Review", *European Journal of Operational Research*, 202 (1), 2010: 16 – 24.

[5] Govindan, K., Rajendran, S., Sarkis, J., & Murugesan, P., "Multi Criteria Decision Making Approaches for Green Supplier Evaluation and Selection: A Literature Review", *Journal of Cleaner Production*, 98, 2015: 66 – 83.

此将模糊理论和 DEMATEL 结合起来的模糊 DEMATEL 方法能够找到关键指标来提高绩效和为供应链管理中供应商选择提供决策支持信息。

二 指标体系

在遭遇"塑化剂"风波、"限酒令"之后，白酒行业面临结构调整和产业升级的压力。如何在激烈的竞争中占有一席之地成为白酒企业需要考虑的重点，而供应商的选择则成为其必须考虑的重要方面。白酒供应商选择和评价需要考虑其指标的合理性，而指标本身具有模糊性和不确定性（动态性）。在传统的供应链中，对供应商的选择和评价一般从经济角度进行考虑。可持续供应链供应商选择需要从经济、社会、环境三个维度进行分析。根据文献分析结果和专家意见，本书对白酒行业的供应链供应商可持续评价从经济、环境和社会三个维度进行分析，其中经济指标、环境指标和社会指标各5个。其指标结构如图4.2所示。

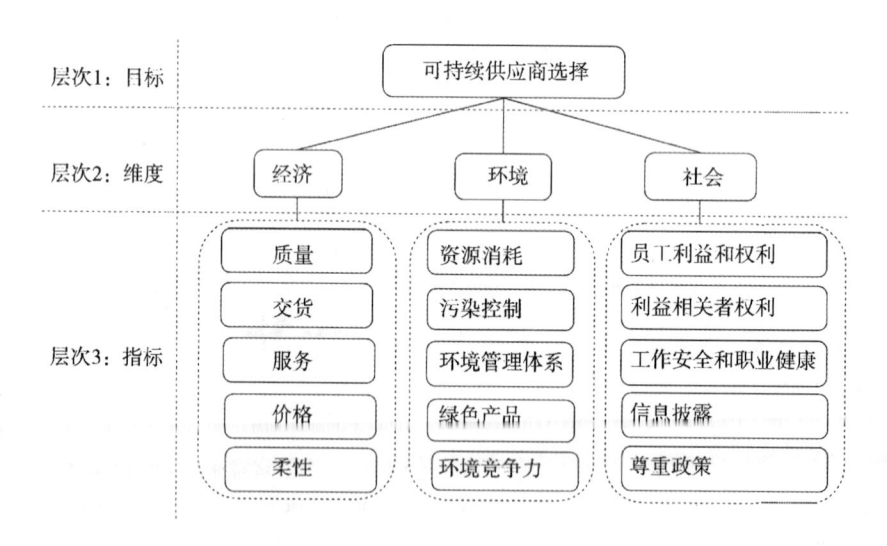

图 4.2 供应商选择可持续指标

（一）经济指标

在白酒行业的供应商选择中，既需要考虑供应商选择的共性，又要考虑白酒行业供应商选择的独特性。因此,根据文献分析结果和专家意见,本书选取了5个经济指标来评估供应商,即质量(Quality,$C11$)、交货(Delivery,$C12$)、服务(Service,$C13$)、价格(Price,$C14$)和柔性(Flexibility,$C15$)。

1. 质量

产品的使用价值是以产品质量为基础的。Dickson 认为质量在所有影响供应商选择的指标中占据最重要的地位[1]。不论是传统的供应商选择,还是可持续供应链视角下的供应商选择,质量因素都当仁不让成为重点考核因素,因为产品质量是企业和供应链生存之本[2]。质量体系是否健全和完善,是衡量供应商质量系统的重要标准之一。质量是供应商选择中学者专家研究最多的指标之一[3]。Chang 等主要指的是产品质量[4]。Amid 等认为质量

---

[1] Dickson, G. W., "An Analysis of Vendor Selection Systems and Decisions", *Journal of Purchasing*, 2 (1), 1966: 5–17.

[2] Ageron, B., Gunasekaran, A., & Spalanzani, A., "Sustainable Supply Management: An Empirical Study", *International Journal of Production Economics*, 140 (1), 2012: 168–182; Shabanpour, H., Yousefi, S., & Saen, R. F., "Future Planning for Benchmarking and Ranking Sustainable Suppliers Using Goal programming and Robust Double Frontiers DEA", *Transportation Research Part D: Transport and Environment*, 50, 2017: 129–143; Shaw, K., Shankar, R., Yadav, S. S., & Thakur, L. S., "Supplier Selection Using Fuzzy AHP and Fuzzy Multi-objective Linear Programming for Developing Low Carbon Supply Chain", *Expert Systems with Applications*, 39 (9), 2012: 8182–8192; Luthra, S., Govindan, K., Kannan, D., Mangla, S. K., & Garg, C. P., "An integrated Framework for Sustainable Supplier Selection and Evaluation in Supply Chains", *Journal of Cleaner Production*, 140, 2017: 1686–1698; Azadi, M., Jafarian, M., Saen, R. F., & Mirhedayatian, S. M., "A New Fuzzy DEA Model for Evaluation of Efficiency and Effectiveness of Suppliers in Sustainable Supply Chain Management Context", *Computers & Operations Research*, 54, 2015: 274–285; Ghadimi, P., & Heavey, C., "Sustainable Supplier Selection in Medical device Industry: Toward Sustainable Manufacturing", *Procedia Cirp*, 15, 2014: 165–170.

[3] Amindoust, A., Ahmed, S., Saghafinia, A., & Bahreininejad, A., "Sustainable Supplier Selection: A ranking Model Based on Fuzzy Inference System", *Applied Soft Computing*, 12 (6), 2012: 1668–1677; Ho, L. H., Feng, S. Y., Lee, Y. C., & Yen, T. M., "Using Modified IPA to Evaluate Supplier's Performance: Multiple Regression Analysis and DEMATEL Approach", *Expert Systems with Applications*, 39 (8), 2012: 7102–7109; Büyüközkan, G., & Çifçi, G., "A Novel Fuzzy Multi-criteria Decision Framework for Sustainable Supplier Selection with in Complete Information", *Computers in Industry*, 62 (2), 2011: 164–174; Gold, S., & Awasthi, A., "Sustainable Global Supplier Selection Extended Towards Sustainability Risks from (1 + n) th Tier Suppliers Using Fuzzy AHP Based Approach", *Ifac-Papersonline*, 48 (3), 2015: 966–971; Azadnia, A. H., Saman, M. Z. M., Wong, K. Y., Ghadimi, P., & Zakuan, N., "Sustainable Supplier Selection Based on Self-organizing Map Neural Network and Multi Criteria Decision Making Approaches", *Procedia-Social and Behavioral Sciences*, 65 (ICIBSoS), 2012: 879–884.

[4] Chang, B., Chang, C. W., & Wu, C. H., "Fuzzy DEMATEL Method for Developing Supplier Selection Criteria", *Expert Systems with Applications*, 38 (3), 2011: 1850–1858.

包括生产能力、缺陷（瑕疵）、全面质量管理[1]，Chen 等将质量看成是投入质量控制、生产能力、可靠性、高收益控制[2]。Chan 和 Kumar 将产品质量分为产品报废率、交货周期延长、质量评估、质量问题的补救[3]。Rezaei 等[4]认为产品质量因素有平均故障率、符合规格、产品精细创新、产品包装。供应商的质量问题对于白酒企业的生存和发展起着至关重要的作用。白酒塑化剂的超标是因为使用了不合标准的包装材料造成的[5]。这里的质量指标主要是指白酒企业的供应商所供给的各类物资的质量。

2. 交货

在 Dickson 和 Weber 的研究中，交货都是排在第二位的重要供应商选择指标[6]，可见交货对于企业有着举足轻重的作用[7]。交货可靠性低就会引起整个供应链的连锁反应，造成大量的资源浪费并导致成本上升，甚至会致使供应链的解体。白酒企业为其供应商设定了交货时间窗，每个供应商必须在规定时间范围内交付公司所订购的商品，超过时间交付将会被拒绝接

---

[1] Amid, A., Ghodsypour, S. H., & O'Brien, C., "A Weighted Max-min Model for Fuzzy Multi-objective Supplier Selection in a Supply Chain", *International Journal of Production Economics*, 131 (1), 2011: 139 – 145.

[2] Chen, P. S., & Wu, M. T., "A Modified Failure Mode and Effects Analysis Method for Supplier Selection Problems in the Supply Chain Risk Environment: A Case Study", *Computers & Industrial Engineering*, 66 (4), 2013: 634 – 642.

[3] Chan, F. T., & Kumar, N., "Global Supplier Development Considering Risk Factors Using Fuzzy Extended AHP-based Approach", *Omega*, 35 (4), 2007: 417 – 431.

[4] Rezaei, J., Fahim, P. B., & Tavasszy, L., "Supplier Selection in the Airline Retail Industry Using a Funnel Methodology: Conjunctive Screening Method and Fuzzy AHP", *Expert Systems with Applications*, 41 (18), 2014: 8165 – 8179.

[5] 赵凤琦:《我国白酒产业可持续发展研究》，博士学位论文，中国社会科学院，2014年；周刚:《论白酒包装材料安全把控的重要性及发展前景》，《科技与企业》2015 年第 22 期。

[6] Dickson, G. W., "An Analysis of Vendor Selection Systems and Decisions", *Journal of Purchasing*, 2 (1), 1966: 5 – 17; Weber, C. A., Current, J. R., & Benton, W. C., "Vendor Selection Criteria and Methods", *European Journal of Operational Research*, 50 (1), 1991: 2 – 18.

[7] Ageron, B., Gunasekaran, A., & Spalanzani, A., "Sustainable Supply Management: An Empirical Study", *International Journal of Production Economics*, 140 (1), 2012: 168 – 182; Azadnia, A. H., Saman, M. Z. M., Wong, K. Y., Ghadimi, P., & Zakuan, N., "Sustainable Supplier Selection Based on Self-organizing Map Neural Network and Multi-criteria Decision Making Approaches", *Procedia-Social and Behavioral Sciences*, 65 (ICIBSoS), 2012: 879 – 884.

收。这一交付条件就考验了供应商的交货准时水平[1]。Rezaei 认为交货指提前期，符合预定的到期日期，符合预订的订单数量[2]，Chang 等提到交货绩效和稳定的交货[3]。Ho 等提到交货可靠性，交货速度[4]，Amid 指按时交货[5]，Chen 等认为交货能力包括产品周期、按时交货、交货提前期[6]。Van der Rhee 等用交货绩效速度来表示原型交付、提前期和按时交货[7]。

3. 服务

服务是供应商选择中的另一个重要指标[8]。Kilincci 等认为服务绩效标准包括细节落实、技术支持、提前期、专业化[9]。Rezaei 等提到支持服务有

---

[1] Amindoust, A., Ahmed, S., Saghafinia, A., & Bahreininejad, A., "Sustainable Supplier Selection: A Ranking Model Based on Fuzzy Inference System", *Applied Soft Computing*, 12 (6), 2012: 1668 – 1677; Sarkis, J., & Dhavale, D. G., "Supplier Selection for Sustainable Operations: A Triple-bottom-line Approach Using a Bayesian Framework", *International Journal of Production Economics*, 166, 2015: 177 – 191; Ghadimi, P., & Heavey, C., "Sustainable Supplier Selection in Medical Device Industry: Toward Sustainable Manufacturing", *Procedia Cirp*, 15, 2014: 165 – 170.

[2] Rezaei, J., Fahim, P. B., & Tavasszy, L., "Supplier Selection in the Airline Retail Industry Using a Funnel Methodology: Conjunctive Screening Method and Fuzzy AHP", *Expert Systems with Applications*, 41 (18), 2014: 8165 – 8179.

[3] Chang, B., Chang, C. W., & Wu, C. H., "Fuzzy DEMATEL Method for Developing Supplier Selection Criteria", *Expert Systems with Applications*, 38 (3), 2011: 1850 – 1858.

[4] Ho, L. H., Feng, S. Y., Lee, Y. C., & Yen, T. M., "Using Modified IPA to Evaluate Supplier's Performance: Multiple Regression Analysis and DEMATEL Approach", *Expert Systems with Applications*, 39 (8), 2012: 7102 – 7109.

[5] Amid, A., Ghodsypour, S. H., & O'Brien, C., "A Weighted Max-min Model for Fuzzy Multi-objective Supplier Selection in a Supply Chain", *International Journal of Production Economics*, 131 (1), 2011: 139 – 145.

[6] Chen, P. S., & Wu, M. T., "A Modified Failure Mode and Effects Analysis Method for Supplier Selection Problems in the Supply Chain Risk Environment: A Case Study", *Computers & Industrial Engineering*, 66 (4), 2013: 634 – 642.

[7] Van der Rhee, B., Verma, R., & Plaschka, G., "Understanding Trade-offs in the Supplier Selection Process: the Role of Flexibility, Delivery, and Value-added Services/support", *International Journal of Production Economics*, 120 (1), 2009: 30 – 41.

[8] Luthra, S., Govindan, K., Kannan, D., Mangla, S. K., & Garg, C. P., "An Integrated Framework for Sustainable Supplier Selection and Evaluation in Supply Chains", *Journal of Cleaner Production*, 140, 2017: 1686 – 1698; Govindan, K., Shankar, K. M., & Kannan, D., "Sustainable Material Selection for Construction Industry——A Hybrid Multi-criteria Decision Making Approach", *Renewable and Sustainable Energy Reviews*, 55, 2016: 1274 – 1288.

[9] Kilincci, O., & Onal, S. A., "Fuzzy AHP Approach for Supplier Selection in a Washing Machine Company", *Expert Systems with Applications*, 38 (8), 2011: 9656 – 9664.

售后服务、提供资料、回购能力[①]。Van der Rhee 等谈到价值增值服务涉及问题解决、组装服务、在线订购[②]。Ho 等谈到售后服务[③]。Amid 等认为服务是按时交货、应对变化、产品开发、财务和组织能力[④]。Chen 等认为服务指标有投诉处理、响应需求、报告生成[⑤]。Chan 等认为服务绩效包括交货时间表、技术和研发支持、应对变化、易于交流[⑥]。Ghadimi 等认为服务包括处理和保持产品、产品标识和可追溯性、客户投诉处理、上市后监管[⑦]。

4. 价格

Weber 发现价格是在供应商选择中谈论最多的一项指标[⑧]。Rezaei 等认为价格因素包括产品价格、上市费（挂牌费）、价格侵蚀、内容相关成本、成本透明度[⑨]。在白酒企业的供应商选择中，价格主要指的是

---

① Rezaei, J., Fahim, P. B., & Tavasszy, L., "Supplier Selection in the Airline Retail Industry Using a Funnel Methodology: Conjunctive Screening Method and Fuzzy AHP", *Expert Systems with Applications*, 41 (18), 2014: 8165 – 8179.

② Van der Rhee, B., Verma, R., & Plaschka, G., "Understanding Trade-offs in the Supplier Selection Process: the Role of Flexibility, Delivery, and Value-added Services/support", *International Journal of Production Economics*, 120 (1), 2009: 30 – 41.

③ Ho, L. H., Feng, S. Y., Lee, Y. C., & Yen, T. M., "Using Modified IPA to Evaluate Supplier's Performance: Multiple Regression Analysis and DEMATEL Approach", *Expert Systems with Applications*, 39 (8), 2012: 7102 – 7109.

④ Amid, A., Ghodsypour, S. H., & O'Brien, C., "A Weighted Maxmin Model for Fuzzy Multi-objective Supplier Selection in a Supply Chain", *International Journal of Production Economics*, 131 (1), 2011: 139 – 145.

⑤ Chen, P. S., & Wu, M. T., "A Modified Failure Mode and Effects Analysis Method for Supplier Selection Problems in the Supply Chain Risk Environment: A Case Study", *Computers & Industrial Engineering*, 66 (4), 2013: 634 – 642.

⑥ Chan, F. T., & Kumar, N., "Global Supplier Development Considering Risk Factors Using Fuzzy Extended AHP-based Approach", *Omega*, 35 (4), 2007: 417 – 431.

⑦ Ghadimi, P., & Heavey, C., "Sustainable Supplier Selection in Medical Device Industry: Toward Sustainable Manufacturing", *Procedia Cirp*, 15, 2014: 165 – 170.

⑧ Weber, C. A., Current, J. R., & Benton, W. C., "Vendor Selection Criteria and Methods", *European Journal of Operational Research*, 50 (1), 1991: 2 – 18.

⑨ Rezaei, J., Fahim, P. B., & Tavasszy, L., "Supplier Selection in the Airline Retail Industry Using a Funnel Methodology: Conjunctive Screening Method and Fuzzy AHP", *Expert Systems with Applications*, 41 (18), 2014: 8165 – 8179.

产品价格[1]。由此可见，价格是供应商选择的重要指标[2]。这里的价格因素主要是指供应商供给的粮食和包装材料的价格，供应商提供的产品价格对于下游企业的产成品价格影响很大。

5. 柔性

柔性的概念最早源于柔性制造系统（FMS），是系统对需求变化的响应能力。在供应商选择和评价中，白酒企业更关心的是供应商对未来变化的响应能力[3]。柔性是供应商选择中用得最多的指标之一[4]。Rezaei 等提到了交付柔性、数量柔性、产品混合柔性和提前期柔性[5]。Chen 等提到了生产柔性[6]。白酒企业的供应商柔性既要考虑外在柔性，又要考虑内在柔性。外在柔性需要考虑生产柔性、产品柔性、混合柔性、时间

---

[1] Chang, B., Chang, C. W., & Wu, C. H., "Fuzzy DEMATEL Method for Developing Supplier Selection Criteria", *Expert Systems with Applications*, 38 (3), 2011: 1850 - 1858; Chan, F. T., & Kumar, N., "Global Supplier Development Considering Risk Factors Using Fuzzy Extended AHP-based Approach", *Omega*, 35 (4), 2007: 417 - 431; Luthra, S., Govindan, K., Kannan, D., Mangla, S. K., & Garg, C. P., "An Integrated Framework for Sustainable Supplier Selection and Evaluation in Supply Chains", *Journal of Cleaner Production*, 140, 2017: 1686 - 1698.

[2] Ageron, B., Gunasekaran, A., & Spalanzani, A., "Sustainable Supply Management: An Empirical Study", *International Journal of Production Economics*, 140 (1), 2012: 168 - 182; Amindoust, A., Ahmed, S., Saghafinia, A., & Bahreininejad, A., "Sustainable Supplier Selection: A Ranking Model Based on Fuzzy Inference System", *Applied Soft Computing*, 12 (6), 2012: 1668 - 1677; Van der Rhee, B., Verma, R., & Plaschka, G., "Understanding Trade-offs in the Supplier Selection Process: the Role of Flexibility, Delivery, and Value-added Services/support", *International Journal of Production Economics*, 120 (1), 2009: 30 - 41; Ho, L. H., Feng, S. Y., Lee, Y. C., & Yen, T. M., "Using Modified IPA to Evaluate Supplier's Performance: Multiple Regression Analysis and DEMATEL Approach", *Expert Systems with Applications*, 39 (8), 2012: 7102 - 7109; Azadi, M., Jafarian, M., Saen, R. F., & Mirhedayatian, S. M., "A new Fuzzy DEA Model for Evaluation of Efficiency and Effectiveness of Suppliers in Sustainable Supply Chain Management Context", *Computers & Operations Research*, 54, 2015: 274 - 285.

[3] 刘蕾、唐小我、丁奕翔：《供应链管理模式下的供应商柔性评价》，《商业研究》2005 年第 15 期。

[4] Ageron, B., Gunasekaran, A., & Spalanzani, A., "Sustainable Supply Management: An Empirical Study", *International Journal of Production Economics*, 140 (1), 2012: 168 - 182; Amindoust, A., Ahmed, S., Saghafinia, A., & Bahreininejad, A., "Sustainable Supplier Selection: A Ranking Model Based on Fuzzy Inference System", *Applied Soft Computing*, 12 (6), 2012: 1668 - 1677.

[5] Rezaei, J., Fahim, P. B., & Tavasszy, L., "Supplier Selection in the Airline Retail Industry Using a Funnel Methodology: Conjunctive Screening Method and Fuzzy AHP", *Expert Systems with Applications*, 41 (18), 2014: 8165 - 8179.

[6] Chen, P. S., & Wu, M. T., "A Modified Failure Mode and Effects Analysis Method for Supplier Selection Problems in the Supply Chain Risk Environment: A Case Study", *Computers & Industrial Engineering*, 66 (4), 2013: 634 - 642; Van der Rhee, B., Verma, R., & Plaschka, G., "Understanding Trade-offs in the Supplier Selection Process: the Role of Flexibility, Delivery, and Value-added Services/support", *International Journal of Production Economics*, 120 (1), 2009: 30 - 41.

柔性。而内在柔性就需要考虑基于柔性的资源储备、技术基于柔性的协调机制和信息系统等几个方面的内容[1]。

（二）环境指标

白酒可持续供应商从环境角度分为资源消耗（resource consumption，$C21$）、污染控制（pollution control，$C22$）、环境管理体系（environmental management system，$C23$）、绿色产品（green product，$C24$）和环境竞争力（environmental competencies，$C25$）5个指标。

1. 资源消耗

资源消耗是绿色供应商选择中的一个重要指标[2]。白酒行业的供应商选择中的资源消耗主要是指产品生产过程中消耗的粮食、电能、水能、天然气等资源，以及原材料和包装材料配送过程中消耗的汽油、柴油等燃料。

2. 污染控制

许多文献都谈到污染控制[3]。污染可分为空气污染、水污染、土地污染、噪声污染等方面。污染控制是指采用技术的、经济的、法律的以及其他管理手段和方法，以杜绝、削减污染物排放的环保措施。污染控制是一项很重要的指标[4]。Ghadimi和Heavey认为污染控制主要涉及固体

---

[1] 刘蕾、唐小我、丁奕翔：《供应链管理模式下的供应商柔性评价》，《商业研究》2005年第15期，第6—8页。

[2] Amindoust, A., Ahmed, S., Saghafinia, A., & Bahreininejad, A., "Sustainable Supplier Selection: A Ranking Model Based on Fuzzy Inference System", *Applied Soft Computing*, 12 (6), 2012: 1668 - 1677; Azadi, M., Jafarian, M., Saen, R. F., & Mirhedayatian, S. M., "A new fuzzy DEA Model for Evaluation of Efficiency and Effectiveness of Suppliers in Sustainable Supply Chain Management Context", *Computers & Operations Research*, 54, 2015: 274 - 285.

[3] Initiative, G. R., Sustainability Reporting Guidelines, Version 3.0", *GRI, Amsterdam*, 2006; Boukherroub, T., Ruiz, A., Guinet, A., & Fondrevelle, J., "An Integrated Approach for Sustainable Supply Chain Planning", *Computers & Operations Research*, 54, 2015: 180 - 194; Chardine-Baumann, E., & Botta-Genoulaz, V., "A Framework for Sustainable Performance Assessment of Supply Chain Management Practices", *Computers & Industrial Engineering*, 76, 2014: 138 - 147.

[4] Bai, C., & Sarkis, J., "Integrating Sustainability into Supplier Selection with Grey System and Rough set Methodologies", *International Journal of Production Economics*, 124 (1), 2010: 252 - 264; Sarkis, J., & Dhavale, D. G., "Supplier Selection for Sustainable Operations: A triple-bottom-line approach Using a Bayesian Framework", *International Journal of Production Economics*, 166, 2015: 177 - 191; Azadi, M., Jafarian, M., Saen, R. F., & Mirhedayatian, S. M., "A New Fuzzy DEA Model for Evaluation of Efficiency and Effectiveness of Suppliers in Sustainable Supply Chain Management Context", *Computers & Operations Research*, 54, 2015: 274 - 285.

废弃物和危险材料的使用①。白酒供应商选择中主要是对供应商处理废弃物（废水、废弃固体、废气）的情况进行评估。

3. 环境管理体系

环境管理体系是可持续供应商选择的重要指标②，它是一个组织内全面管理体系的组成部分，包括为制定、实施、实现、评审和保持环境方针所需的组织机构、规划活动、机构职责、惯例、程序、过程和资源。还包括组织的环境方针、目标和指标等管理方面的内容。白酒企业要求其供应商通过 ISO 14000 环境管理体系标准，它是创建绿色企业的有效工具。可以通过标准的认证，对企业持续地开展环境管理工作及对企业的可持续发展起到有效的推动作用③。

4. 绿色产品

绿色产品能直接促使人们的消费观念和生产方式发生转变，其主要特点是以市场调节方式来实现环境保护目标。公众以购买绿色产品为时尚，促进企业以生产绿色产品作为获取经济利益的途径。白酒供应商的绿色产品是指生产过程及其本身节能、节水、低污染、低毒、可再生、可回收的这类产品④。

5. 环境竞争力

环境竞争力是指供应商使用环境友好型材料、实施清洁技术、减少污染效应的能力，也指企业或其产品在国际国内市场环境中所表现出来

---

① Ghadimi, P., & Heavey, C., "Sustainable Supplier Selection in Medical Device Industry: Toward Sustainable Manufacturing", *Procedia Cirp*, 15, 2014: 165 – 170.

② Sarkis, J., & Dhavale, D. G., "Supplier Selection for Sustainable Operations: A triple-bottom-line approach Using a Bayesian Framework", *International Journal of Production Economics*, 166, 2015: 177 – 191.

③ Curkovic, S., & Sroufe, R., "Using ISO 14001 to Promote a Sustainable Supply Chain Strategy", *Business Strategy and the Environment*, 20 (2), 2011: 71 – 93.

④ Amindoust, A., Ahmed, S., Saghafinia, A., & Bahreininejad, A., "Sustainable Supplier Selection: A Ranking Model Based on Fuzzy Inference System", *Applied Soft Computing*, 12 (6), 2012: 1668 – 1677; Azadi, M., Jafarian, M., Saen, R. F., & Mirhedayatian, S. M., "A New Fuzzy DEA Model for Evaluation of Efficiency and Effectiveness of Suppliers in Sustainable Supply Chain Management Context", *Computers & Operations Research*, 54, 2015: 274 – 285.

的环境保护方面的能力①。白酒供应商的环境竞争力不只局限于产品本身,而是渗透到产品的原料采购、制造、包装销售、产品回收等产品生命周期的全过程。

(三) 社会指标

社会指标分为员工利益和权利 (the interests and rights of employees, $C31$)、利益相关者权利 (stakeholders' rights, $C32$)、工作安全和职业健康 (work safety and labor health, $C33$)、信息披露 (information disclosure, $C34$)、尊重政策 (respect for the policy, $C35$) 5 个方面。

1. 员工利益和权利

员工利益和权利是主要的社会指标。它包括享受社会保险和福利的权利、获得劳动报酬的权利、节假日休息的权利、获得劳动安全和保护的权利等。

2. 利益相关者权利

企业利益相关者包括股东、企业员工、债权人、供应商、零售商、消费者、竞争者、政府、公众利益群体等②。利益相关者权利是指以上这些利益相关者的合法权利能够得到保护。

3. 工作安全和职业健康

工作安全和职业健康涉及安全的工作环境和员工的身心健康③。

---

① Luthra, S., Govindan, K., Kannan, D., Mangla, S. K., & Garg, C. P., "An Integrated Framework for Sustainable Supplier Selection and Evaluation in Supply Chains", *Journal of Cleaner Production*, 140, 2017: 1686 – 1698.

② Azadnia, A. H., Saman, M. Z. M., Wong, K. Y., Ghadimi, P., & Zakuan, N., "Sustainable Supplier Selection Based on Self-organizing Map Neural Network and Multi Criteria Decision Making Approaches", *Procedia-Social and Behavioral Sciences*, 65 (ICIBSoS), 2012: 879 – 884.

③ Amindoust, A., Ahmed, S., Saghafinia, A., & Bahreininejad, A., "Sustainable Supplier Selection: A Ranking Model Based on Fuzzy Inference System", *Applied Soft Computing*, 12 (6), 2012: 1668 – 1677; Azadi, M., Jafarian, M., Saen, R. F., & Mirhedayatian, S. M., "A New Fuzzy DEA Model for Evaluation of Efficiency and Effectiveness of Suppliers in Sustainable Supply Chain Management Context", *Computers & Operations Research*, 54, 2015: 274 – 285; Luthra, S., Govindan, K., Kannan, D., Mangla, S. K., & Garg, C. P., "An Integrated Framework for Sustainable Supplier Selection and Evaluation in Supply Chains", *Journal of Cleaner Production*, 140, 2017: 1686 – 1698; Shabanpour, H., Yousefi, S., & Saen, R. F., "Future Planning for Benchmarking and Ranking Sustainable Suppliers Using Goal Programming and Robust Double Frontiers DEA", *Transportation Research Part D: Transport and Environment*, 50, 2017: 129 – 143.

Ghadimi 和 Heavey 认为健康安全包括安全审计与评估，职业健康安全管理体系（OHSAS）18001 以及规范健康和安全条件[1]。

4. 信息披露

信息披露主要是指公众公司以招股说明书、上市公告书以及定期报告和临时报告等形式，把公司及与公司相关的信息，向投资者和社会公众公开披露的行为，为顾客、利益相关者提供材料使用、工作环境、资金流向、生产过程中碳排放和有害物质残留等相关信息。

5. 尊重政策

尊重政策是指供应商是否尊重环境管理体系、员工职业健康体系和安全体系等，以及不招用童工、不歧视员工和消费者等。

三 模糊决策实验与评价实验室方法

DEMATEL（Decision Making Trial and Evaluation Laboratory，决策实验与评价实验室）方法起源于日内瓦巴特尔纪念研究中心用于研究和解决结构复杂的问题[2]。DEMATEL 是一个全面综合的工具，用于构建和分析涉及复杂因素之间因果关系的结构模型。当评价问题时可以很清楚地看到其相互关系。该方法以矩阵工具和图论为基础，通过聚集专家或群组的知识和经验判断，构建复杂因素之间因果关系的可视化结构[3]，得出每个因素的中心度和原因度，分析因素的所属种类（原因组或结果组）以更好地理解和解决所要研究的问题。在 DEMATEL 方法中指标被分成原因组和结果组，原因组对结果组有影响，这种影响使用指标权重

---

[1] Ghadimi, P., & Heavey, C., "Sustainable Supplier Selection in Medical Device Industry: Toward Sustainable Manufacturing", *Procedia Cirp*, 15, 2014: 165 – 170.

[2] Gabus, A., & Fontela, E., "World Problems, an Invitation to Further Thought Within the Framework of DEMATEL", *Battelle Geneva Research Center*, *Geneva*, *Switzerland*, 1972: 1 – 8; Lin, R. J., "Using fuzzy DEMATEL to Evaluate the Green Supply Chain Management Practices", *Journal of Cleaner Production*, 40, 2013: 32 – 39.

[3] Wu, W. W., & Lee, Y. T., "Developing Global Managers'Competencies Using the Fuzzy DEMATEL Method", *Expert Systems with Applications*, 32 (2), 2007: 499 – 507.

来评估[1]。该数学模型适用于较多的学术领域,如战略分析、能力评估、方案分析、选择等,它已被证明是一个用来决策复杂问题的有用方法。

在现实世界中,有许多问题需要处理模糊、不精确和不确定的信息[2],因而难以提供数字精确的信息[3],决策者的判断通常是模糊的,因此模糊理论很适合用来表达相应的语言变量。将模糊理论和 DEMATEL 方法结合起来形成的模糊 DEMATEL 方法对于供应商选择来说可以找到关键指标来提高绩效,同时为供应商选择提供决策支持信息。模糊 DEMATEL 方法具体步骤如下所示。

步骤 1:确定要素

根据文献综述内容和专家意见,确定系统中有 n 个影响因素需要考虑。

步骤 2:确定直接影响程度

确定系统要素间的直接影响关系的有无及其关系的强弱,构造有向图。假设有 H 个专家提供建议,有 n 个影响因素需要考虑。每个利益相关者确定他(她)所认为的影响因素。两者之间的强弱用 0—4 的整数来表示。其中分别用"没有影响(0)""影响很低(1)""影响低(2)""影响高(3)"和"影响很高(4)"来表示[4]。图 4.3 展示了这种影响图的示例。每个字母表示系统中的一个因素。从 c 到 d 的箭头表示 c 对 d 有影响效果,其效果的强度为 3。DEMATEL 可以将系统因素之间的结

---

[1] Uygun, Ö., Kaçamak, H., & Kahraman, Ü. A., "An Integrated DEMATEL and Fuzzy ANP Techniques for Evaluation and Selection of Outsourcing Provider for a Telecommunication Company", *Computers & Industrial Engineering*, 86, 2015: 137 – 146; Dalalah, D., Hayajneh, M., & Batieha, F., "A Fuzzy Multi-criteria Decision Making Model for Supplier Selection", *Expert Systems with Applications*, 38 (7), 2011: 8384 – 8391.

[2] Abdullah, L., & Zulkifli, N., "Integration of Fuzzy AHP and Interval Type – 2 Fuzzy DEMATEL: An Application to Human Resource Management", *Expert Systems with Applications*, 42 (9), 2015: 4397 – 4409.

[3] Chen, C. T., "Extensions of the TOPSIS for Group Decision-making Under Fuzzy Environment", *Fuzzy Sets and Systems*, 114 (1), 2000: 1 – 9.

[4] Chang, B., Chang, C. W., & Wu, C. H., "Fuzzy DEMATEL Method for Developing Supplier Selection Criteria", *Expert Systems with Applications*, 38 (3), 2011: 1850 – 1858.

构关系转换成系统的可理解映射。我们用表 4.2 表示评价和转化专家判断的语言变量。三角模糊数 (l,m,u)，其中 $l \leq m \leq u$。假设 $[x_{ij}^k] = (l_{ij}^k, m_{ij}^k, u_{ij}^k)$，其中 $1 \leq k \leq K$，是第 k 个专家要素 i 对要素 j 的影响度。

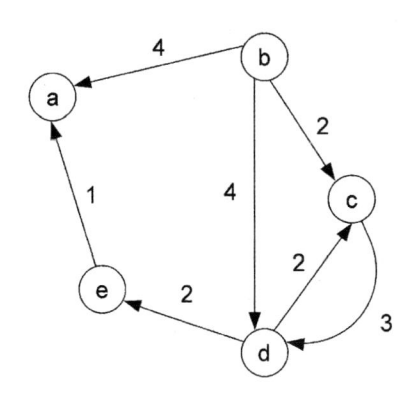

图 4.3 影响图示例

表 4.2 模糊 DEMATEL 方法语言变量

语言变量	相应的三角模糊数
没有影响	(0, 0.1, 0.3)
影响很低	(0.1, 0.3, 0.5)
影响低	(0.3, 0.5, 0.7)
影响高	(0.5, 0.7, 0.9)
影响很高	(0.7, 0.9, 1.0)

步骤 3：构建模糊初始影响矩阵

每个专家给的分数可以形成一个 $n \times n$ 非负答应矩阵，其中 $X^k = [x_{ij}^k] = (l_{ij}^k, m_{ij}^k, u_{ij}^k)$，$k = 1, 2, \cdots, H$。因此，$X^1, X^2, \cdots, X^H$ 是 H 个专家的回答矩阵。每个答应矩阵的对角元素 $X^k = [x_{ij}^k]_{n \times n}$ 都设为 0，意味着没有影响。

$$b_{ij} = \frac{1}{H}\sum_{k=1}^{H} x_{ij}^{k} \tag{4.1}$$

步骤 4：去模糊化得到直接影响矩阵

要将三角模糊数转化为具体数值，去模糊化是很有必要的。用公式（4.2）的去模糊化方法可以得到直接影响矩阵[1]。

$$a_{ij} = \frac{1}{3}(l_{ij}^{k} + m_{ij}^{k} + u_{ij}^{k}) \tag{4.2}$$

矩阵 $A = [a_{ij}]_{n \times n}$ 也称为初始直接影响矩阵。此外，我们可以通过绘制影响图来绘制系统中每对因素之间的因果效应。

步骤 5：计算规范化直接影响矩阵

通过以下方法对直接影响矩阵 A 进行归一化来获得归一化的初始直接关系矩阵 $D = [d_{ij}]_{n \times n}$。

$$s = \max(\max_{1 \leqslant i \leqslant n}\sum_{j=1}^{n} a_{ij}) \tag{4.3}$$

则：

$$D = \frac{A}{s} \tag{4.4}$$

矩阵 A 的每一行 j 的总和表示因子对其他因素施加的直接影响。因此 $\max_{1 \leqslant i \leqslant n}\sum_{j=1}^{n} a_{ij}$ 代表了受其他因素影响最大的因素。正标量 s 取极值和的最大值，矩阵 D 是通过将 A 中每个元素除以标量获得的。矩阵 D 的每个元素 d_{ij} 都在 0 和 1 之间。

步骤 6：确定综合影响矩阵

综合影响矩阵 $T = [t_{ij}]_{n \times n}$，$i, j = 1, 2, \cdots, n$ 可以通过使用公式（4.5）获得。

$$T = \lim_{m \to \infty}(D + D^{2} + \cdots + D^{m}) = D(I - D)^{-1} \tag{4.5}$$

其中 I 表示单位矩阵。

---

[1] Luthra, S., Govindan, K., Kharb, R. K., & Mangla, S. K., "Evaluating the Enablers in Solar Power Developments in the Current Scenario Using Fuzzy DEMATEL: An Indian Perspective", *Renewable and Sustainable Energy Reviews*, 63, 2016: 379–397.

步骤 7：计算要素的影响度和被影响度

向量 $R = (R_1, R_2, \cdots, R_n)$ 与 $C = (C_1, C_2, \cdots, C_n)$ 分别表示矩阵 T 的行和及矩阵的列和。

$$R_i = \sum_{j=1}^{n} t_{ij} \tag{4.6}$$

$$C_i = \sum_{i=1}^{n} t_{ij} \tag{4.7}$$

其中，$t_{ij}(i, j = 1, 2, \cdots, n)$ 为 T 中元素，t_{ij} 表示要素 j 受到要素 i 的综合影响程度。R_i 表示行的总和，表明各行对应要素对其他要素的总和影响值，称为影响度。C_i 表示列的总和，表示各列对应要素受其他各要素影响的综合值，称为被影响度。

步骤 8：计算要素的中心度与原因度

$R_i + C_i$ 是系统要素的影响度与被影响度之和，表示中心度。根据中心度可判断出要素在系统中的重要程度。若要素的中心度越高，则说明此要素在整个系统中的重要程度越高，供应商的改善意愿较大。$R_i - C_i$ 是系统要素的影响度与被影响度的差，表示原因度。原因度可以表示要素在系统中的位置。如原因度 $R_i - C_i$ 大于 0，则代表此要素是原因类，对其他指标有影响。如原因度 $R_i - C_i$ 小于 0，则表示此要素是结果类，受其他因素的影响。

步骤 9：绘制因果关系图

根据 $R_i + C_i$，$R_i - C_i$ 绘制因果关系图，其中 $R_i + C_i$ 表示横坐标，$R_i - C_i$ 表示纵坐标。以 $(R_i + C_i, R_i - C_i)$ 为坐标绘制因果图，并进行结果分析。据此可以清晰地识别出要素间的关系及其重要性，并可以找出供应商改善意愿大且改善效果好的要素，为提升供应链整体竞争能力提供理论指导。

四 实际应用

四川省的白酒企业 A 认为原有的供应商评价体系已经不适合公众对企业的期望和要求。企业 A 使用的是固态酿酒法，每年的酒类原材料占营业成本比重高达76%。企业A前五名的供应商占年度采购总额比例的62.27%。其中，第一名为27.13%，第二名为21.36%，第三名为7.29%，第四名为3.47%，第五名为3.02%。企业A原有的供应商评价体系主要是从经济方面来进行评估，看重价格和质量，而对于供应商是否对环境有保护，是否履行其相应的社会责任则没有制定相关指标体系。近些年由于市场竞争压力加大，而白酒行业的"塑化剂"风波等严重影响到了白酒行业的生存，因此该公司决定对现有的供应商评价体系进行重新思考，制定出包含经济指标、环境指标和社会指标在内的供应商评价体系。为了评价供应商的可持续指标，企业A选择了一支由10人组成的专家团队。其中，负责企业供应商协调的副总经理一位、技术部代表一位、采购经理一位、生产部代表一位、质保部代表一位、财务部代表一位、学者教授一位、供应商两位（其中一位是包装材料供应商、一位是粮食供应商）和客户代表一位。所有的专家高度熟悉他们各自的领域，并精通决策。根据文献分析结果和专家意见，我们确定了相应的指标体系，并对指标体系进行了选择评估。

（一）选择方法

选用改进的模糊DEMATEL方法，对供应商的选择指标进行了评价选择。其步骤如下所示。

1. 确定指标

根据文献分析结果和专家意见，选择了关于经济、环境和社会三个维度的15个可持续供应商指标。其指标体系如图4.2所示。

2. 确定直接影响程度

运用表4.2所示的模糊语言变量，各专家分别将15个指标的相互影响关系表示出来。

3. 构建模糊初始影响矩阵

通过公式（4.1）求11个专家的模糊语言变量的平均值，可以得到模糊初始直接影响矩阵，如表4.3和表4.4所示。

表 4.3　模糊初始影响矩阵

	C11	C12	C13	C14	C15	C21	C22	C23
C11	(0.00,0.10,0.30)	(0.65,0.85,0.97)	(0.51,0.70,0.85)	(0.70,0.90,1.00)	(0.41,0.61,0.78)	(0.38,0.57,0.75)	(0.35,0.55,0.75)	(0.41,0.61,0.80)
C12	(0.45,0.65,0.81)	(0.00,0.10,0.30)	(0.63,0.83,0.96)	(0.57,0.77,0.94)	(0.41,0.61,0.79)	(0.35,0.55,0.74)	(0.32,0.52,0.69)	(0.37,0.57,0.75)
C13	(0.50,0.70,0.88)	(0.55,0.75,0.90)	(0.00,0.10,0.30)	(0.65,0.85,0.97)	(0.55,0.75,0.92)	(0.23,0.43,0.61)	(0.39,0.59,0.76)	(0.35,0.55,0.74)
C14	(0.65,0.85,0.97)	(0.59,0.79,0.94)	(0.66,0.86,0.98)	(0.00,0.10,0.30)	(0.50,0.70,0.87)	(0.41,0.61,0.78)	(0.46,0.66,0.83)	(0.37,0.57,0.75)
C15	(0.32,0.52,0.72)	(0.43,0.63,0.82)	(0.59,0.79,0.94)	(0.52,0.72,0.89)	(0.00,0.10,0.30)	(0.39,0.59,0.78)	(0.46,0.66,0.84)	(0.46,0.66,0.83)
C21	(0.54,0.74,0.88)	(0.41,0.61,0.78)	(0.35,0.55,0.74)	(0.59,0.79,0.94)	(0.43,0.63,0.79)	(0.00,0.10,0.30)	(0.52,0.72,0.88)	(0.61,0.81,0.95)
C22	(0.39,0.59,0.77)	(0.23,0.43,0.63)	(0.33,0.52,0.70)	(0.37,0.57,0.76)	(0.20,0.39,0.59)	(0.28,0.48,0.68)	(0.00,0.10,0.30)	(0.66,0.86,0.98)
C23	(0.39,0.59,0.77)	(0.27,0.46,0.65)	(0.30,0.50,0.70)	(0.35,0.55,0.75)	(0.20,0.39,0.59)	(0.35,0.55,0.74)	(0.52,0.72,0.85)	(0.00,0.10,0.30)
C24	(0.52,0.72,0.89)	(0.27,0.46,0.66)	(0.35,0.54,0.73)	(0.32,0.48,0.67)	(0.16,0.35,0.55)	(0.45,0.63,0.80)	(0.43,0.61,0.77)	(0.45,0.65,0.81)
C25	(0.41,0.61,0.79)	(0.25,0.45,0.65)	(0.34,0.54,0.74)	(0.35,0.55,0.75)	(0.25,0.45,0.65)	(0.55,0.75,0.90)	(0.61,0.81,0.94)	(0.59,0.79,0.92)
C31	(0.35,0.55,0.75)	(0.35,0.55,0.74)	(0.41,0.61,0.79)	(0.32,0.52,0.72)	(0.35,0.55,0.75)	(0.14,0.32,0.52)	(0.42,0.61,0.78)	(0.34,0.54,0.73)
C32	(0.50,0.70,0.86)	(0.34,0.54,0.74)	(0.32,0.52,0.72)	(0.21,0.41,0.61)	(0.26,0.46,0.66)	(0.25,0.45,0.65)	(0.30,0.50,0.69)	(0.25,0.45,0.65)
C33	(0.43,0.63,0.81)	(0.35,0.55,0.75)	(0.50,0.70,0.86)	(0.35,0.55,0.75)	(0.32,0.52,0.72)	(0.13,0.30,0.50)	(0.44,0.63,0.78)	(0.48,0.68,0.85)
C34	(0.50,0.70,0.88)	(0.43,0.63,0.80)	(0.50,0.70,0.88)	(0.52,0.72,0.88)	(0.52,0.72,0.89)	(0.50,0.70,0.87)	(0.48,0.68,0.86)	(0.48,0.68,0.85)
C35	(0.37,0.57,0.77)	(0.22,0.41,0.61)	(0.34,0.54,0.74)	(0.18,0.37,0.57)	(0.21,0.41,0.61)	(0.37,0.57,0.77)	(0.45,0.65,0.83)	(0.43,0.63,0.80)

表4.4 模糊初始影响矩阵续

	C24	C25	C31	C32	C33	C34	C35
C11	(0.46, 0.66, 0.85)	(0.48, 0.68, 0.85)	(0.59, 0.79, 0.94)	(0.66, 0.86, 0.98)	(0.38, 0.57, 0.75)	(0.54, 0.74, 0.90)	(0.48, 0.68, 0.84)
C12	(0.35, 0.55, 0.74)	(0.55, 0.75, 0.89)	(0.57, 0.77, 0.92)	(0.63, 0.83, 0.95)	(0.45, 0.65, 0.81)	(0.50, 0.70, 0.85)	(0.46, 0.66, 0.82)
C13	(0.39, 0.59, 0.77)	(0.55, 0.75, 0.90)	(0.57, 0.77, 0.93)	(0.61, 0.81, 0.95)	(0.39, 0.59, 0.79)	(0.57, 0.77, 0.94)	(0.57, 0.77, 0.93)
C14	(0.46, 0.66, 0.83)	(0.50, 0.70, 0.85)	(0.46, 0.66, 0.85)	(0.59, 0.79, 0.94)	(0.35, 0.55, 0.75)	(0.35, 0.55, 0.74)	(0.37, 0.57, 0.75)
C15	(0.45, 0.65, 0.80)	(0.55, 0.75, 0.89)	(0.52, 0.72, 0.88)	(0.57, 0.77, 0.93)	(0.45, 0.65, 0.80)	(0.46, 0.66, 0.83)	(0.46, 0.66, 0.84)
C21	(0.48, 0.68, 0.86)	(0.61, 0.81, 0.95)	(0.35, 0.55, 0.75)	(0.43, 0.63, 0.82)	(0.41, 0.61, 0.77)	(0.45, 0.65, 0.80)	(0.54, 0.74, 0.90)
C22	(0.57, 0.77, 0.93)	(0.65, 0.85, 0.95)	(0.50, 0.70, 0.86)	(0.48, 0.68, 0.85)	(0.59, 0.79, 0.93)	(0.52, 0.72, 0.88)	(0.57, 0.77, 0.94)
C23	(0.55, 0.75, 0.91)	(0.45, 0.65, 0.82)	(0.34, 0.54, 0.73)	(0.35, 0.55, 0.73)	(0.46, 0.66, 0.82)	(0.37, 0.57, 0.77)	(0.37, 0.57, 0.75)
C24	(0.00, 0.10, 0.30)	(0.39, 0.57, 0.75)	(0.37, 0.57, 0.75)	(0.39, 0.59, 0.76)	(0.39, 0.57, 0.75)	(0.40, 0.59, 0.77)	(0.43, 0.63, 0.82)
C25	(0.57, 0.77, 0.92)	(0.00, 0.10, 0.30)	(0.50, 0.70, 0.87)	(0.46, 0.66, 0.83)	(0.61, 0.81, 0.95)	(0.50, 0.70, 0.86)	(0.54, 0.74, 0.90)
C31	(0.32, 0.52, 0.71)	(0.37, 0.57, 0.76)	(0.00, 0.10, 0.30)	(0.39, 0.59, 0.77)	(0.45, 0.65, 0.81)	(0.32, 0.52, 0.71)	(0.38, 0.57, 0.75)
C32	(0.30, 0.50, 0.69)	(0.34, 0.54, 0.73)	(0.34, 0.54, 0.74)	(0.00, 0.10, 0.30)	(0.32, 0.52, 0.72)	(0.26, 0.46, 0.66)	(0.25, 0.41, 0.61)
C33	(0.49, 0.68, 0.84)	(0.50, 0.70, 0.86)	(0.66, 0.86, 0.97)	(0.57, 0.77, 0.92)	(0.00, 0.10, 0.30)	(0.45, 0.65, 0.81)	(0.57, 0.77, 0.92)

续表

	C24	C25	C31	C32	C33	C34	C35
C34	(0.48, 0.68, 0.85)	(0.34, 0.54, 0.74)	(0.39, 0.59, 0.76)	(0.45, 0.65, 0.81)	(0.54, 0.74, 0.88)	(0.00, 0.10, 0.30)	(0.39, 0.59, 0.77)
C35	(0.48, 0.68, 0.86)	(0.45, 0.65, 0.85)	(0.50, 0.70, 0.86)	(0.43, 0.63, 0.83)	(0.37, 0.57, 0.75)	(0.34, 0.54, 0.73)	(0.00, 0.10, 0.30)

4. 去模糊化得到直接影响矩阵

用公式（4.2）对模糊初始影响矩阵去模糊化，可以得到直接影响矩阵，如表 4.5 所示。

表 4.5　　　　　　　　　　直接关系矩阵

	C11	C12	C13	C14	C15	C21	C22	C23	C24	C25	C31	C32	C33	C34	C35
C11	0.133	0.821	0.685	0.867	0.6	0.57	0.555	0.606	0.658	0.673	0.773	0.836	0.57	0.724	0.667
C12	0.633	0.133	0.806	0.761	0.603	0.567	0.509	0.404	0.548	0.733	0.755	0.803	0.633	0.685	0.734
C13	0.694	0.736	0.133	0.821	0.742	0.421	0.582	0.548	0.585	0.736	0.758	0.791	0.591	0.761	0.758
C14	0.821	0.773	0.836	0.133	0.691	0.6	0.652	0.567	0.652	0.685	0.658	0.773	0.552	0.548	0.567
C15	0.518	0.624	0.773	0.709	0.133	0.588	0.655	0.652	0.63	0.733	0.706	0.758	0.63	0.652	0.655
C21	0.6	0.548	0.773	0.615	0.706	0.133	0.739	0.788	0.758	0.791	0.624	0.597	0.63	0.691	0.585
C22	0.585	0.427	0.515	0.57	0.394	0.482	0.133	0.836	0.758	0.815	0.688	0.67	0.77	0.706	0.761
C23	0.585	0.461	0.5	0.555	0.394	0.548	0.697	0.133	0.739	0.636	0.533	0.545	0.648	0.573	0.567
C24	0.709	0.467	0.536	0.491	0.358	0.624	0.603	0.636	0.133	0.573	0.567	0.582	0.57	0.588	0.624
C25	0.603	0.445	0.536	0.552	0.445	0.736	0.785	0.767	0.755	0.133	0.691	0.652	0.788	0.688	0.724
C31	0.555	0.548	0.603	0.518	0.555	0.324	0.603	0.533	0.515	0.57	0.133	0.585	0.633	0.515	0.57
C32	0.688	0.536	0.518	0.409	0.464	0.445	0.497	0.445	0.497	0.533	0.536	0.133	0.518	0.464	0.424
C33	0.621	0.552	0.688	0.552	0.518	0.309	0.615	0.67	0.67	0.688	0.833	0.755	0.133	0.633	0.755
C34	0.694	0.618	0.694	0.706	0.709	0.691	0.676	0.67	0.67	0.536	0.582	0.633	0.718	0.133	0.585
C35	0.573	0.412	0.536	0.376	0.409	0.573	0.639	0.618	0.676	0.645	0.688	0.627	0.567	0.533	0.133

5. 计算规范化直接影响矩阵

用公式（4.3）对直接影响矩阵求行和，找到最大值，然后用直接影响矩阵除以这个最大值，即用公式（4.4）得到规范化直接影响矩阵。结果如表 4.6 所示。

表4.6　　　　　　　　　　　　　规范化直接影响矩阵

	C11	C12	C13	C14	C15	C21	C22	C23	C24	C25	C31	C32	C33	C34	C35
C11	0.014	0.084	0.07	0.089	0.062	0.059	0.057	0.062	0.068	0.069	0.079	0.086	0.059	0.074	0.068
C12	0.065	0.014	0.083	0.078	0.062	0.058	0.052	0.041	0.056	0.075	0.078	0.082	0.065	0.07	0.075
C13	0.071	0.076	0.014	0.084	0.076	0.043	0.06	0.056	0.06	0.076	0.078	0.081	0.061	0.078	0.078
C14	0.084	0.079	0.086	0.014	0.071	0.062	0.067	0.058	0.067	0.07	0.068	0.079	0.057	0.056	0.058
C15	0.053	0.064	0.079	0.073	0.014	0.06	0.067	0.067	0.065	0.075	0.072	0.078	0.065	0.067	0.067
C21	0.062	0.056	0.079	0.063	0.072	0.014	0.076	0.081	0.078	0.081	0.064	0.061	0.065	0.071	0.06
C22	0.06	0.044	0.053	0.059	0.04	0.049	0.014	0.086	0.078	0.084	0.071	0.069	0.079	0.072	0.078
C23	0.06	0.047	0.051	0.057	0.04	0.056	0.072	0.014	0.076	0.065	0.055	0.056	0.067	0.059	0.058
C24	0.073	0.048	0.055	0.05	0.037	0.064	0.062	0.065	0.014	0.059	0.058	0.06	0.059	0.06	0.064
C25	0.062	0.046	0.055	0.057	0.046	0.076	0.081	0.079	0.078	0.014	0.071	0.067	0.081	0.071	0.074
C31	0.057	0.056	0.062	0.053	0.057	0.033	0.062	0.055	0.053	0.059	0.014	0.06	0.065	0.053	0.059
C32	0.071	0.055	0.053	0.042	0.048	0.046	0.051	0.046	0.051	0.055	0.055	0.014	0.053	0.048	0.044
C33	0.064	0.057	0.071	0.057	0.053	0.032	0.063	0.069	0.069	0.071	0.086	0.078	0.014	0.065	0.078
C34	0.071	0.063	0.071	0.072	0.073	0.071	0.069	0.069	0.069	0.055	0.06	0.06	0.065	0.014	0.074
C35	0.059	0.042	0.055	0.039	0.042	0.059	0.066	0.063	0.069	0.066	0.071	0.064	0.058	0.055	0.014

6. 确定综合影响矩阵

单位矩阵 I 减规范化矩阵 D，得到表4.7。然后对 $I-D$ 求逆，得到表4.8。然后再用规范化矩阵 D 乘以 $I-D$ 的逆得到综合影响矩阵，也就是用公式（4.5）可以得到综合影响矩阵，如表4.9所示。

表4.7　　　　　　　　　　　　　　$I-D$

	C11	C12	C13	C14	C15	C21	C22	C23	C24	C25	C31	C32	C33	C34	C35
C11	0.986	-0.084	-0.07	-0.089	-0.062	-0.059	-0.057	-0.062	-0.068	-0.069	-0.079	-0.086	-0.059	-0.074	-0.068
C12	-0.065	0.986	-0.083	-0.078	-0.062	-0.058	-0.052	-0.041	-0.056	-0.075	-0.078	-0.082	-0.065	-0.07	-0.075
C13	-0.071	-0.076	0.986	-0.084	-0.076	-0.043	-0.06	-0.056	-0.06	-0.076	-0.078	-0.081	-0.061	-0.078	-0.078
C14	-0.084	-0.079	-0.086	0.986	-0.071	-0.062	-0.067	-0.058	-0.067	-0.07	-0.068	-0.079	-0.057	-0.056	-0.058
C15	-0.053	-0.064	-0.079	-0.073	0.986	-0.06	-0.067	-0.067	-0.065	-0.075	-0.072	-0.078	-0.065	-0.067	-0.067
C21	-0.062	-0.056	-0.079	-0.063	-0.072	0.986	-0.076	-0.081	-0.078	-0.081	-0.064	-0.061	-0.065	-0.071	-0.06
C22	-0.06	-0.044	-0.053	-0.059	-0.04	-0.049	0.986	-0.086	-0.078	-0.084	-0.071	-0.069	-0.079	-0.072	-0.078
C23	-0.06	-0.047	-0.051	-0.057	-0.04	-0.056	-0.072	0.986	-0.076	-0.065	-0.055	-0.056	-0.067	-0.059	-0.058
C24	-0.073	-0.048	-0.055	-0.05	-0.037	-0.064	-0.062	-0.065	0.986	-0.059	-0.058	-0.06	-0.059	-0.06	-0.064
C25	-0.062	-0.046	-0.055	-0.057	-0.046	-0.076	-0.081	-0.079	-0.078	0.986	-0.071	-0.067	-0.081	-0.071	-0.074
C31	-0.057	-0.056	-0.062	-0.053	-0.057	-0.033	-0.062	-0.055	-0.053	-0.059	0.986	-0.06	-0.065	-0.053	-0.059
C32	-0.071	-0.055	-0.053	-0.042	-0.048	-0.046	-0.051	-0.046	-0.051	-0.055	-0.055	0.986	-0.053	-0.048	-0.044
C33	-0.064	-0.057	-0.071	-0.057	-0.053	-0.032	-0.063	-0.069	-0.069	-0.071	-0.086	-0.078	0.986	-0.065	-0.078
C34	-0.071	-0.063	-0.071	-0.072	-0.073	-0.071	-0.069	-0.069	-0.069	-0.055	-0.06	-0.06	-0.065	0.986	-0.074
C35	-0.059	-0.042	-0.055	-0.039	-0.042	-0.059	-0.066	-0.063	-0.069	-0.066	-0.071	-0.064	-0.058	-0.055	0.986

表 4.8　　　　　　　　　　　　　$I-D$ 的逆

	C11	C12	C13	C14	C15	C21	C22	C23	C24	C25	C31	C32	C33	C34	C35
C11	1.679	0.678	0.735	0.718	0.629	0.62	0.712	0.712	0.743	0.759	0.774	0.791	0.709	0.724	0.744
C12	0.7	1.588	0.719	0.682	0.606	0.596	0.682	0.667	0.705	0.736	0.744	0.76	0.689	0.694	0.723
C13	0.728	0.666	1.676	0.709	0.638	0.602	0.71	0.702	0.731	0.76	0.768	0.782	0.707	0.722	0.748
C14	0.733	0.663	0.736	1.637	0.627	0.612	0.709	0.697	0.73	0.748	0.751	0.773	0.696	0.696	0.723
C15	0.696	0.64	0.721	0.683	1.565	0.604	0.701	0.696	0.719	0.743	0.746	0.761	0.695	0.697	0.722
C21	0.716	0.645	0.734	0.686	0.631	1.57	0.722	0.722	0.745	0.762	0.751	0.76	0.708	0.713	0.729
C22	0.677	0.599	0.672	0.645	0.569	0.573	1.627	0.69	0.707	0.725	0.718	0.727	0.684	0.678	0.707
C23	0.617	0.548	0.61	0.587	0.517	0.528	0.621	1.563	0.643	0.645	0.64	0.65	0.613	0.606	0.627
C24	0.625	0.546	0.61	0.578	0.512	0.532	0.609	0.608	1.581	0.636	0.64	0.65	0.602	0.604	0.629
C25	0.693	0.614	0.688	0.658	0.587	0.609	0.704	0.699	0.722	1.675	0.734	0.74	0.7	0.69	0.718
C31	0.59	0.536	0.596	0.562	0.513	0.487	0.589	0.578	0.598	0.615	1.577	0.63	0.589	0.577	0.604
C32	0.561	0.498	0.547	0.512	0.469	0.463	0.538	0.529	0.554	0.568	0.573	1.541	0.537	0.532	0.547
C33	0.673	0.604	0.68	0.637	0.574	0.55	0.665	0.666	0.69	0.704	0.724	0.727	1.615	0.663	0.698
C34	0.708	0.637	0.711	0.68	0.618	0.61	0.7	0.695	0.72	0.721	0.731	0.742	0.691	1.643	0.724
C35	0.605	0.534	0.602	0.56	0.51	0.521	0.606	0.6	0.627	0.635	0.644	0.647	0.596	0.592	1.574

表 4.9　　　　　　　　　　　　　综合影响矩阵

	C11	C12	C13	C14	C15	C21	C22	C23	C24	C25	C31	C32	C33	C34	C35
C11	0.679	0.678	0.735	0.718	0.629	0.62	0.712	0.712	0.743	0.759	0.774	0.791	0.709	0.724	0.744
C12	0.7	0.588	0.719	0.682	0.606	0.596	0.682	0.667	0.705	0.736	0.744	0.76	0.689	0.694	0.723
C13	0.728	0.666	0.676	0.709	0.638	0.602	0.71	0.702	0.731	0.76	0.768	0.782	0.707	0.722	0.748
C14	0.733	0.663	0.736	0.637	0.627	0.612	0.709	0.697	0.73	0.748	0.751	0.773	0.696	0.696	0.723
C15	0.696	0.64	0.721	0.683	0.565	0.604	0.701	0.696	0.719	0.743	0.746	0.761	0.695	0.697	0.722
C21	0.716	0.645	0.734	0.686	0.631	0.57	0.722	0.722	0.745	0.762	0.751	0.76	0.708	0.713	0.729
C22	0.677	0.599	0.672	0.645	0.569	0.573	0.627	0.69	0.707	0.725	0.718	0.727	0.684	0.678	0.707
C23	0.617	0.548	0.61	0.587	0.517	0.528	0.621	0.563	0.643	0.645	0.64	0.65	0.613	0.606	0.627
C24	0.625	0.546	0.61	0.578	0.512	0.532	0.609	0.608	0.581	0.636	0.64	0.65	0.602	0.604	0.629
C25	0.693	0.614	0.688	0.658	0.587	0.609	0.704	0.699	0.722	0.675	0.734	0.74	0.7	0.69	0.718
C31	0.59	0.536	0.596	0.562	0.513	0.487	0.589	0.578	0.598	0.615	0.577	0.63	0.589	0.577	0.604
C32	0.561	0.498	0.547	0.512	0.469	0.463	0.538	0.529	0.554	0.568	0.573	0.541	0.537	0.532	0.547
C33	0.673	0.604	0.68	0.637	0.574	0.55	0.665	0.666	0.69	0.704	0.724	0.727	0.615	0.663	0.698
C34	0.708	0.637	0.711	0.68	0.618	0.61	0.7	0.695	0.72	0.721	0.731	0.742	0.691	0.643	0.724
C35	0.605	0.534	0.602	0.56	0.51	0.521	0.606	0.6	0.627	0.635	0.644	0.647	0.596	0.592	0.574

7. 计算指标的影响度和被影响度

用公式（4.6）对综合矩阵求行和，得到影响度 R，用公式（4.7）对综合矩阵求列和，得到被影响度 C。其结果如表 4.10 所示。

表 4.10　　　　　　　　　　模糊 DEMATEL 计算结果

指标	R	C	$R+C$	$R-C$	排序
质量（$C11$）	10.726	10.001	20.727	0.726	1
交货（$C12$）	10.291	8.997	19.289	1.294	8
服务（$C13$）	10.648	10.035	20.684	0.613	2
价格（$C14$）	10.532	9.533	20.065	0.999	5
柔性（$C15$）	10.388	8.565	18.953	1.823	13
资源消耗（$C21$）	10.594	8.479	19.073	2.115	11
污染控制（$C22$）	9.999	9.897	19.896	0.103	6
环境管理体系（$C23$）	9.014	9.823	18.837	-0.809	14
绿色产品（$C24$）	8.961	10.214	19.174	-1.253	9
环境竞争力（$C25$）	10.232	10.43	20.662	-0.198	3
员工利益和权利（$C31$）	8.64	10.513	19.152	-1.873	10
利益相关者权利（$C32$）	7.969	10.682	18.65	-2.713	15
工作安全和职业健康（$C33$）	9.869	9.831	19.7	0.039	7
信息披露（$C34$）	10.329	9.832	20.161	0.497	4
尊重政策（$C35$）	8.853	10.216	19.07	-1.363	12

8. 计算指标的中心度与原因度

$R_i + C_i$ 是系统要素的影响度与被影响度之和，表示中心度。$R_i - C_i$ 是系统要素的影响度与被影响度的差，表示原因度。其结果如表 4.12 所示。

9. 绘制因果关系图

根据 $R_i + C_i$，$R_i - C_i$ 绘制因果关系图，其中 $R_i + C_i$ 表示横坐标，$R_i - C_i$ 表示纵坐标。以 $(R_i + C_i, R_i - C_i)$ 为坐标绘制因果图，并进行结果分析。其结果如图 4.4 所示。

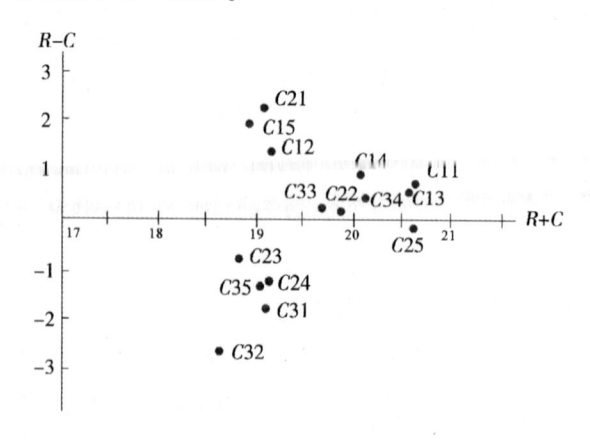

图 4.4　因果关系图

(二) 讨论分析

通过模糊 DEMATEL 方法对白酒企业 A 的供应商评价指标进行分析，得出了相应的结果。现在对供应商选择指标从重要度分析、原因要素分析和结果要素分析三个方面进行讨论。

1. 重要度分析

通过对白酒企业供应链上的供应商指标进行可持续分析，从中心度可以看到供应商评价指标的重要度排序。这些指标按 $R+C$ 重要性排序为：$C11 > C13 > C25 > C34 > C14 > C22 > C33 > C12 > C24 > C31 > C21 > C35 > C15 > C23 > C32$。通过模糊 *DEMATEL* 分析得出，质量（$C11$）、服务（$C13$）、环境竞争力（$C25$）、信息披露（$C34$）和价格（$C14$）分别以值 20.727、20.684、20.662、20.161 和 20.065 排在最重要指标的前五位。而柔性（$C15$）、环境管理体系（$C23$）、利益相关者权利（$C32$）分别以值 18.953、18.831 和 18.650 处于重要度排序的后三位。

如原因度 $R_i - C_i$ 大于 0，则代表此要素是原因类，对其他指标有影响。根据表 4.10，质量（$C11$）、交货（$C12$）、服务（$C13$）、价格（$C14$）、柔性（$C15$）、资源消耗（$C21$）、污染控制（$C22$）、工作安全和职业健康（$C33$）和信息披露（$C34$）均属于原因类指标。而如果原因度 $R_i - C_i$ 小于 0，则表示此要素是结果类，受其他因素的影响。表 4.10 中，环境管理体系（$C23$）、绿色产品（$C24$）、环境竞争力（$C25$）、尊重政策（$C35$）、员工利益和权利（$C31$）和利益相关者权利（$C32$）属于结果类指标。

白酒企业需要从三个维度 15 个指标中改善供应商选择绩效。从研究中看出，采购方管理人员要重点关注供应商的质量（$C11$）、服务（$C13$）、环境竞争力（$C25$）、信息披露（$C34$）和价格（$C14$）。从图 4.4 看出，资源消耗（$C21$）和柔性（$C15$）是最重要的两个原因要素。它们直接影响其他要素。尽管它们不是最重要的指标要素，但是它们能为管理决策者提供参考，选出具有可持续发展能力的供应商。这也说明采购企业要关注供应商的资源消耗情况和相关柔性指标。

2. 原因要素分析

原因度分析是很重要的一类分析，因此在白酒企业的供应商选择中需要重视它。从图 4.4 看出，资源消耗（$C21$）具有最高的 $R-C$ 值 2.115，意味着资源消耗（$C21$）对整个系统具有很强的影响力。然而它的中心度（$R+C$）值 19.073 却相对较低，影响度为 10.594，意味着供应商的资源消耗对其他指标有着重要影响力的同时受其他要素影响较小。

柔性（$C15$）是排在第二位的原因度，值为 1.823。但是其中心度值是 18.953，影响度为 10.388，说明它更易于直接影响其他要素，而受其他要素影响相对较小。对于白酒企业的供应商来说，是否具有柔性，对企业后期的可持续发展具有重要的影响。交货（$C12$）以原因度 1.294 排在第三位。其中心度值是 19.289，影响度为 10.291。说明交货是原因要素，对其他要素具有一定的影响力，同时也受其他因素的影响。价格（$C14$）的原因度 0.999 排在第四位。其中心度为 20.065，在重要性上排第五。质量（$C11$）的原因度 0.726 紧排其后，质量的中心度为 20.727，排在重要度的第一位，这与 Chang 等[1]的研究结论一致。服务（$C13$）的原因度为 0.613。中心度为 20.684，排在重要度的第二位。信息披露（$C34$）的原因度为 0.497。中心度为 20.161，排在重要度的第四位。污染控制（$C22$）的原因度为 0.103，中心度为 19.896，在重要度排序上排第六。工作安全和职业健康（$C33$）的原因度为 0.039，中心度为 19.700。

3. 结果要素分析

系统中的结果要素很容易受到其他要素的影响。然而，尽管这些结果要素对整个系统没有直接影响，但是仍对整个系统有着重要贡献。在所有的结果要素中，利益相关者权利（$C32$）以 $R-C$ 值 -2.713 处于结果要素的最低点，这表示此要素受其他要素的影响最大。在白酒企业的供应商选

---

[1] Chang, B., Chang, C. W., & Wu, C. H., "Fuzzy DEMATEL Method for Developing Supplier Selection Criteria", *Expert Systems with Applications*, 38 (3), 2011: 1850-1858.

择中,其供应商的其他各项指标越好,意味着对它的利益相关者权利越有益。其他结果要素如下,员工利益和权利($C31$)的$R-C$值为-1.873,尊重政策($C35$)的$R-C$值为-1.363,绿色产品($C24$)的$R-C$值为-1.253,环境管理体系($C23$)的$R-C$值为-0.809,环境竞争力($C25$)的$R-C$值为-0.198。结果要素中质量($C11$)具有最高的$R+C$值20.727,说明这个要素是最重要的结果要素。

五 本章小结

白酒企业的供应商选择对白酒企业可持续发展起着重要的作用。根据文献分析结果和专家意见,我们确定了白酒行业的供应商可持续选择指标。从经济、环境和社会三个维度考虑,其中每个角度分别选取了5个指标,因此总共有15个可持续供应商选择指标。运用模糊DEMATEL方法进行评价选择。最后将该算法应用到四川省一家白酒企业的可持续供应商选择中。结果表明该方法是有效的。研究的贡献总结如下:(1)首次在白酒供应链中从经济、环境和社会三个维度考虑可持续供应商的选择指标。(2)构建了白酒行业的供应商可持续选择的三个维度的指标体系。(3)将本书提出的方法应用于四川省的一家白酒企业的可持续供应商选择中,结果表明该算法和模型是可行的、有效的。

第五章 白酒可持续供应链风险管控模型及应用

供应链风险问题会影响供应链的稳定性,使供应链整体竞争实力下降,并最终导致供应链上的企业遭受巨大损失。风险问题是任何企业在任何发展阶段都会面临的重要问题。近年来全球供应链风险事件频繁爆发,对全球供应链产生较大影响。1999 年,苹果因为中国台湾地震短缺 DRAM 芯片而失去大量顾客[1]。2000 年,芯片厂火灾导致爱立信损失 4 亿欧元的销售额,市场份额由之前的 12% 降至 9%[2]。2001 年,"9·11"事件导致福特、丰田等汽车生产线停产。路虎公司在 2001 年因其供应商破产解雇了 1400 名员工。2005 年"苏丹红"事件导致麦当劳和肯德基损失严重。2006 年,因为火灾,戴尔召回了由索尼生产的 400 万个笔记本电脑电池[3]。2008 年的"三聚氰胺"事件造成中国直接损失 200 亿元。2011 年日本福岛核电站事故,对全球精密零部件的整个产业供应链都造成了严重影响。2011 年,泰国洪水造成重大损失。

---

[1] Chen, P. S., & Wu, M. T., "A Modified Failure Mode and Effects Analysis Method for Supplier Selection Problems in the Supply Chain Risk Environment: A Case Study", *Computers & Industrial Engineering*, 66 (4), 2013: 634–642.

[2] Jüttner, U., Peck, H., & Christopher, M., "Supply Chain Risk Management: Outlining an Agenda for Future Research", *International Journal of Logistics: Research and Applications*, 6 (4), 2003: 197–210.

[3] Tang, C., & Tomlin, B., "The Power of Flexibility for Mitigating Supply Chain Risks", *International Journal of Production Economics*, 116 (1), 2008: 12–27.

由于洪水淹没建筑物及农田等设施，造成重大经济损失，被形容为"慢海啸"。2015年天津港爆炸事件冲击全球供应链体系。造成12万多辆汽车和7000多个集装箱受损，直接经济损失达68.66亿元。过去20年来，各种风险事件使供应链运营中断，对企业的短期绩效带来了很严重的影响[1]。供应链中断可能导致经济损失、使公司形象受损、危害健康和安全等，会对公司的金融绩效产生长远的负面效应[2]。由此可见，在全球经济一体化的今天，供应链风险无处不在，人们对于风险管理也越来越重视。

一　维度方法

目前，保险学、管理学、统计学、经济学、决策理论学等领域都从理论和实践两个角度对风险进行了深入而广泛的研究。无论是学术研究者还是企业实践者，都对风险与风险管理给予了高度重视。

（一）风险维度

传统的方法对供应链风险的管理侧重在经济维度上。但是随着企业、政府、消费者、公众等对环境保护和社会责任的重视，风险管理的维度也逐渐拓展到经济、环境和社会等维度。在原有的经济风险分析中，尽管没有明确提出环境保护或社会责任，但是有些学者在研究的过程中都或多或少地考虑到了相关影响因素。

1. 传统的风险维度

风险发生是因为对未来的不确定，意味着意想不到的事件发生。日益发展的全球运营一方面大幅降低成本，另一方面使供应链更容易遭受风险。整合绩效和风险管理是增加股东价值的关键杠杆。Hahn和Kuhn

---

[1] Tang, C. S., "Perspectives in Supply Chain Risk Management", *International Journal of Production Economics*, 103 (2), 2006: 451 – 488.

[2] Zeng, B., & Yen, B. P. C., "Rethinking the Role of Partnerships in Global Supply Chains: A Risk-based Perspective", *International Journal of Production Economics*, 185, 2017: 52 – 62.

认为风险源分为需求不确定（数量、价格）、供应不确定（成本、提前期、能力）、资源中断、质量问题、利率水平、供应商偿付能力和外汇汇率①。Lavastre 等通过对 50 家不同的法国公司的 142 位总经理和物流供应链经理的研究表明，有效的供应链风险管理是基于协同和合作伙伴关系的供应链②。Braunscheidel 等提出中断、延迟、系统、预测、知识产权、采购、应收账款、库存、能力是 9 个供应链风险来源，识别出过程、控制、需求、供应、环境 5 个风险源。认为供应链经理对风险的态度一般分为风险厌恶、风险中性、风险偏好③。Chan 和 Kumar 将风险因素分为地理位置、政治稳定、经济和恐怖主义④。在风险管理中，通常情况下，破坏性事件（如破产、自然灾害等）都会考虑到，但是动态环境（如顾客偏好的改变、技术转型等）的持续改变却经常被忽略⑤。

Vilko 和 Hallikas 等划分了三种形式的风险，即内在风险，从组织中产生的；供应链风险，组织外的但是在供应链中的；外在风险，是供应链之外的环境引起的。他们将风险分为供应风险、运营风险、需求风险、安全风险、宏观风险、政策风险、竞争风险和资源风险。认为供应链风险的标准定义是：$Risk = P(Probability) \times L(Loss)$。风险是损失发生的概率（$P$）和其结果的严重度（$L$）的函数⑥。Tang 和 Tomlin 总结了 6 类主要的供应链风险，即供应风险、流程风险、需求风险、知识产权

---

① Hahn, G. J., & Kuhn, H., "Value-based Performance and Risk Management in Supply Chains: A Robust Optimization Approach", *International Journal of Production Economics*, 139 (1), 2012: 135 – 144.

② Lavastre, O., Gunasekaran, A., & Spalanzani, A., "Supply Chain Risk Management in French Companies", *Decision Support Systems*, 52 (4), 2012: 828 – 838.

③ Braunscheidel, M. J., & Suresh, N. C., "The Organizational Antecedents of a Firm's Supply Chain Agility for Risk Mitigation and Response", *Journal of Operations Management*, 27 (2), 2009: 119 – 140.

④ Chan, F. T., & Kumar, N., "Global Supplier Development Considering Risk Factors Using Fuzzy Extended AHP-based Approach", *Omega*, 35 (4), 2007: 417 – 431.

⑤ Trkman, P., & McCormack, K., "Supply Chain Risk in Turbulent Environments—A Conceptual Model for Managing Supply Chain Network Risk", *International Journal of Production Economics*, 119 (2), 2009: 247 – 258.

⑥ Vilko, J. P., & Hallikas, J. M., "Risk Assessment in Multimodal Supply Chains", *International Journal of Production Economics*, 140 (2), 2012: 586 – 595.

风险、行为风险和社会风险。其研究结果认为柔性可以缓解供应链风险[①]。Dong 和 Cooper 对风险进行了详细的划分，分为飓风、地震、政治政策、战争、金融危机、恐怖主义、汇率波动、供应商破产、供应商的不准确装船、供应商透明度低、合同违约、供应中断、低供应商整合、供应商锁定、运输供应商的分裂、运输瓶颈、市场需求转型、不准确出货给客户、不准确的需求预测、订单波动、紧急订单、产品在途破坏、保修政策、信息扭曲、客户流失、缺乏技术工人、工资上涨、技术升级和机器故障[②]。Thun 和 Hoenig 分析调查了 67 家德国汽车行业的生产工厂，调查了供应链脆弱性和供应链风险的关键驱动力。识别出的供应链风险有供应商失败、供应商质量问题、石油危机、恐怖袭击、罢工、信息技术系统故障、意外事故（如火灾）、自然灾害；机器故障、进出口限制、交通运输中断、交付链中断、技术变更、原材料价格增加、客户需求变动[③]。Venkatesh 等确定的风险变量有全球化、原料及产品质量标准、稀缺资源、供应商的不确定性、缺乏协调、员工行为方面、基础设施风险、进度的延迟/提前期、需求的不确定性、客户不满意、金融风险和安全[④]。Tang 和 Musa 将风险划分为物流、生产、交付、供应链范围、资金流风险、信息流风险、知识外包七个维度[⑤]。Hendricks 和 Singhal 根据 1989—2000 年发表的 827 次中断公告样本，研究了供应链中断对长期股票价格效应和股权风险的影响。股票价格影响从破产公告日期之前一年到两年之间开始检查。在这段时间内，经历中断

[①] Tang, C., & Tomlin, B., "The Power of Flexibility for Mitigating Supply Chain Risks", *International Journal of Production Economics*, 116（1），2008：12 - 27.

[②] Dong, Q., & Cooper, O., "An Orders-of-Magnitude AHP Supply Chain Risk Assessment Framework", *International Journal of Production Economics*, 182, 2016：144 - 156.

[③] Thun, J. H., & Hoenig, D., "An Empirical Analysis of Supply Chain Risk Management in the German Automotive Industry", *International Journal of Production Economics*, 131（1），2011：242 - 249.

[④] Venkatesh, V. G., Rathi, S., & Patwa, S., "Analysis on Supply Chain Risks in Indian Apparel Retail Chains and Proposal of Risk Prioritization Model Using Interpretive Structural Modeling", *Journal of Retailing and Consumer Services*, 26, 2015：153 - 167.

[⑤] Tang, O., & Musa, S. N., "Identifying Risk Issues and Research Advancements in Supply Chain Risk Management", *International Journal of Production Economics*, 133（1），2011：25 - 34.

的公司的平均异常股票收益率接近33%—40%。在公告前一年，公告日期和公告后一年，观察到大部分公司业绩不佳。此外，证据表明，企业不能迅速从破坏的负面影响中恢复。公司的股权风险在公告日期上也显著增加。公告后一年的权益风险较公告前一年的权益风险高13.50%[1]。Hendricks和Singhal报告称企业遭受供应链中断经历相对于其行业基准低33%—40%的股票回报。Mohammaddust等将供应链风险分为延迟风险、中断风险、质量风险和预测风险四类，并提出了相应的应对策略[2]。Assefa等通过对欧洲农产品供应链中的农民、批发商、加工商和零售商的访谈，发现价格与预期水平偏差超过10%—15%就会被大多数供应链成员认为是价格波动。并提出了四种价格波动管理策略：生存（survive）、调整（adapt）、控制（control）和对冲（hedge）[3]。供应链缓解和控制策略分为主动和被动两类[4]。在全球供应链环境下，采取有效的风险管理策略变得越来越具挑战性。

2. 绿色的风险维度

随着人们对环境保护的重视，风险因素中开始考虑环保或者说与绿色相关的风险维度和指标。Lintukangas等从165家芬兰公司收集的实证数据用于检查企业的风险管理能力与采用绿色供应管理实践之间的联系。基于回归分析，发现质量和品牌风险管理能力与采用绿色供应管理正相关，而价格和成本风险管理能力具有相反的效果。其将风险划分为

---

[1] Hendricks, K. B., & Singhal, V. R., "An Empirical Analysis of the Effect of Supply Chain Disruptions on Long-Run Stock Price Performance and Equity Risk of the Firm", *Production and Operations Management*, 14 (1), 2005: 35–52.

[2] Mohammaddust, F., Rezapour, S., Farahani, R. Z., Mofidfar, M., & Hill, A., "Developing Lean and Responsive Supply Chains: A Robust Model for Alternative Risk Mitigation Strategies in Supply Chain Designs", *International Journal of Production Economics*, 183, 2017: 632–653.

[3] Assefa, T. T., Meuwissen, M. P., & Lansink, A. G. O., "Price Risk Perceptions and Management Strategies in Selected European Food Supply Chains: An Exploratory Approach", *NJAS-Wageningen Journal of Life Sciences*, 80, 2017: 15–26.

[4] Ghadge, A., Dani, S., Ojha, R., & Caldwell, N., "Using Risk Sharing Contracts for Supply Chain Risk Mitigation: A Buyer-supplier Power and Dependence Perspective", *Computers & Industrial Engineering*, 103, 2017: 262–270.

知识产权风险、品牌形象风险、质量风险、价格风险、外包风险、全球化、原料和产品质量标准、资源稀缺、供应商不确定性、缺乏协调、员工的行为方面、基础设施风险、交货时间延迟、需求不确定性、客户不满意、财务风险、安全[①]。Zhao 等在绿色供应链管理中用多目标优化方法降低由危险物质、碳排放和经济成本引起的最低内生风险[②]。Cousins 等探讨了与环境相关的风险[③]。

3. 可持续的风险维度

尽管越来越多的学者和企业界人士开始关注供应链可持续性与风险之间的联系，但是关于这方面的研究还很少[④]。有些学者只聚焦于环境风险研究，有些学者局限于某些特定的方面，认为任何风险管理战略适用于可持续性相关的风险研究[⑤]。然而这些研究中的风险概念具有局限性，仅仅从财务管理角度关注最小化可持续绩效的负面效应。Foerstl 等通过提出的可持续供应商风险管理开创了这个领域的研究[⑥]。Hoffman 等研究了供应链问题会引起可持续相关风险，但是缺少对供应

---

① Lintukangas, K., Köhkänen, A. K., & Ritala, P., "Supply Risks as Drivers of Green Supply Management Adoption", *Journal of Cleaner Production*, 112, 2016: 1901 – 1909.

② Zhao, R., Liu, Y., Zhang, N., & Huang, T., "An Optimization Model for Green Supply Chain Management by Using a Big Data Analytic Approach", *Journal of Cleaner Production*, 142, 2017: 1085 – 1097.

③ Cousins, P. D., Lamming, R. C., & Bowen, F., "The Role of Risk in Environment-related Supplier Initiatives", *International Journal of Operations & Production Management*, 24 (6), 2004: 554 – 565.

④ Giannakis, M., & Papadopoulos, T., "Supply Chain Sustainability: A Risk Management Approach", *International Journal of Production Economics*, 171, 2016: 455 – 470; William Blackburn, *The Sustainability Handbook: The Complete Management Guide to Achieving Social, Economic and Environmental Responsibility*, Routledge, 2012.

⑤ Anderson, D. R., & Anderson, K. E., "Sustainability Risk Management", *Risk Management and Insurance Review*, 12 (1), 2009: 25; Anderson, D. R., "The Critical Importance of Sustainability Risk Management", *Risk Management*, 53 (4), 2006: 66.

⑥ Foerstl, K., Reuter, C., Hartmann, E., & Blome, C., "Managing Supplier Sustainability Risks in a Dynamically Changing Environment——Sustainable Supplier Management in the Chemical Industry", *Journal of Purchasing and Supply Management*, 16 (2), 2010: 118 – 130.

链可持续相关风险的集成分析和发展相关的风险管理策略[1]。Pullman 等考虑到可持续性的三重底线和 Brundtland 定义,将风险划分为经济风险、环境风险和社会风险。这些与可持续性相关的风险与典型的供应链风险在很多方面都不同。可持续风险管理考虑到供应链运营在自然生态系统、公司声誉、金融风险方面以及遵从法律而不是破坏的后果。在环境维度,风险指导原则需满足共享生态系统质量的需求。社会维度则是指对员工、客户、商业伙伴、政府和社会的责任交付[2]。经济维度则是指由金融环境、公司和个人欺诈行为、经济持续增长的努力引起的货币风险[3]。

United Nations Global Compact and BSR（2010）提出常见的可持续相关风险有温室气体、自然灾害、事故、能源消耗、包装浪费、在物流和运输过程中的环境破坏。其他可持续风险可能包括对某一公司产品的抵制、由于环境事故而被起诉；不遵从法律规定或者由不人道的行为、不公平雇用和工作实践引起的社会评价风险；由商品和能源涨价引起的燃料短缺。BSR 报告谈及了一系列的商业丑闻,包括童工/强迫性劳动、虐待动物、负面环境影响、限价、行贿指责、欺骗和专利侵权。这些风险对于很多企业来说是很重要的,因为他们对公司的名誉造成损害,进而会引起很大的金融损失[4]。Giannakis 和 Papadopoulos 通过广泛的文献回顾和个人访谈,确定了经济、环境和社会三个维度的风险因素,具体指标如表 5.1 所示。使用 FMEA 方法评估所选风险的相对重要性,案

---

[1] Hofmann, H., Busso, C., Bode, C., & Henke, M., "Sustainability-related Supply Chain Risks: Conceptualization and Management", *Business Strategy and the Environment*, 23 (3), 2014: 160 – 172.

[2] Pullman, M. E., Maloni, M. J., & Carter, C. R., "Food for Thought: Social Versus Environmental Sustainability Practices and Performance Outcomes", *Journal of Supply Chain Management*, 45 (4), 2009: 38 – 54.

[3] Marcel Jeucken, *Sustainability in Finance: Banking on the Planet*, Eburon Uitgeverij BV, 2004.

[4] Un Global Compact., "Supply Chain Sustainability: A Practical Guide for Continuous Improvement", *Sustainability the Journal of Record*, 4 (3): 2010: 480 – 497.

例分析显示内生环境风险是其中与可持续相关的最重要的风险[1]。最近的一些研究表明，如果一个公司在运营中能够将经济因素与负责任的因素结合起来，它们就可以获得长期的竞争优势[2]。

表 5.1　　　　　　　　可持续相关供应链风险

维度	来源	指标
环境风险	内生	能源消耗，环境事故，温室气体，未遵守可持续法规，污染（空气、水、土地），产品废弃物，不必要的包装
	外生	自然灾害（洪水、地震），热浪，干旱，水短缺
社会风险	内生	童工/强迫性劳动，歧视（种族、性别、宗教、年龄、政治），不健康/危险的工作环境，不人性化的对待/骚扰，不公平的工资待遇，对待动物不人道，超长工时/工作生活不平衡
	外生	人口结构方面的挑战/人口老龄化，流行病，社会不稳定/不安定
经济风险	内生	反垄断索赔，行贿指责/贪污受贿，虚假索赔/不诚实，专利侵权，价格操纵的指控，逃税避税
	外生	抵制，能源价格变动，金融危机，诉讼

资料来源：Giannakis, M., & Papadopoulos, T., "Supply Chain Sustainability: A Risk Management Approach", *International Journal of Production Economics*, 171, 2016: 455–470。

（二）管理方法

随着对供应链脆弱性的日益重视，用于分析供应链风险管理的有效数学工具现在正受到广泛关注。Wu 等运用大数据方法（社会媒体、定量定性数据）、模糊和灰色 DEMATEL 方法对台湾发光二极管产业的供应链风险和不确定性进行了广泛的研究，结果显示能力和运营比其他供应链属性具有更大的影响[3]。Zhao 等用大数据分析方法对绿色供应链风

---

[1] Giannakis, M., & Papadopoulos, T., "Supply Chain Sustainability: A Risk Management Approach", *International Journal of Production Economics*, 171, 2016: 455–470.

[2] Kramer, M. R., & Porter, M., "Creating Shared Value", *Harvard Business Review*, 89 (1/2), 2011: 62–77.

[3] Wu, K. J., Liao, C. J., Tseng, M. L., Lim, M. K., Hu, J., & Tan, K., "Toward Sustainability: Using Big Data to Explore the Decisive Attributes of Supply Chain Risks and Uncertainties", *Journal of Cleaner Production*, 142, 2017: 663–676.

险管理的相关参数进行了分析①。Sherwin 等将故障树分析方法用于识别延迟风险，并在低产量高价值的供应链中积极提出具有成本效益的缓解策略②。Chan 和 Kumar 应用模糊扩展层次分析法（FEAHP）在考虑风险的情况下对全球供应商发展进行了分析③。Kauppi 等应用信息处理理论和互补理论，表明供应链整体风险管理方法与经营绩效正相关④。Helbig 等扩展了地缘政治供应风险评估下的生命周期可持续评估框架，并将这个方法应用到聚丙烯腈碳纤维供应链⑤。

Babazadeh 等用扩展—约束方法和帕累托最优研究表明对基于风险的供应链网络设计投入高投资成本是必要的⑥。Tapiero 通过使 Neyman-Pearson 位数风险框架得出各方承担的风险取决于组织结构、动机和供应链成员之间的权利关系⑦。Govindan 和 Fattahi 通过使用不同的风险度量和最小化目标的加权平均风险目标，分别获得风险规避和稳健的解决方案⑧。Dong 和 Cooper 开发了一个基于事前供应链风险关系评估的数

---

① Zhao, R., Liu, Y., Zhang, N., & Huang, T., "An Optimization Model for Green Supply Chain Management by Using a Big Data Analytic Approach", *Journal of Cleaner Production*, 142, 2017: 1085 – 1097.

② Sherwin, M. D., Medal, H., & Lapp, S. A., "Proactive Cost-effective Identification and Mitigation of Supply Delay Risks in a Low Volume High Value Supply Chain Using Fault-tree Analysis", *International Journal of Production Economics*, 175, 2016: 153 – 163.

③ Chan, F. T., & Kumar, N., "Global Supplier Development Considering Risk Factors Using Fuzzy Extended AHP-based Approach", *Omega*, 35 (4), 2007: 417 – 431.

④ Kauppi, K., Longoni, A., Caniato, F., & Kuula, M., "Managing Country Disruption Risks and Improving Operational Performance: Risk Management Along Integrated Supply Chains", *International Journal of Production Economics*, 182, 2016: 484 – 495.

⑤ Helbig, C., Gemechu, E. D., Pillain, B., Young, S. B., Thorenz, A., Tuma, A., & Sonnemann, G., "Extending the Geopolitical Supply Risk Indicator: Application of Life Cycle Sustainability Assessment to the Petrochemical Supply Chain of Polyacrylonitrile-based Carbon Fibers", *Journal of Cleaner Production*, 137, 2016: 1170 – 1178.

⑥ Babazadeh, R., Razmi, J., Pishvaee, M. S., & Rabbani, M., "A Sustainable Second-Generation Biodiesel Supply Chain Network Design Problem Under Risk", *Omega*, 66, 2017: 258 – 277.

⑦ Tapiero, C. S., "Consumers Risk and Quality Control in a Collaborative Supply Chain", *European Journal of Operational Research*, 182 (2), 2007: 683 – 694.

⑧ Govindan, K., & Fattahi, M., "Investigating Risk and Robustness Measures for Supply Chain Network Design Under Demand Uncertainty: A Case Study of Glass Supply Chain", *International Journal of Production Economics*, 183, 2017: 680 – 699.

量级的层次分析法模型（Orders-of-magnitude AHP，OM – AHP），并用案例验证了方法的有效性[1]。Lintukangas 等提出了 ISM 和模糊 MICMAC 方法的风险优先级（RPN）计算的新模型[2]。Giannakis 和 Louis 发展了一个基于决策支持系统的多代理框架来管理供应链风险[3]。Wu 和 Olson 在供应链风险中考虑了供应链中的机会约束规划（CCP），提出数据包络分析（DEA）和多目标规划（MOP）模型[4]。Venkatesh 等介绍了 Delphi 技术解释性结构建模（ISM）、风险优先级（RPN）计算、模糊 MICMAC 方法[5]。Goh 等提出了一个多阶段全球供应链网络问题的随机模型，使用 Moreau-Yosida 正则化提供了一种新的解决方法[6]。Xia 和 Chen 提出了基于 ANP 的风险决策模型[7]。Zeng 和 Yen 提出了一个供应链风险系统模型，能够传达基于风险的全球供应链伙伴关系观点。通过分析推断，表明合作伙伴之间的协作水平有助于提高供应链的弹性[8]。Tuncel 和 Alpan 用 FMECA（Failure Mode，Effects and Criticality Analysis）技术调查了供应链网络中的中断因素[9]。

上述很多方法是在风险发生后对其进行分析。供应链风险管理重在

---

[1] Dong, Q., & Cooper, O., "An Orders-of-magnitude AHP Supply Chain Risk Assessment Framework", *International Journal of Production Economics*, 182, 2016: 144 – 156.

[2] Lintukangas, K., Kähkönen, A. K., & Ritala, P., "Supply Risks as Drivers of Green Supply Management Adoption", *Journal of Cleaner Production*, 112, 2016: 1901 – 1909.

[3] Giannakis, M., & Louis, M., "A Multi-agent Based Framework for Supply Chain Risk Management", *Journal of Purchasing and Supply Management*, 17 (1), 2011: 23 – 31.

[4] Wu, D., & Olson, D. L., "Supply Chain Risk, Simulation, and Vendor Selection", *International Journal of Production Economics*, 114 (2), 2008: 646 – 655.

[5] Venkatesh, V. G., Rathi, S., & Patwa, S., "Analysis on Supply Chain Risks in Indian Apparel Retail Chains and Proposal of Risk Prioritization Model Using Interpretive Structural Modeling", *Journal of Retailing and Consumer Services*, 26, 2015: 153 – 167.

[6] Goh, M., Lim, J. Y., & Meng, F., "A Stochastic Model for Risk Management in Global Supply Chain Networks", *European Journal of Operational Research*, 182 (1), 2007: 164 – 173.

[7] Xia, D., & Chen, B., "A Comprehensive Decision-making Model for Risk Management of Supply Chain", *Expert Systems With Applications*, 38 (5), 2011: 4957 – 4966.

[8] Zeng, B., & Yen, B. P. C., "Rethinking the Role of Partnerships in Global Supply Chains: A Risk-based Perspective", *International Journal of Production Economics*, 185, 2017: 52 – 62.

[9] Tuncel, G., & Alpan, G., "Risk Assessment and Management for Supply Chain Networks: A Case Study", *Computers in Industry*, 61 (3), 2010: 250 – 259.

事前的预警和预防，而不是事后的控制。失效模式与影响分析（Failure Mode and Effects Analysis，FMEA）是根据已有经验，系统地应用管理工具来发现并评估供应链中潜在的失效风险及后果，找到可以避免或减少这些潜在失效风险发生的措施，并形成相应的文件[①]；从而可以长期提高供应链的可靠性和安全性，增强供应链整体绩效水平。

（三）白酒风险

企业不仅要关注供应链的效率，更要关注其风险。如果发生意外的事情，所有的供应链成员都将受到影响，其结果将可能导致重大损失[②]。近年来，白酒企业面临的风险也愈加复杂和多样化。白酒企业的成长与发展以及产业集群优势的提升与供应链风险密切相关[③]。

白酒面临洋酒和其他酒类替代品的竞争，国家政策因素也对白酒销量有一定的影响。白酒市场需求具有很大的不确定性，使得白酒供应链供需匹配的难度非常大[④]。"勾兑门"事件、"塑化剂"风波等给白酒行业的发展带来严重的负面影响。在多重打击下，白酒销售业绩下降、行业整体效益下滑。据统计，2012年和2013年全国白酒销售率分别为98.1%和95.6%，期末库存和年初相比分别增长了20.1%和46.5%。部分白酒市场出现产能过剩、供大于求的局面，导致库存积压严重，严重影响了白酒行业的发展。王保谦等通过 Z 计分（Z-score）财务预警模型，对中国白酒行业的上市公司财务状况进行分析，分析发现2012年的白酒事件对白酒上市公司有较大的影响。据2013年财务统计，19

[①] Kolich, M., "Using Failure Mode and Effects Analysis to Design a Comfortable Automotive Driver Seat", *Applied Ergonomics*, 45 (4), 2014: 1087-1096.

[②] Chen, P. S., & Wu, M. T., "A Modified Failure Mode and Effects Analysis Method for Supplier Selection Problems in the Supply Chain Risk Environment: A Case Study", *Computers & Industrial Engineering*, 66 (4), 2013: 634-642.

[③] Peng, "Risk Management Situation and Strategic Analysis of Supply Chains of Small and Medium Enterprises in Luzhou Liquor Industry Development Zone", 《国际技术管理》2016年第7期。

[④] 王群智、向琴:《白酒行业供应链运作及风险研究》，《交通运输工程与信息学报》2016年第2期。

家白酒上市公司中有 12 家受到了影响[①]。吴昊和平瑛绘制出白酒生产过程的故障树，结合专家访谈法与相关生产数据建立起风险系数模型，识别出其中的关键风险因素，为事后管理向事前管理、过程管理转变提供依据，也为进行白酒生产风险评估与建立风险管理体系奠定了基础[②]。朱红和胡方用综合安全评估法（FSA）对滚装船运输白酒槽罐车风险进行评估[③]。田江等提出了相应的风险评价体系，有效降低了信用风险[④]。Zhu 等探究了酒精在全国食品服务行业的使用[⑤]。有的文章研究酒精与健康风险[⑥]。面对激烈的市场竞争，白酒企业采取不同的策略，带来各种业绩和风险[⑦]。

综上所述，白酒企业的风险管理研究相对较少，上升到供应链高度的文章就更少，而从经济、环境、社会三个维度对白酒风险的可持续性进行分析的文章少之又少，这些都说明白酒行业的供应链风险管理研究还不成熟。因此，对它进行研究具有重要的理论和实践价值。

[①] 王保谦、黄晓芬、朱永淦：《Z-score 模型下白酒上市公司财务风险实证分析》，《技术与市场》2015 年第 12 期。

[②] 吴昊、平瑛：《我国白酒企业生产链风险识别研究》，《食品工业》2013 年第 11 期。

[③] 朱红、胡方：《基于综合安全评估法的滚装船专船专运白酒槽罐车风险评估》，《中国水运月刊》2016 年第 6 期。

[④] 田江、陈晨、徐胜明：《基于供应链合作企业的物流金融服务模式创新与风险控制——以 a 集团为例》，《物流工程与管理》2015 年第 6 期。

[⑤] Zhu, J., Tews, M. J., Stafford, K., & George, R. T., "Alcohol and Illicit Substance Use in the Food Service Industry: Assessing Self-selection and Job-related Risk Factors", *Journal of Hospitality & Tourism Research*, 35 (1), 2011: 45 - 63.

[⑥] Delobelle, P., Sanders, D., Puoane, T., & Freudenberg, N., "Reducing the Role of the Food, Tobacco, and Alcohol Industries in Noncommunicable Disease Risk in South Africa", *Health Education & Behavior*, 43 (1_ suppl), 2016: 70S - 81S; Miller, P. "Energy Drinks and Alcohol: Research Supported by Industry May be Downplaying Harms", *BMJ*, 347, 2013: 1 - 2; Roche, A. M., Lee, N. K., Battams, S., Fischer, J. A., Cameron, J., & McEntee, A., "Alcohol Use Among Workers in Male-dominated Industries: A Systematic Review of Fisk Factors", *Safety Science*, 78, 2015: 124 - 141.

[⑦] Yan-Ping, N., Ya-Nan, S. U., & Xin, W., "Investment Risk Evaluation of Liquor Listed Companies Based on Cluster Analysis", *Journal of Hebei University of Science and Technology* (Social Sciences), 2015.

二 风险辨析

结合文献分析结果和专家意见，本书将白酒企业的可持续供应链风险分为经济、环境和社会三个维度共 30 个风险因素，如表 5.2 所示。其中经济风险有价格操纵的指控、逃税避税、抵制、供给变动、金融危机、法律风险、需求变动、产品风险、财务风险、信息风险、合作关系风险、物流风险、管理风险和全球化。环境风险有环境事故，污染，自然灾害，雾霾、热浪、干旱，产品废弃物，不符合可持续发展的法律，温室气体和水质风险。社会风险有不健康的工作环境、不公平的福利待遇、超时工作、流行病、品牌形象风险、政策风险、文化风险和道德风险。选用的可持续供应链风险管理框架如图 5.1 所示。

表 5.2　　　　　　　　　　可持续供应链风险

维度	指标	维度	指标
经济	价格操纵的指控	环境	污染
	逃税避税		自然灾害
	抵制		雾霾、热浪、干旱
	供给变动		产品废弃物
	金融危机		不符合可持续发展的法律
	法律风险		温室气体
	需求变动		水质风险
	产品风险	社会	不健康的工作环境
	财务风险		不公平的福利待遇
	信息风险		超时工作
	合作关系风险		流行病
	物流风险		品牌形象风险
	管理风险		政策风险
	全球化		文化风险
环境	环境事故		道德风险

图 5.1 可持续供应链风险管理框架

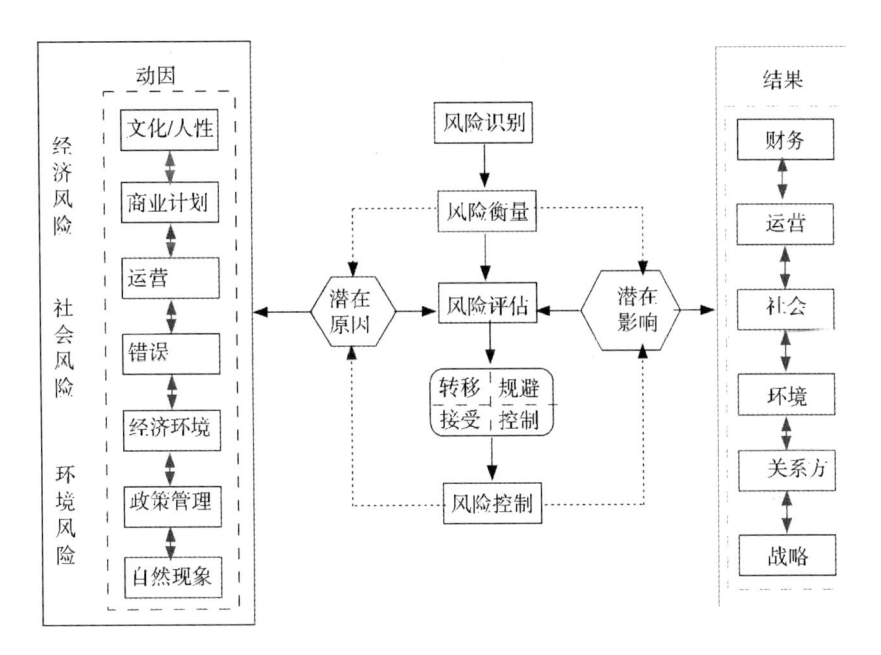

（一）经济风险

价格操纵是指以获取不当利益或转嫁风险为目的，利用其资金、信息等优势或者滥用职权操纵市场，影响交易价格，制造市场假象，诱导或者致使投资者在不了解事实真相的情况下做出投资决定，扰乱市场秩序的行为，即买方或卖方通过共谋互惠定价[1]。价格和成本是购买决策的主要决定因素[2]。价格和成本可能是实施可持续供应链的障碍，因为要增加相应的管理和监控成本；也可能是实施可持续供应链的动力，因为可以降低能源消耗和减少浪费和污染[3]。而价格风险涉及价格变动风

---

[1] Giannakis, M., & Papadopoulos, T., "Supply Chain Sustainability: A Risk Management Approach", *International Journal of Production Economics*, 171, 2016: 455-470.

[2] Holweg, M., Reichhart, A., & Hong, E., "On Risk and Cost in Global Sourcing", *International Journal of Production Economics*, 131 (1), 2011: 333-341.

[3] Lintukangas, K., Kähkönen, A. K., & Ritala, P., "Supply Risks as Drivers of Green Supply Management Adoption", *Journal of Cleaner Production*, 112, 2016: 1901-1909.

险、价格敏感、商品价格①、商品/可替代能源价格波动②、原材料价格增加③等多个因素。价格变动属于需求不确定性④。前几年，白酒高端产品的价格累积涨幅比较高，造成人心浮动，引发相关产业价格的上涨应借鉴价格上限规制制定白酒价格⑤。

逃税避税是为了减轻税收负担，从一个健全的财务计划中以欺诈手段非法尝试减少税收金额⑥。市场竞争压力加大，部分经营艰难的白酒企业有逃税避税的行为，这对整个白酒行业来说都是有负面社会效应的⑦。

抵制通常是因为社会、道德或政治的原因，采用停止使用、购买或惩罚组织的方式表达抗议⑧。白酒属于食品饮料范畴，因其产品的独特性，产品质量问题或是饮用过度、饮用不当都会造成健康安全问题，而一旦出现问题，公众对白酒产品就会出现抵触情绪，"塑化剂"风波就给白酒行业带来了巨大冲击⑨。

供给变动风险是指因白酒企业的供应商提供的产品不合规格、原材料价格上涨等导致的供给问题。比如"塑化剂"风波就是因为白酒供

---

① Braunscheidel, M. J., & Suresh, N. C., "The Organizational Antecedents of a Firm's Supply Chain Agility for Risk Mitigation and Response", Journal of Operations Management, 27 (2), 2009: 119 – 140; Trkman, P., & McCormack, K., "Supply Chain Risk in Turbulent Environments—A Conceptual Model for Managing Supply Chain Network Risk", International Journal of Production Economics, 119 (2), 2009: 247 – 258; Aqlan, F., & Lam, S. S., "A fuzzy-based Integrated Framework for Supply Chain Risk Assessment", International Journal of Production Economics, 161, (2015): 54 – 63.

② Tang, O., & Musa, S. N., "Identifying Risk Issues and Research Advancements in Supply Chain Risk Management", International Journal of Production Economics, 133 (1), 2011: 25 – 34.

③ Thun, J. H., & Hoenig, D., "An Empirical Analysis of Supply Chain Risk Management in the German Automotive Industry", International Journal of Production Economics, 131 (1), 2011: 242 – 249.

④ Hahn, G. J., & Kuhn, H., "Value-based Performance and Risk Management in Supply Chains: A Robust Optimization Approach", International Journal of Production Economics, 139 (1), 2012: 135 – 144; Ghadge, A., Dani, S., Ojha, R., & Caldwell, N., "Using Risk Sharing Contracts for Supply Chain Risk Mitigation: A Buyer-supplier Power and Dependence Perspective", Computers & Industrial Engineering, 103, 2017: 262 – 270.

⑤ 赵凤琦：《我国白酒产业可持续发展研究》，博士学位论文，中国社会科学院，2014年。

⑥ Giannakis, M., & Papadopoulos, T., "Supply Chain Sustainability: A Risk Management Approach", International Journal of Production Economics, 171, 2016: 455 – 470.

⑦ 赵凤琦：《我国白酒产业可持续发展研究》，博士学位论文，中国社会科学院，2014年。

⑧ Giannakis, M., & Papadopoulos, T., "Supply Chain Sustainability: A Risk Management Approach", International Journal of Production Economics, 171, 2016: 455 – 470.

⑨ 赵凤琦：《我国白酒产业可持续发展研究》，博士学位论文，中国社会科学院，2014年。

应商提供的包装材料有问题导致的①。

金融危机是指因泡沫、银行恐慌、股市崩盘、货币危机等原因突然损失大部分金融资产的名义价值②。也指高现金转换周期、低市场占有率、低利润率、降低收入等③。

法律风险是由于一国法律及法律制度是不断完善的,因此企业面临的法律环境也会不断变化。一旦这种法律环境对经营企业的某一方不利时,会诱发相应的风险。其中的诉讼风险是发生争议/诉讼或其他法律纠纷,或发生影响可持续发展的概率④。

需求变动风险指需求预测误差、牛鞭效应、产品生命周期短、新进入者的风险等⑤。全球经济一体化的到来,加剧了市场竞争,加大了市场预测的难度,洋酒、其他酒类替代品的竞争,以及人们对健康饮酒的要求,导致客户对白酒的需求变化也越来越大。

产品风险指设计变化、质量问题(塑化剂)、产品质量标准等方面的风险⑥,也指新产品风险⑦,涉及产品生命周期缩短⑧、产品在途

---

① 赵凤琦:《我国白酒产业可持续发展研究》,博士学位论文,中国社会科学院,2014年。

② Giannakis, M., & Papadopoulos, T., "Supply Chain Sustainability: A Risk Management Approach", *International Journal of Production Economics*, 171, 2016: 455 – 470.

③ Venkatesh, V. G., Rathi, S., & Patwa, S., "Analysis on Supply Chain Risks in Indian apparel Retail Chains and Proposal of Risk Prioritization Model Using Interpretive Structural Modeling", *Journal of Retailing and Consumer Services*, 26, 2015: 153 – 167.

④ Giannakis, M., & Papadopoulos, T., "Supply Chain Sustainability: A Risk Management Approach", *International Journal of Production Economics*, 171, 2016: 455 – 470.

⑤ Venkatesh, V. G., Rathi, S., & Patwa, S., "Analysis on Supply Chain Risks in Indian apparel Retail Chains and Proposal of Risk Prioritization Model Using Interpretive Structural Modeling", *Journal of Retailing and Consumer Services*, 26, 2015: 153 – 167.

⑥ Venkatesh, V. G., Rathi, S., & Patwa, S., "Analysis on Supply Chain Risks in Indian Apparel Retail Chains and Proposal of Risk Prioritization Model Using Interpretive Structural Modeling", *Journal of Retailing and Consumer Services*, 26, 2015: 153 – 167; Chopra, S., & Sodhi, M. S., "Supply-chain Breakdown", *MIT Sloan management review*, 46 (1), 2004: 53 – 61; Aqlan, F., & Lam, S. S., "A Fuzzy-based Integrated Framework for Supply Chain Risk Assessment", *International Journal of Production Economics*, 161, 2015: 54 – 63.

⑦ Venkatesh, V. G., Rathi, S., & Patwa, S., "Analysis on Supply Chain Risks in Indian apparel Retail Chains and Proposal of Risk Prioritization Model Using Interpretive Structural Modeling", *Journal of Retailing and Consumer Services*, 26, 2015: 153 – 167.

⑧ Venkatesh, V. G., Rathi, S., & Patwa, S., "Analysis on Supply Chain Risks in Indian Apparel Retail Chains and Proposal of Risk Prioritization Model Using Interpretive Structural Modeling", *Journal of Retailing and Consumer Services*, 26, 2015: 153 – 167; Chopra, S., & Sodhi, M. S., "Supply-chain Breakdown", *MIT Sloan management review*, 46 (1), 2004: 53 – 61; Aqlan, F., & Lam, S. S., "A Fuzzy-based Integrated Framework for Supply Chain Risk Assessment", *International Journal of Production Economics*, 161, 2015: 54 – 63.

破坏[1]、产品/服务的直接风险[2]、产品和工艺设计风险[3]、季节性产品[4]等。质量问题又是其中一个重要的方面[5]。质量问题通常可以追溯到供应商。实施质量管理标准的公司更有可能采用环境管理标准。核心公司的质量风险管理能力会影响其可持续供应链的实践。产品可能在生产中或运输中（材料质量）被破坏，由于供应链上的供应商缺少相关知识、能力或决策，不正确的信息会导致供应链上顾客的要求得不到满足[6]。

财务风险指供应商财务不稳定的风险、财务质量风险[7]，以及供应链合作伙伴的财务实力[8]。

信息风险是指信息在传递过程中出现信息失真的可能性会变大，比如产生牛鞭效益。上下游企业之间的信息出现延迟或错误，会导致各种损失和客户流失[9]。

合作关系风险主要是合作企业在很多问题上产生纠纷引起的。最直接的原因是合作企业的企业文化、核心价值观、管理理念、员工素质、财务实力等不同，这些不同的企业看待事物的角度不同，从而应对问题

---

[1] Dong, Q., & Cooper, O., "An Orders-of-magnitude AHP Supply Chain Risk Assessment Framework", *International Journal of Production Economics*, 182, 2016: 144–156.

[2] Lintukangas, K., Kähkönen, A. K., & Ritala, P., "Supply Risks as Drivers of Green Supply Management Adoption", *Journal of Cleaner Production*, 112, 2016: 1901–1909.

[3] Tang, O., & Musa, S. N., "Identifying Risk Issues and Research Advancements in Supply Chain risk Management", *International Journal of Production Economics*, 133 (1), 2011: 25–34.

[4] Neiger, D., Rotaru, K., & Churilov, L., "Supply Chain Risk Identification with Value-focused Process Engineering", *Journal of Operations Management*, 27 (2), 2009: 154–168.

[5] Aqlan, F., & Lam, S. S., "Supply Chain Optimization Under Risk and Uncertainty: A Case Study for High-end Server Manufacturing", *Computers & Industrial Engineering*, 93, 2016: 78–87; Hahn, G. J., & Kuhn, H., "Value-based Performance and Risk Management in Supply Chains: A Robust Optimization Approach", *International Journal of Production Economics*, 139 (1), 2012: 135–144; Thun, J. H., & Hoenig, D., "An Empirical Analysis of Supply Chain Risk Management in the German Automotive Industry", *International Journal of Production Economics*, 131 (1), 2011: 242–249; Lintukangas, K., Kähkönen, A. K., & Ritala, P., "Supply Risks as Drivers of Green Supply Management Adoption", *Journal of Cleaner Production*, 112, 2016: 1901–1909.

[6] Mohammaddust, F., Rezapour, S., Farahani, R. Z., Mofidfar, M., & Hill, A., "Developing Lean and Responsive Supply Chains: A Robust Model for Alternative Risk Mitigation Strategies in Supply Chain Designs", *International Journal of Production Economics*, 183, 2017: 632–653.

[7] Vilko, J. P., & Hallikas, J. M., "Risk Assessment in Multimodal Supply Chains", *International Journal of Production Economics*, 140 (2), 2012: 586–595.

[8] Tang, O., & Musa, S. N., "Identifying Risk Issues and Research Advancements in Supply Chain Risk Management", *International Journal of Production Economics*, 133 (1), 2011: 25–34.

[9] 赵凤琦：《我国白酒产业可持续发展研究》，博士学位论文，中国社会科学院，2014年。

的方式也不同,导致白酒企业的供应链出现混乱[①]。

物流风险来源有单一采购风险,采购灵活性风险,供应产品监控/质量和供给能力、供应商选择/外包问题[②]。信息不共享、物流问题(比如运输能力、运输成本等),或者相关人员操作错误、设备出现问题,或者由于灾害性天气在库存、运输、配送等过程中出现衔接失误,这些问题都可能导致物流运作失败[③]。

管理风险是指管理运作过程中因信息不对称、管理不善、判断失误等影响管理的水平。可以从管理者的素质、组织结构、企业文化、管理过程四个角度来看待管理风险[④]。

全球化是指汇率波动、设计转移、市场竞争、法律与政治风险、政策变迁等[⑤]。全球化是以经济全球化为核心的包含各个国家和民族在经济、政治、文化、科技、生活方式、价值观念等多领域、多层次相互联系和制约的多元化概念。

(二) 环境风险

环境事故是由公司运营、机器或工作人员造成的影响环境的事故[⑥]。

[①] Tang, O., & Musa, S. N., "Identifying Risk Issues and Research Advancements in Supply Chain Risk Management", *International Journal of Production Economics*, 133 (1), 2011: 25 – 34.

[②] Ibid..

[③] Hallikas, J., Virolainen, V. M., & Tuominen, M., "Risk Analysis and Assessment in Network Environments: A Dyadic Case Study", *International Journal of Production Economics*, 78 (1), 2002: 45 – 55; Aqlan, F., & Lam, S. S., "A Fuzzy-based Integrated Framework for Supply Chain Risk Assessment", *International Journal of Production Economics*, 161, 2015: 54 – 63.

[④] Trkman, P., & McCormack, K., "Supply Chain Risk in Turbulent Environments—A Conceptual Model for Managing Supply Chain Network Risk", *International Journal of Production Economics*, 119 (2), 2009: 247 – 258.

[⑤] Venkatesh, V. G., Rathi, S., & Patwa, S., "Analysis on Supply Chain Risks in Indian Apparel Retail Chains and Proposal of Risk Prioritization Model Using Interpretive Structural Modeling", *Journal of Retailing and Consumer Services*, 26, 2015: 153 – 167; Lavastre, O., Gunasekaran, A., & Spalanzani, A., "Supply Chain Risk Management in French Companies", *Decision Support Systems*, 52 (4), 2012: 828 – 838; Thun, J. H., & Hoenig, D., "An Empirical Analysis of Supply Chain Risk Management in the German Automotive Industry", *International Journal of Production Economics*, 131 (1), 2011: 242 – 249.

[⑥] Giannakis, M., & Papadopoulos, T., "Supply Chain Sustainability: A Risk Management Approach", *International Journal of Production Economics*, 171, 2016: 455 – 470.

污染是指由于运营或产品导致的空气、水或土壤污染[①]。在白酒供应链中主要指生产过程中排放的锅底水、洗瓶废水或酒糟对环境造成的负面影响,或是生产和配送过程中的碳排放对空气造成的污染[②]。

自然灾害是指由于洪水、地震等引起的中断[③]。自然灾害是破坏性事件[④]。尽管灾难性事件发生的可能性很低,但是一旦发生将产生严重的后果[⑤]。

产品废弃物是指在生产、配送或消费过程中产生的不需要的不能使用的物质[⑥]。在白酒供应链中,废弃物主要是指锅底水、酒糟、洗瓶水等,这些可以通过变废为宝或循环利用来解决。

不符合可持续发展的法律是指不遵守环境、就业或财务条例[⑦]。比如企业不遵守劳动法、不遵守环境法规等,都会给企业带来严重的风险。

温室气体是指排放在空气中的气体导致温室效应[⑧]。白酒行业中主要是指生产过程和配送过程中的碳排放。

---

① Stephanie Graham, "Perspectives on Information Management in Sustainable Supply Chains", *Business for Social Responsibility*, 2009.

② 赵凤琦:《我国白酒产业可持续发展研究》,博士学位论文,中国社会科学院,2014年。

③ Braunscheidel, M. J., & Suresh, N. C., "The Organizational Antecedents of a Firm's Supply Chain Agility for Risk Mitigation and Response", *Journal of Operations Management*, 27 (2), 2009: 119–140; Mohammaddust, F., Rezapour, S., Farahani, R. Z., Mofidfar, M., & Hill, A., "Developing Lean and Responsive Supply Chains: A Robust model for Alternative Risk Mitigation Strategies in Supply Chain Designs", *International Journal of Production Economics*, 183, 2017: 632–653.

④ Aqlan, F., & Lam, S. S., "Supply Chain Optimization Under Risk and Uncertainty: A Case Study for High-end Server Manufacturing", *Computers & Industrial Engineering*, 93, 2016: 78–87; Trkman, P., & McCormack, K., "Supply Chain Risk in Turbulent Environments—A Conceptual Model for Managing Supply Chain Network Risk", *International Journal of Production Economics*, 119 (2), 2009: 247–258; Thun, J. H., & Hoenig, D., "An empirical Analysis of Supply Chain Risk Management in the German Automotive Industry", *International Journal of Production Economics*, 131 (1), 2011: 242–249; Aqlan, F., & Lam, S. S., "A Fuzzy-based Integrated Framework for Supply Chain Risk Assessment", *International Journal of Production Economics*, 161, 2015: 54–63.

⑤ Knemeyer, A. M., Zinn, W., & Eroglu, C., "Proactive Planning for Catastrophic Events in Supply Chains", *Journal of Operations Management*, 27 (2), 2009: 141–153.

⑥ Giannakis, M., & Papadopoulos, T., "Supply Chain Sustainability: A Risk Management Approach", *International Journal of Production Economics*, 171, 2016: 455–470.

⑦ Ibid..

⑧ Anderson, D. R., & Anderson, K. E., "Sustainability Risk Management", *Risk Management and Insurance Review*, 12 (1), 2009: 25–38.

雾霾、热浪、干旱是因天气造成的不利环境影响[1]。对于白酒供应链来说，这些天气因素不仅影响产品配送，也会影响消费者对白酒的需求。

水质风险涉及水短缺风险[2]、水资源利用[3]、水污染等。白酒生产对水质的要求很高，水源一旦受到污染，将对白酒企业造成严重的打击。

(三) 社会风险

不健康（危险）的工作环境主要指在不健康的工作场所工作或使用有害材料威胁员工健康和安全[4]。

不公平的福利待遇，一是会影响员工的积极性；二是会造成社会对企业产生负面印象，影响产品的销售[5]。

超时工作（工作生活不平衡）是指超越法定要求的繁重工作量和工作要求[6]。

流行病是一种在全世界范围内或在非常大的范围内发生的流行病，跨越国际界限，通常影响大量的人[7]。

品牌形象风险会影响到企业的形象。组织的品牌形象是企业的一项宝贵资产[8]。强大的品牌可以为公司提供财务优势，强化公司市场地位。形象是公司展示给其客户和其他利益相关者的战略决策[9]。任何

---

[1] Halldórsson, Á., Kotzab, H., & Skjøtt-Larsen, T., "Supply Chain Management on the Crossroad to Sustainability: A Blessing or a Curse?", *Logistics Research*, 1 (2), 2009: 83 – 94.

[2] Giannakis, M., & Papadopoulos, T., "Supply Chain Sustainability: A Risk Management Approach", *International Journal of Production Economics*, 171, 2016: 455 – 470.

[3] Chan, F. T., & Kumar, N., "Global Supplier Development Considering Risk Factors Using Fuzzy Extended AHP-based Approach", *Omega*, 35 (4), 2007: 417 – 431.

[4] Halldórsson, Á., Kotzab, H., & Skjøtt-Larsen, T., "Supply Chain Management on the Crossroad to Sustainability: A Blessing or a Curse?", *Logistics Research*, 1 (2), 2009: 83 – 94.

[5] Giannakis, M., & Papadopoulos, T., "Supply Chain Sustainability: A Risk Management Approach", *International Journal of Production Economics*, 171, 2016: 455 – 470.

[6] Ibid..

[7] Halldórsson, Á., Kotzab, H., & Skjøtt-Larsen, T., "Supply Chain Management on the Crossroad to Sustainability: A Blessing or a Curse?", *Logistics Research*, 1 (2), 2009: 83 – 94.

[8] Lintukangas, K., Kähkönen, A. K., & Ritala, P., "Supply Risks as Drivers of Green Supply Management Adoption", *Journal of Cleaner Production*, 112, 2016: 1901 – 1909.

[9] Maloni, M. J., & Brown, M. E., "Corporate Social Responsibility in the Supply Chain: An Application in the Food Industry", *Journal of Business Ethics*, 68 (1), 2006: 35 – 52.

影响企业形象的事件都会降低品牌价值，降低销售额，从而影响股东利润[①]。

政策风险方面，国家政策是企业运营的指示灯，一旦政策变动，白酒企业的日常经营活动就有可能发生变化，这种变化对于白酒行业供应链来说可能是负面影响[②]。

文化风险一般是指文化差异给企业带来的影响，可通过培训和明确经营责任来降低[③]。在白酒供应链中，一是指供应链企业之间因为文化差异导致的风险；二是白酒自身面临的文化风险，白酒形象严肃刻板，以"中年"形象示人，不能赢得年轻人的青睐，会导致白酒市场的萎缩[④]。随着中国全面步入人口老龄化社会，白酒消费群体可能逐渐减少，导致白酒行业长期总体规模萎缩[⑤]。

道德风险是指在信息不对称的情况下，白酒企业中的合作方不能监督另一方的行动或当监督成本太高时，一方行为的变化使另一方的利益受到损害，导致合约破裂，让整个供应链面临中断的危机[⑥]。部分白酒企业在生产与经营中不诚信行为时有发生，例如制假售假、以次充好、合同违约、债务违约等[⑦]。

---

① Lange, D., Lee, P. M., & Dai, Y., "Organizational Reputation: A Review", *Journal of Management*, 37 (1), 2011: 153 – 184.

② Venkatesh, V. G., Rathi, S., & Patwa, S., "Analysis on Supply Chain Risks in Indian Apparel Retail Chains and Proposal of Risk Prioritization Model Using Interpretive Structural Modeling", *Journal of Retailing and Consumer Services*, 26, 2015: 153 – 167; Vilko, J. P., & Hallikas, J. M., "Risk Assessment in Multimodal Supply Chains", *International Journal of Production Economics*, 140 (2), 2012: 586 – 595; Dong, Q., & Cooper, O., "An Orders-of-magnitude AHP Supply Chain Risk Assessment Framework", *International Journal of Production Economics*, 182, 2016: 144 – 156.

③ Tang, O., & Musa, S. N., "Identifying Risk Issues and Research Advancements in Supply Chain Risk Management", *International Journal of Production Economics*, 133 (1), 2011: 25 – 34; Aqlan, F., & Lam, S. S., "A Fuzzy-based Integrated Framework for Supply Chain Risk Assessment", *International Journal of Production Economics*, 161, 2015: 54 – 63.

④ 赵凤琦：《我国白酒产业可持续发展研究》，博士学位论文，中国社会科学院，2014年。

⑤ 同上。

⑥ Hallikas, J., Virolainen, V. M., & Tuominen, M., "Risk Analysis and Assessment in Network Environments: A Dyadic Case Study", *International Journal of Production Economics*, 78 (1), 2002: 45 – 55.

⑦ 赵凤琦：《我国白酒产业可持续发展研究》，博士学位论文，中国社会科学院，2014年。

三 失效模式与影响分析方法

失效模式与影响分析（Failure Mode and Effects Analysis，FMEA）是在产品出售之前，用于确定、识别和消除在系统、设计、过程以及服务中已知与潜在的失效、问题、错误的技术方法，它包括系统 FMEA、设计 FMEA、过程 FMEA、服务 FMEA[1]。FMEA 是广泛使用的安全可靠的风险分析工具[2]。它最重要的特性之一就是事前预防，而不是事后才进行补救，自始至终强调及时性。其工作流程如图 5.2 所示。

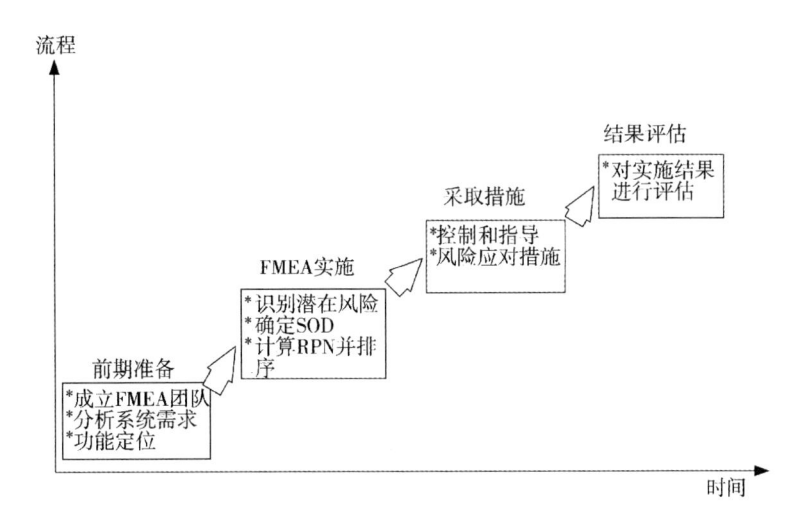

图 5.2 FMEA 工作流程

FMEA 作为一种可靠性分析方法起源于美国[3]。早在 20 世纪 50 年

---

[1] Kolich, M., "Using Failure Mode and Effects Analysis to Design a Comfortable Automotive Driver Seat", *Applied Ergonomics*, 45 (4), 2014: 1087 – 1096.

[2] Feili, H. R., Akar, N., Lotfizadeh, H., Bairampour, M., & Nasiri, S., "Risk Analysis of Geothermal Power Plants Using Failure Modes and Effects Analysis (FMEA) Technique", *Energy Conversion and Management*, 72, 2013: 69 – 76.

[3] Liu, H. C., Liu, L., & Liu, N., "Risk Evaluation Approaches in Failure Mode and Effects Analysis: A Literature Review", *Expert Systems with Applications*, 40 (2), 2013: 828 – 838.

代初，美国飞机制造公司在研制主操作系统时就采用了 FMEA 方法，取得了良好的效果①。到了 20 世纪六七十年代，FMEA 方法开始广泛地应用于航空、航天、兵器、船舶等军用系统的研制中，并逐渐渗透到汽车、医疗设备、机械等民用工业领域。目前，在航天、航空、船舶、兵器、机械、电子、汽车、家用电器等领域，FMEA 方法均获得了相当程度的普及，为确保产品可靠性起到了重要作用。FMEA 方法经过长久发展与完善，已成为系统研发、设计与使用中非常重要的可靠性分析工具。FMEA 方法使用很广泛，Pillay 介绍了 FMEA 的步骤②。Wang 等发展了模糊 FMEA 方法用于风险的评估③。Afshari 将 FMEA 方法用于评估环保建筑，分析了相关科技、金融、组织、社会和环境因素④。FMEA 还可用于驾驶座设计⑤、供应商选择⑥、渔船评估⑦、应急部门的决策⑧和地热发电厂风险分析⑨。

---

① Bowles, J. B., & Peláez, C. E., "Fuzzy Logic Prioritization of Failures in a System Failure Mode, Effects and Criticality Analysis", *Reliability Engineering & System Safety*, 50 (2), 1995: 203-213.

② Pillay, A., & Wang, J., "Modified Failure Mode and Effects Analysis Using Approximate Reasoning", *Reliability Engineering & System Safety*, 79 (1), 2003: 69-85.

③ Wang, Y. M., Chin, K. S., Poon, G. K. K., & Yang, J. B., "Risk Evaluation in Failure Mode and Effects Analysis Using Fuzzy Weighted Geometric Mean", *Expert Systems with Applications*, 36 (2), 2009: 1195-1207.

④ Afshari, H., Issa, M. H., & Radwan, A., "Using Failure Mode and Effects Analysis to Evaluate Barriers to the Greening of Existing Buildings Using the Leadership in Energy and Environmental Design Rating System", *Journal of Cleaner Production*, 127, 2016: 195-203.

⑤ Kolich, M., "Using Failure Mode and Effects Analysis to Design a Comfortable Automotive Driver Seat", *Applied Ergonomics*, 45 (4), 2014: 1087-1096.

⑥ Chen, P. S., & Wu, M. T., "A Modified Failure Mode and Effects Analysis Method for Supplier Selection Problems in the Supply Chain Risk Environment: A Case Study", *Computers & Industrial Engineering*, 66 (4), 2013: 634-642.

⑦ Chin, K. S., Wang, Y. M., Poon, G. K. K., & Yang, J. B., "Failure Mode and Effects Analysis Using a Group-based Evidential Reasoning Approach", *Computers & Operations Research*, 36 (6), 2009: 1768-1779.

⑧ Chanamool, N., & Naenna, T., "Fuzzy FMEA Application to Improve Decision-making Process in an Emergency Department", *Applied Soft Computing*, 43, 2016: 441-453.

⑨ Feili, H. R., Akar, N., Lotfizadeh, H., Bairampour, M., & Nasiri, S., "Risk Analysis of Geothermal Power Plants Using Failure Modes and Effects Analysis (FMEA) Technique", *Energy Conversion and Management*, 72, 2013: 69-76.

失效模式与影响分析的主要目的是通过分析识别并阻止那些能到达用户手中的已知的和潜在的问题。为了达到这个目的，每一个识别出的失效模式的风险都需要被评估和给出优先次序，从而使得适宜的正确操作能对不同的失效模式实施。一个失效模式的优先级是通过风险优先数（Risk Priority Number，RPN）来进行风险分析的。它由相关专家对各故障模式的发生频度（Occurrence Probability Ranking，O）、影响严重程度（Effect Severity Ranking，S）和检测难易程度（Detection Difficulty Ranking，D）打分，然后连乘得到 RPN，公式表示为：$RPN = O \times S \times D$。这三个维度的元素——频度 O、严重度 S 和检测难易度 D 通过使用区间为 1—10 的等级（也称为排序或得分）来进行所有的评估，具体评估标准和对应的等级如表 5.3、表 5.4 和表 5.5 所示[1]。其中，失效频度（Occurrence）描述的是引起某个失效模式发生的原因的发生可能性，因此，失效频率越高，该失效模式越容易发生。严重度（Severity）描述的是，如果一个失效模式没有被检测到，且未被修正的情况下，该失效模式对系统最终输出结果所产生影响的严重程度，因此，严重度越高，该失效模式造成的影响越严重。检测难易度（Detection）描述的是某个失效模式能被检测到的可能性，而在这个维度中，通常不可被检测度越高，该失效模式越不易被检测到，因此，检测难易度有时也被标记为不可被检测度（Lack of Detection）。这三个维度的标准阈值都是 1—10[2]。RPN 值越高说明风险越大，指标越重要，越需要修正。

---

[1] Chin, K. S., Wang, Y. M., Poon, G. K. K., & Yang, J. B., "Failure Mode and Effects Analysis Using a Group-based Evidential Reasoning Approach", *Computers & Operations Research*, 36 (6), 2009: 1768–1779; Silva, M. M., de Gusmão, A. P. H., Poleto, T., e Silva, L. C., & Costa, A. P. C. S., "A Multidimensional Approach toInformation Security Risk Management Using FMEA and Fuzzy Theory", *International Journal of Information Management*, 34 (6), 2014: 733–740.

[2] Kolich, M., "Using Failure Mode and Effects Analysis to Design a Comfortable Automotive Driver Seat", *Applied Ergonomics*, 45 (4), 2014: 1087–1096; Dağsuyu, C., Göçmen, E., Narll, M., & Kokangül, A., "Classical and Fuzzy FMEA Risk Analysis in a Sterilization Unit", *Computers & Industrial Engineering*, 101, 2016: 286–294.

表 5.3　　　　　　　　　　故障发生频度评价标准

等级	失效发生的可能性	失效概率
10	极高：失效几乎是不可避免的	>1/2
9	很高：失效极有可能发生	1/3
8	高：反复发生的失效	1/8
7	较高：较反复发生的失效	1/20
6	中等高：偶尔发生的失效	1/80
5	中等：相对偶尔发生的失效	1/400
4	相对低：相对很少发生的失效	1/2000
3	低：相对很少发生的失效	1/15000
2	很低：失效不太可能发生	1/150000
1	极低：失效几乎不可能发生	1/1500000

资料来源：Wang, Y. M., Chin, K. S., Poon, G. K. K., & Yang, J. B., "Risk Evaluation in Failure Mode and Effects Analysis Using Fuzzy Weighted Geometric Mean", *Expert Systems with Applications*, 36 (2), 2009: 1195-1207; Silva, M. M., de Gusmão, A. P. H., Poleto, T., e Silva, L. C., & Costa, A. P. C. S., "A Multidimensional Approach to Information Security Risk Management Using FMEA and Fuzzy Theory", *International Journal of Information Management*, 34 (6), 2014: 733-740。

表 5.4　　　　　　　　　　严重度评估标准

等级	严重度等级	评定标准
10	无警告的严重危害	非常严重的实效模式，在不能通过各种测试察觉出的情况下，危害到白酒供应链安全，损害企业声誉
9	有警告的严重危害	非常严重的实效模式，可以通过各种测试察觉出危险的发生，危害到白酒供应链安全，损害企业声誉
8	很高	供应链不能运作，丧失基本功能，顾客很不满意
7	高	供应链能运作，但性能下降，顾客很不满意
6	中等	供应链能运作，但部分环节不能运作，顾客感觉很不方便
5	低	供应链能运作，但部分环节性能下降，顾客感觉有些不方便
4	很低	供应链部分环节出现问题，大多数顾客发现缺陷
3	轻微	供应链部分环节出现问题，约一半顾客发现有缺陷
2	很轻微	供应链部分环节有轻微问题，很少有顾客发现缺陷
1	无	供应链没有任何问题，无影响

资料来源：Wang, Y. M., Chin, K. S., Poon, G. K. K., & Yang, J. B., "Risk Evaluation in Failure Mode and Effects Analysis Using Fuzzy Weighted Geometric Mean", *Expert Systems with Applications*, 36 (2), 2009: 1195-1207; Silva, M. M., de Gusmão, A. P. H., Poleto, T., e Silva, L. C., & Costa, A. P. C. S., "A Multidimensional Approach to Information Security Risk Management Using FMEA and Fuzzy Theory", *International Journal of Information Management*, 34 (6), 2014: 733-740。

表 5.5 检测难易度评价标准

等级	探测性	评定标准
10	绝对不可能	没有已知的控制方法能找到失效模式
9	很微小	现行控制方法找出失效模式的可能性很微小
8	微小	现行控制方法找出失效模式的可能性微小
7	很低	现行控制方法找出失效模式的可能性很低
6	低	现行控制方法找出失效模式的可能性低
5	中等	现行控制方法找出失效模式的可能性中等
4	中上	现行控制方法找出失效模式的可能性中等偏上
3	高	现行控制方法找出失效模式的可能性高
2	很高	现行控制方法找出失效模式的可能性很高
1	几乎确定	现行控制方法几乎肯定找出失效模式

资料来源：Wang, Y. M., Chin, K. S., Poon, G. K. K., & Yang, J. B., "Risk Evaluation in Failure Mode and Effects Analysis Using Fuzzy Weighted Geometric Mean", *Expert Systems with Applications*, 36 (2), 2009: 1195 - 1207; Silva, M. M., de Gusmão, A. P. H., Poleto, T., e Silva, L. C., & Costa, A. P. C. S., "A Multidimensional Approach to Information Security Risk Management Using FMEA and Fuzzy Theory", *International Journal of Information Management*, 34 (6), 2014: 733 - 740。

四 案例探讨

白酒企业的供应链潜在失效模式管理重在事前预警和预防，而不是事后的控制[1]。我们选择的案例是四川地区的一家白酒企业 A，因其面临的市场竞争压力加大，风险因素增多，为尽量减少供应链运营中的风险，决定制定一个对整个企业的供应链风险进行全面分析的评估体系。在开展风险管理之前，需要成立一个专门的工作小组，由于小组成员的构成及其工作方法对风险管理工作的效率有较大的影响[2]，因此小组成员的选择就变得尤为重要。鉴于此，这个风险小组由 11 位专家组成，有总经理

---

[1] Wang, Y. M., Chin, K. S., Poon, G. K. K., & Yang, J. B., "Risk Evaluation in Failure Mode and Effects Analysis Using Fuzzy Weighted Geometric Mean", *Expert Systems with Applications*, 36 (2), 2009: 1195 - 1207.

[2] Tarí, J. J., & Sabater, V., "Quality Tools and Techniques: Are They Necessary for Quality Management?", *International Journal of Production Economics*, 92 (3), 2004: 267 - 280.

1位、学者专家2位、环境专家2位、供应商2位、客户2位、供应链经理2位。所有的专家高度熟悉他们各自的领域,精通决策。选用 FMEA 方法进行风险管控。对企业 A 的风险管理分为四个阶段,分别是风险识别、风险衡量、风险评估和风险控制。其框架如图 5.3 所示。

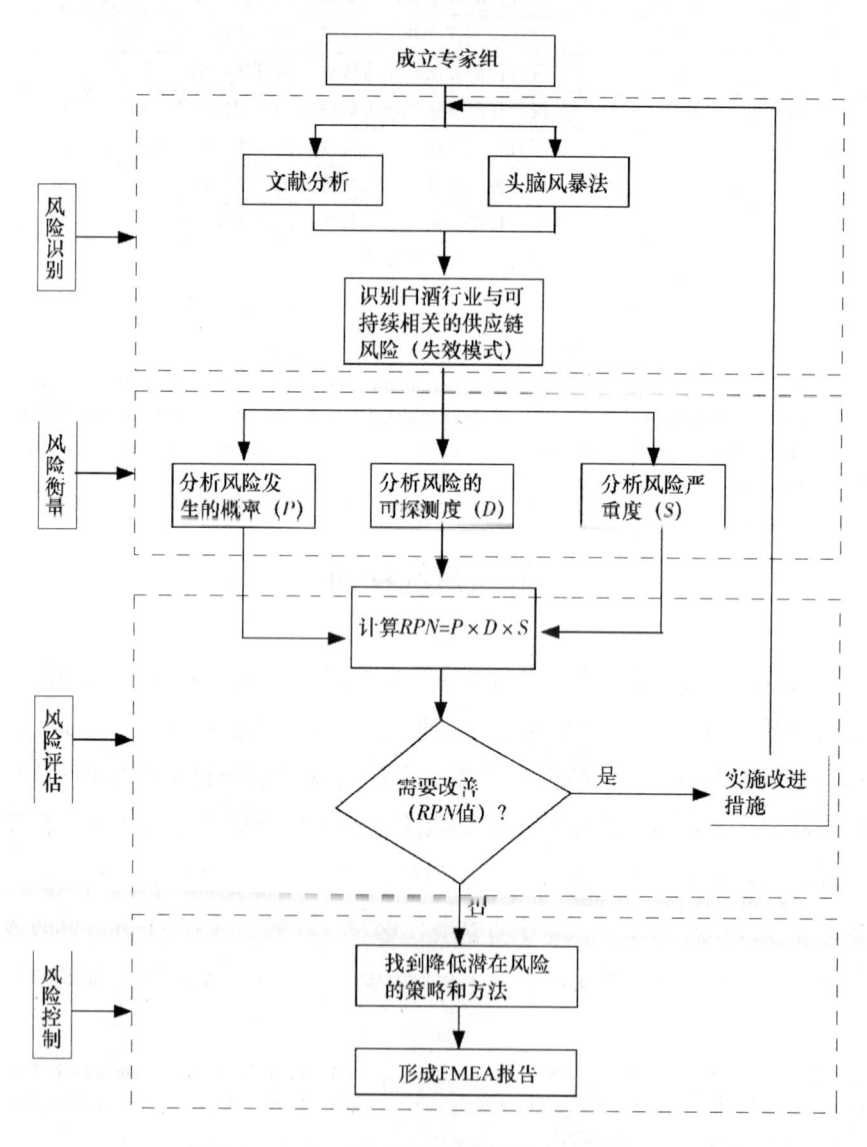

图 5.3　FMEA 方法下的可持续供应链管理流程

（一）风险识别

综合文献分析结果和专家意见，最后得出三个维度的 30 个指标。风险评估专家选择了白酒生产厂的总经理 1 位、供应链经理 2 位、学者专家 2 位、环境专家 2 位、供应商 2 位、客户 2 位，总计 11 位。其中经济风险有 14 个，分别是价格操纵的指控、逃税避税、抵制、供给变动、金融危机、法律风险、需求变动、产品风险、财务风险、信息风险、合作关系风险、物流风险、管理风险和全球化。环境风险有 8 个，分别是环境事故，污染，自然灾害（洪水、地震），雾霾、热浪、干旱，产品废弃物，不符合可持续发展的法律，温室气体，水质风险。社会风险有 8 个，分别是不健康的工作环境、不公平的福利待遇、超时工作、流行病、品牌形象风险、政策风险、文化风险和道德风险（如表 5.2 所示）。

（二）风险衡量

将 FMEA 技术应用于白酒供应链的可持续风险评价中。FMEA 方法可以系统衡量评价风险因素，不需要复杂的统计方法。专家组根据表 5.3、表 5.4 和表 5.5 给三个维度的 30 个指标打分，给出每个指标的发生频度 O、严重度 S、检测难易度 D。其分值如表 5.9 所示。企业 A 的供应链网络比较复杂，引起的风险因素也比较多，而且这些因素都具有不确定性。对风险的发生频度、严重度和检测难易度分析如下。

1. 发生频度分析

对企业 A 的供应链风险因素的发生频度进行由高到低排序，排前十位的如表 5.6 所示。

从表 5.6 的排序可以看出，极易发生的风险排名在前五的有供给变动、全球化、信息风险、需求变动和物流风险。经济维度的风险有 14 项，在发生频度排序表中占了 7 项，其中有 6 项占据了前六位。不难看出，在企业 A 构建的白酒可持续供应链中，问题最多的是经济相关方面

表5.6 发生频度排序

排序	风险	发生频度 O
1	供给变动	5.91
2	全球化	5.82
3	信息风险	5.55
4	需求变动	5.27
5	物流风险	5.27
6	合作关系风险	5.27
7	温室气体	5.00
8	雾霾、热浪、干旱	5.00
9	超时工作	4.91
10	金融危机	4.64

的。这些问题集中在供给变动、全球化、信息风险、需求变动、物流风险、合作关系风险和金融危机。这种情况可能主要源于整个经济大环境，也可能是企业 A 对于供应链的整合管理还不够完善，需要继续努力。环境维度的风险有 8 项，发生频度排序表中出现了两项，分别是排在第七、第八位的温室气体和雾霾、热浪、干旱。这与加工企业的特点有关，也与企业 A 所在的区位有关。近年来，四川等地冬季发生雾霾的时间、天数和严重度都有所增加，给相关企业供应链带来了一定程度的影响。社会维度的风险有 8 项，但是在发生频度排序表中的只出现了一项，即超时工作。这与企业 A 的供应链有关，在有些环节可能会出现超时工作的情况。

2. 严重度分析

对企业 A 的供应链风险严重度从高到低进行排序，排前十位的如表5.7 所示。从表5.7 可以看出，严重度排第一的是自然灾害，排第二的是环境事故，排第三的是品牌形象风险，排第四的是产品风险。其中，经济维度方面的风险中产品风险排在严重度的第四位。"塑化剂"风波给整个白酒行业带来了一场大地震，可见产品风险的影响力之大。抵制排在第七位。如果出现消费者对某种产品的抵制，那么将会带来严重的后果。环境维度方面的风险在严重度排序表中占据了5个席位，它们是自然灾害、环境事故、水质风险、污染和不符合可持续发展的法律。自然灾害的发生往往是没有任何预警的，它的突发性会引起供应链的突然中断。自然灾害一旦发生，造成的损失一般是很严重的。供应链上的企业不可能阻止自然灾害的发生，可以做到的是在灾害发生后拿出相应的应急预案。社会维度方面有3个风险因素进了严重度排序表，分别是品牌形象风险、流行病和政策风险。品牌形象一旦受到损害，很难将流失的消费者再次吸引过来，将会给供应链带来可怕的后果。流行病如果没有控制好，也会给整个链条上的企业带来严重的后果。

表5.7　　　　　　　　　　　　严重度排序表

排序	风险	严重度 S
1	自然灾害	8.09
2	环境事故	7.91
3	品牌形象风险	7.55
4	产品风险	7.36
5	水质风险	7.36
6	流行病	7.18
7	抵制	7.00
8	政策风险	7.00
9	污染	6.91
10	不符合可持续发展的法律	6.82

3. 检测难易度分析

对企业A的供应链风险检测难易度从高到低进行排序，排在前十的汇总如表5.8所示。检测难易度是将风险或潜在风险检测出来的难易程度，得分越高表明越难被检测到。从表5.8可以看出自然灾害和道德风险带来的失效是很难被检测出来的。其中经济维度方面的风险在检测难易度排序表中有4项，分别是产品风险、抵制、金融危机和合作关系风险。环境维度方面在检测难易度排序表中有1项，即自然灾害。因为自然灾害一般是突发性的，企业不可能提前预知何时何地会发生何种灾害，这种灾害会给企业带来哪种程度的损失。社会维度方面占据检测难易度排序表前十的有 5 项，它们是道德风险、文化风险、品牌形象风险、流行病和政策风险。

表 5.8　　　　　　　　　　检测难易度排序

排序	风险	检测难易度 D
1	自然灾害	8.27
2	道德风险	7.55
3	文化风险	7.45
4	品牌形象风险	7.45
5	产品风险	7.36
6	流行病	6.82
7	政策风险	6.64
8	抵制	6.27
9	金融危机	6.00
10	合作关系风险	5.82

（三）风险评估

随着三个维度的发生频度、严重度和检测难易度确定下来，运用 FMEA 中求风险顺序数的方法求出各个分析因子的风险顺序数。风险顺序数越大，相应风险因子的风险越大。算出风险顺序数后，可以根据风险数的大小给出改善顺序。其结果如表 5.9 所示。FMEA 风险评价表由评价维度、风险因素、发生频度 O、严重度 S、检测难易度 D、风险顺序数 RPN、改善顺序七个部分组成。其中维度按照可持续供应链的三重底线方法分为经济、环境和社会。风险因素根据每个维度中的失效模式确定。发生频度 O、严重度 S、检测难易度 D 是 FMEA 评价小组依据经验以及历史数据打分得出，风险顺序数 RPN 是发生频度 O、严重度 S、检测难易度 D 三者的乘积。改善顺序数是按照风险顺序数数值从高到低排序得到的。

表 5.9　　　　　　　　　　　　风险评价表

评价维度	风险因素	发生频度 O	严重度 S	检测难易度 D	风险顺序数 RPN	改善顺序
经济	价格操纵的指控	3.91	5.45	4.18	89.17	22
	逃税避税	4.09	5.55	4.09	92.81	19
	抵制	3.09	7.00	6.27	135.72	14
	供给变动	5.91	5.09	3.91	117.60	17
	金融危机	4.64	6.73	6.00	187.14	5
	法律风险	4.36	4.73	4.45	91.89	20
	需求变动	5.27	6.18	5.00	162.98	11
	产品风险	3.73	7.36	7.36	202.10	2
	财务风险	4.00	5.73	3.36	77.06	24
	信息风险	5.55	5.82	5.18	167.19	8
	合作关系风险	5.27	6.18	5.82	189.64	4
	物流风险	5.27	5.09	5.36	143.98	13
	管理风险	4.55	6.27	4.73	134.79	15
	全球化	5.82	5.91	4.82	165.65	9
	平均值	4.68	5.94	5.04	139.84	—
环境	环境事故	3.45	7.91	5.27	144.06	12
	污染	3.64	6.91	4.00	100.50	18
	自然灾害	2.55	8.09	8.27	170.38	7
	雾霾、热浪、干旱	5.00	5.09	3.55	90.25	21
	产品废弃物	4.18	4.82	3.64	73.27	26
	不符合可持续发展的法律	3.73	6.82	2.91	73.93	25
	温室气体	5.00	4.55	3.45	78.51	23
	水质风险	3.00	7.36	2.73	60.25	29
	平均值	3.82	6.44	4.23	98.89	—

续表

评价维度	风险因素	发生频度 O	严重度 S	检测难易度 D	风险顺序数 RPN	改善顺序
社会	不健康的工作环境	3.18	6.73	2.73	58.38	30
	不公平的福利待遇	4.09	4.91	3.18	63.90	27
	超时工作	4.91	4.55	2.82	62.89	28
	流行病	2.73	7.18	6.82	133.55	16
	品牌形象风险	3.09	7.55	7.45	173.86	6
	政策风险	3.55	7.00	6.64	164.70	10
	文化风险	4.00	6.91	7.45	206.02	1
	道德风险	4.36	6.00	7.55	197.55	3
	平均值	3.74	6.35	5.58	132.61	—
总体平均值		4.20	6.18	4.97	126.99	—

以下对企业 A 的风险顺序数从高到低进行排序，排前十位的如表 5.10 所示。分析得出，排在第一位的是文化风险。这与中国现阶段的情况相似，白酒文化受到了严重的冲击，给白酒行业带来不可估量的影响。排名第二的是产品风险，众所周知的"塑化剂"风波给白酒行业带来了严重的损害。白酒属于食品类，产品质量一旦出现严重的问题，会影响整个白酒行业的发展。可以看出，在 14 个经济风险中，排在风险顺序数前十的有 5 项，它们是产品风险、合作关系风险、金融危机、信息风险和全球化。在 8 个环境风险中，排在风险顺序数前十的有 1 项，即自然灾害。在 8 个社会风险中，排在风险顺序数前十的有 4 项，它们是文化风险、道德风险、品牌形象风险和政策风险。可以看出，对白酒行业影响最大的是经济风险，其次是社会风险，最后是环境风险。

表 5.10 风险顺序数排序表

排序	风险	风险顺序数 RPN
1	文化风险	206.02
2	产品风险	202.10
3	道德风险	197.55
4	合作关系风险	189.64
5	金融危机	187.14
6	品牌形象风险	173.86
7	自然灾害	170.38
8	信息风险	167.19
9	全球化	165.65
10	政策风险	164.70

（四）风险控制

风险管理的最后一个阶段是提出相应的应对策略来降低或消除风险因素。这一阶段，11 位专家的意见得到了充分的尊重。这些专家被要求对风险策略进行讨论和提出有效的策略。他们提供了风险规避、风险转移、风险减轻和风险接受四种应对策略。鉴于企业的要求，这里简单列举出来，如表 5.11 和 表 5.12 所示。可以看出，风险减轻策略和风险规避策略是用得最多的可持续风险应对策略，这与白酒企业的供应链特点有关。

（五）结果分析

通过使用 FMEA 方法，由专家根据历史数据和分析给每个因素打分。然后将 11 位专家打的每个指标的发生频度、严重度和检测难易度的分数分别加起来，再除以专家人数求得每一个指标值的平均数。最后将每个指标的发生频度、严重度和检测难易度分别相乘，得到每个指标的 RPN 值，如表 5.9 所示。白酒企业的供应链风险管理从经济、环境和社会三个维度选取了 30 个指标进行风险评估。其中经济风险 14 项、环境风险 8 项、社会风险 8 项。

表 5.11　　　　　　　　　　　　风险应对策略

维度	可持续风险	应对策略	实践
经济	价格操纵的指控	规避	市场调查（试行价）
		减轻	行业标准
		接受	处罚低
	逃税避税	规避	依法纳税
	抵制	减轻	进行审计确保合规
		接受	处罚低
	供给变动	减轻	做好市场调查
		转移	对冲（期货）
	金融危机	减轻	和政府、金融机构合作
		转移	通过证券等确保流动性
	法律风险	规避	发展跟踪和评估法律事项系统
		减轻	及时积极跟进法律事项
	需求变动	减轻	信息系统、白酒文化
		接受	—
	产品风险	规避	对设计产品进行评价、质量体系
		减轻	应急预案
	财务风险	规避	完善财务体系、人员素质高
		减轻	内部严控
	信息风险	规避	建立完善信息平台、人员素质高
		减轻	相应约束措施
		接受	损失低
	合作关系风险	规避	严格考查合作伙伴、完善合同
		减轻	处罚条例
	物流风险	规避	选择合适的物流商
		减轻	保险、及时沟通
	管理风险	规避	完善管理制度、严格进行人员考评
		减轻	制定相应奖惩措施
	全球化	减轻	柔性供应链
		接受	有利的情况下，或是损失小

表 5.12 风险应对策略（续）

维度	可持续风险	应对策略	实践
环境	环境事故	规避	远离危险源、严格执行规章制度
		减轻	为潜在环境问题做好应急预案
		转移	为潜在环境事故购买保险
	污染	规避	制定相应政策法规
		减轻	可持续废弃物处理
	自然灾害	减轻	供应链应急预案
		转移	保险
	雾霾、热浪、干旱	减轻	应急预案、建立柔性供应链
		转移	保险
	产品废弃物	规避	回收再利用
		减轻	可持续废弃物处理
	不符合可持续发展的法律	规避	参与符合可持续发展的法规
		减轻	上下游参与可持续发展规划
	温室气体	规避	使用清洁能源、选择可持续发展的供应商
		减轻	使用产生温室气体少的设备设施
			要求上下游企业加入低碳项目
	水质风险	规避	使用安全的水质
		减轻	做好水质的检测工作
社会	不健康的工作环境	规避	员工培训、环境考评
		减轻	安全指示、应急计划、全员医疗保险
	不公平的福利待遇	规避	制定最低公平工作标准
		减轻	人事、工会等组织做好监控
	超时工作	规避	制定工作时间表
		减轻	完善制度
	流行病	规避	事前预警
		减轻	应急预案
	品牌形象风险	规避	制定严格的规章制度
		减轻	应急预案、及时回应公众
	政策风险	减轻	做好产品和服务
		接受	—
	文化风险	减轻	做好产品和服务
		转移	多元化
		接受	—
	道德风险	规避	严格考察合作伙伴
		减轻	相应的约束措施

从表 5.9 可以看出，可持续相关风险的发生频度平均值是 4.20，严重度平均值是 6.18，检测难易度平均值是 4.97。从这三个维度的风险顺序数平均值可以看出，经济平均 RPN 值为 139.84，风险最大；环境平均 RPN 值为 98.89，风险最小；社会平均 RPN 值为 132.61，风险居中。这与已有的研究有所不同，Giannakis 等得出的结论是环境风险最大，经济次之，社会风险最小[①]。这与具体的背景有关。白酒行业供应链可持续发展现阶段面临的最大问题是经济可持续，即如何在激烈的国际国内竞争环境中生存下去。然后是社会风险，因为文化因素，政策调整的原因，"酒驾""限酒令"等的出台，白酒消费文化受到了前所未有的冲击。改革开放以来，中国一直很重视白酒企业的污染处理问题和环境保护问题，因此，白酒企业的环境风险相对较小。

从经济风险来看，产品风险、道德风险、合作关系风险、金融危机、信息风险和全球化是经济方面的主要风险。从环境分析来看，自然灾害、环境事故和污染是其中最主要的风险因素。从社会维度来看，文化风险、品牌形象风险、政策风险、流行病是其中主要的风险因素。从调查中可以看出，排名前十的可持续相关风险是文化风险、产品风险、道德风险、合作关系风险、金融危机、品牌形象风险、自然灾害、信息风险、全球化、政策风险。因为案例来自中国白酒企业，因此气候特点、社会经济规章制度等反映了这个国度的特点。不健康的工作环境、水质风险、超时工作、不公平的福利待遇、产品废弃物、不符合可持续发展的法律处于相对较低的风险值，这也与中国现阶段的发展情况有关。案例中的白酒企业是一家规模较大的企业，一直很重视环境保护和维护员工的合法权益。

白酒企业的可持续供应链需要不断完善和降低相应的负面风险。风险有时也是一种机会，全球化会带来竞争优势。但是供应商不良的工作环境则可能给企业带来负面影响，不会导致供应链的中断。因此，风险

---

① Giannakis, M., & Papadopoulos, T., "Supply Chain Sustainability: A Risk Management Approach", *International Journal of Production Economics*, 171, 2016: 455–470.

应对策略要充分考虑到利益相关者（股东、员工、顾客、政府和非政府组织）。我们在风险应对策略方面选用了风险规避、风险转移、风险减轻和风险接受，从研究结果得出风险规避和风险减轻是白酒供应链用得最多的应对策略。

五　本章小结

针对白酒企业供应链面临的经济、环境和社会风险，根据文献分析结果和专家意见，我们确定了30个相应的风险因子。运用FMEA方法对这30个风险因子进行了分析，从发生频度、严重度和检测难易度三个角度分别进行了分析，对风险顺序数进行了评价。然后针对各个不同的风险分别提出了相应的应对策略，得出风险规避和风险减轻策略应用最多。白酒企业的供应链风险研究相对较少，从经济、环境和社会三个可持续维度进行风险评估的文献就更少了。FMEA方法是一种事前对风险进行评估的方法，我们通过选取四川某白酒企业的供应链为例，应用FMEA方法对其风险进行了分析和评价，得出排在前五位的风险是文化风险、产品风险、道德风险、合作关系风险和金融危机。而处于最后三项的风险是不健康的工作环境、水质风险和超时工作。本书的研究方法可以为其他行业的供应链风险研究提供理论参考，也可以为其他白酒企业的供应链风险管理提供借鉴。

第六章 白酒可持续供应链绩效评价模型及应用

类似于大多数企业的运营，白酒行业可持续供应链管理需要寻求具体的绩效目标，如经济、环境、社会或综合绩效目标。这些目标可以由多个绩效指标来衡量。传统的绩效评价更多的是考虑经济绩效指标，如质量、可靠性、柔性、成本和响应性。随着可持续发展的观念进入供应链管理视野，各利益相关方面临的挑战更加严峻。这是因为传统的常规指标已经不足以评估可持续供应链的绩效，需要建立更全面系统的绩效评估体系。在多维指标的前提下，评价指标间更容易出现相互冲突的情况，如果要提高某一维度的绩效水平，则有可能需要另一个维度的绩效去平衡这种冲突。比如生产环保产品的同时，可能意味着采购成本的增加。因此，需要建立经济、环境和社会均衡的可持续供应链评价框架。学术界和企业界近年来高度关注可持续供应链管理的研究。白酒行业发展对经济、环境和社会有着重要的影响。然而，对于白酒行业的供应链绩效水平进行评价的文献还很少，而同时从经济、环境和社会三个维度进行可持续供应链评价研究的就更少了。这里用三重底线方法确定经济效益、环境保护和社会责任的可持续指标，并构建一个混合多属性决策框架对指标进行评估，同时对选择方案进行排序。最后，将所提出的方法应用于四川省一家白酒企业的可持续供应链评价案例进行研究。

一 评价研究

随着对环境保护、社会责任和经济效益均衡的关注，可持续供应链绩效评价的研究越来越受重视。

（一）评价维度

大部分可持续供应链管理（SSCM）模型倾向于只关注经济或环境方面的问题[1]。很少有文章同时研究可持续发展两个维度，而同时将可持续发展的三个维度集成的文章就更少了[2]。这里将重点研究那些在供应链管理中同时考虑两个或三个可持续维度的文章。

Chaabane 等提出了一个用于可持续供应链设计的混合整数线性规划框架，并评估了铝行业在各种成本和运营策略下如何实现经济和环境目标之间的权衡[3]。Eskandarpour 等关注整合了可持续发展因素的供应链网络设计问题中的优化模型和技术[4]。Chardine-Baumann 和 Botta-Genou-

---

[1] Seuring, S., Müller, M., "From a Literature Review to a Conceptual Framework for Sustainable Supply Chain Management", *Journal of Cleaner Production*, 16 (15), 2008: 1699 – 1710; Boukherroub, T., Ruiz, A., Guinet, A., & Fondrevelle, J., "An Integrated Approach for Sustainable Supply Chain Planning", *Computers & Operations Research*, 54, 2015: 180 – 194; Chardine-Baumann, E., & Botta-Genoulaz, V., "A Framework for Sustainable Performance Assessment of Supply Chain Management Practices", *Computers & Industrial Engineering*, 76, 2014: 138 – 147; Matos, S., & Hall, J., "Integrating Sustainable Development in the Supply Chain: The Case of Life Cycle Assessment in Oil and Gas and Agricultural Biotechnology", *Journal of Operations Management*, 25 (6), 2007: 1083 – 1102.

[2] Seuring, S., Müller, M., "From a Literature Review to a Conceptual Framework for Sustainable Supply Chain Management", *Journal of Cleaner Production*, 16 (15), 2008: 1699 – 1710.

[3] Chaabane, A., Ramudhin, A., & Paquet, M., "Design of Sustainable Supply Chains Under the Emission Trading Scheme", *International Journal of Production Economics*, 135 (1), 2012: 37 – 49.

[4] Eskandarpour, M., Dejax, P., Miemczyk, J., & Péton, O., "Sustainable Supply Chain Network Design: An Optimization-oriented Review", *Omega*, 54, 2015: 11 – 32.

laz 提出了可持续性绩效特征和评估的框架①。Bouherroub 等提出了一种将可持续发展原则运用于供应链建模的综合方法，并将其应用于加拿大木材产业的案例分析②。在评估和选择可持续供应商时，Sarkis 和 Davalale 提出了基于贝叶斯框架和蒙特卡罗马尔科夫链（MCMC）模拟的三重底线方法，使用特殊方法对供应商进行选择排序③。Gopal 和 Thakkar 研究得出社会绩效和环境绩效与经济绩效具有正相关的关系④。Shen 研究了目前纺织服装业的可持续供应链，并将研究结果应用于 H&M 案例研究，站在瑞典的角度评估社会福祉、环境福祉和经济福利⑤。You 等分析了三个可持续性维度的帕累托前沿⑥。Matos 和 Hall 通过将生命周期评估（LCA）方法应用于两个案例研究来评估可持续发展⑦。Yusuf 等研究了可持续性对英国石油和天然气供应链的运营和业务绩效的影响⑧。Berning 和 Venter 应用相关的供应商理论来研究在可持续供应链管

---

① Chardine-Baumann, E., & Botta Genoulaz, V., "A Framework for Sustainable Performance Assessment of Supply Chain Management Practices", *Computers & Industrial Engineering*, 76, 2014: 138 – 147.

② Boukherroub, T., Ruiz, A., Guinet, A., & Fondrevelle, J., "An Integrated Approach for Sustainable Supply Chain Planning", *Computers & Operations Research*, 54, 2015: 180 – 194.

③ Sarkis, J., & Dhavale, D. G., "Supplier Selection for Sustainable Operations: A Triple-bottom-line Approach Using a Bayesian Framework", *International Journal of Production Economics*, 166, 2015: 177 – 191.

④ Gopal, P. R. C., & Thakkar, J., "Sustainable Supply Chain Practices: An Empirical Investigation on Indian Automobile Industry", *Production Planning & Control*, 27 (1), 2016: 49 – 64.

⑤ Shen, B., "Sustainable Fashion Supply Chain: Lessons from H&M", *Sustainability*, 6 (9), 2014: 6236 – 6249.

⑥ You, F., Tao, L., Graziano, D. J., & Snyder, S. W., "Optimal Design of Sustainable Cellulosic Biofuel Supply Chains: Multiobjective Optimization Coupled with life Cycle Assessment and Input-output Analysis", *AIChE Journal*, 58 (4), 2012: 1157 – 1180.

⑦ Matos, S., & Hall, J., "Integrating Sustainable Development in the Supply Chain: The Case of Life Cycle Assessment in Oil and Gas and Agricultural Biotechnology", *Journal of Operations Management*, 25 (6), 2007: 1083 – 1102.

⑧ Yusuf, Y. Y., Gunasekaran, A., Musa, A., El-Berishy, N. M., Abubakar, T., & Ambursa, H. M., "The UK Oil and Gas Supply Chains: An Empirical Analysis of Adoption of Sustainable Measures and Performance Outcomes", *International Journal of Production Economics*, 146 (2), 2013: 501 – 514.

理中的零售商发展情况[1]。Schaltegger 等提出了一个研究学者和供应链从业人员可用于识别并评估经济、环境和社会绩效指标的多维框架[2]，随后 Varsei 和 Polyakovskiy 研究了葡萄酒供应链，并提出了一个包含经济、环境和社会目标的可持续葡萄酒供应链网络设计的通用模型[3]。Balfaqih 等发现供应链管理中的绩效评价是一个富有成果的研究领域[4]。我们总结了部分供应链可持续发展维度研究情况，如表 6.1 所示。

表 6.1　　供应链可持续发展维度和指标

参考文献	类型	维度	指标
Chaabane 等（2012）[5]	设计	经济	供应链总成本
		环境	温室气体
Eskandarpour 等（2015）[6]	综述	环境	温室气体、废弃物、能源使用、物料回收等
		社会	工作条件、社会承诺、客户问题
Boukherroub 等（2015）[7]	规划	经济	可靠性、响应性、柔性、财务状况、质量
		环境	资源消耗、气候变化、污染、有害物质
		社会	健康与安全、创造就业机会和财富、工作条件

---

[1] Berning, A., & Venter, C., "Sustainable Supply Chain Engagement in a Retail Environment", *Sustainability*, 7 (5), 2015: 6246–6263.

[2] Schaltegger, S., Burritt, R., Varsei, M., Soosay, C., Fahimnia, B., & Sarkis, J., "Framing Sustainability Performance of Supply Chains with Multidimensional Indicators", *Supply Chain Management: An International Journal*, 19 (3), 2014: 242–257.

[3] Varsei, M., & Polyakovskiy, S., "Sustainable Supply Chain Network Design: A Case of the Wine Industry in Australia", *Omega*, 66, 2017: 236–247.

[4] Balfaqih, H., Nopiah, Z. M., Saibani, N., & Al-Nory, M. T., "Review of Supply Chain Performance Measurement Systems: 1998–2015", *Computers in Industry*, 82, 2016: 135–150; Beske-Janssen, P., Johnson, M. P., & Schaltegger, S., "20 Years of Performance Measurement in Sustainable Supply Chain Management—What has been Achieved?", *Supply Chain Management: An International Journal*, 20 (6), 2015: 664–680.

[5] Chaabane, A., Ramudhin, A., & Paquet, M., "Design of Sustainable Supply Chains under the Emission Trading Scheme", *International Journal of Production Economics*, 135 (1), 2012: 37–49.

[6] Eskandarpour, M., Dejax, P., Miemczyk, J., & Péton, O., "Sustainable Supply Chain Network Design: An Optimization-oriented Review", *Omega*, 54, 2015: 11–32.

[7] Boukherroub, T., Ruiz, A., Guinet, A., & Fondrevelle, J., "An Integrated Approach for Sustainable Supply Chain Planning", *Computers & Operations Research*, 54, 2015: 180–194.

续表

参考文献	类型	维度	指标
Chardine-Baumann 和 Botta-Genoulaz（2014）①	评价	经济	可靠性、响应性、柔性、财务状况、质量
		环境	环境管理、资源使用、污染、危险品、自然环境
		社会	工作条件、人权、社会承诺、客户问题、商业互动
Sarkis 和 Dhavale（2015）②	供应商选择	经济	预期成本差异、标准或合同成本、采购产品或服务的质量、按时交货
		环境	供应商能源效率、破坏环境的相关惩罚、环境和污染控制技术的使用
		社会	慈善捐款、社区责任、员工流动率
Matos 和 Hall（2007）③	评价	经济	组织结构方面：互补资产（融资渠道、市场、内部专业知识、规模经济）、公司能力、能力知识、知识产权保护、其他专用机制
		环境	废气排放、排水质量、能源消耗、水资源使用、废弃物管理、土地破坏和复垦多样性
		社会	工作岗位、提高/转移到当地社区的知识、健康和安全、当地社区的健康和安全、机会均等和多样性、潜在负面影响、利益相关者、利益相关者参与满意度
You 等（2012）④	设计	经济	供应链总成本、生物燃料销售激励和副产品信贷
		环境	每年二氧化碳排放
		社会	应计当地就业（以全职一年计）

---

① Chardine-Baumann, E., & Botta-Genoulaz, V., "A Framework for Sustainable Performance Assessment of Supply Chain Management Practices", *Computers & Industrial Engineering*, 76, 2014: 138–147.

② Sarkis, J., & Dhavale, D. G., "Supplier Selection for Sustainable Operations: A Triple-bottom-line Approach Using a Bayesian Framework", *International Journal of Production Economics*, 166, 2015: 177–191.

③ Matos, S., & Hall, J., "Integrating Sustainable Development in the Supply Chain: The Case of Life Cycle Assessment in Oil and Gas and Agricultural Biotechnology", *Journal of Operations Management*, 25 (6), 2007: 1083–1102.

④ You, F., Tao, L., Graziano, D. J., & Snyder, S. W., "Optimal Design of Sustainable Cellulosic Biofuel Supply Chains: Multiobjective Optimization Coupled with Life Cycle Assessment and Input-output Analysis", *AIChE Journal*, 58 (4), 2012: 1157–1180.

续表

参考文献	类型	维度	指标
Varsei 和 Polyakovskiy (2016)①	设计	经济	供应链总成本
		环境	温室气体排放
		社会	失业率、当地生产总值
Schaltegger 等（2014）②	评价	经济	供应链总成本、服务水平
		环境	温室气体排放、耗水量、能源消耗、废弃物的产生、危险和有毒物质的使用
		社会	劳动实践和体面工作、人权、社会、产品责任

综上所述，已有的供应链管理绩效评估研究提到三个可持续维度的文章只有这些文献③；所有其他文献都集中于供应链设计或规划等方面。这里第一个目的是确定白酒供应链的可持续性评估维度。通过综合研究分析，确定了三个可持续性维度，即经济效益、环境保护和社会福利。

（二）评价方法

考虑多个可持续发展指标的绩效评价方法是多维度的④。有很多重

---

① Varsei, M. , & Polyakovskiy, S. , "Sustainable Supply Chain Network Design: A Case of the Wine Industry in Australia", *Omega*, 66, 2017: 236 – 247.

② Schaltegger, S. , Burritt, R. , Varsei, M. , Soosay, C. , Fahimnia, B. , & Sarkis, J. , "Framing Sustainability Performance of Supply Chains with Multidimensional Indicators", *Supply Chain Management: An International Journal*, 19 (3), 2014: 242 – 257.

③ Chardine-Baumann, E. , & Botta-Genoulaz, V. , "A Framework for Sustainable Performance Assessment of Supply Chain Management Practices", *Computers & Industrial Engineering*, 76, 2014: 138 – 147; Matos, S. , & Hall, J. , "Integrating Sustainable Development in the Supply Chain: The Case of Life Cycle Assessment in Oil and Gas and Agricultural Biotechnology", *Journal of Operations Management*, 25 (6), 2007: 1083 – 1102; Sarkis, J. , & Dhavale, D. G. , "Supplier Selection for Sustainable Operations: A Triple-bottom-line Approach Using a Bayesian Framework", *International Journal of Production Economics*, 166, 2015: 177 – 191; Schaltegger, S. , Burritt, R. , Varsei, M. , Soosay, C. , Fahimnia, B. , & Sarkis, J. , "Framing Sustainability Performance of Supply Chains with Multidimensional Indicators", *Supply Chain Management: An International Journal*, 19 (3), 2014: 242 – 257.

④ Boukherroub, T. , Ruiz, A. , Guinet, A. , & Fondrevelle, J. , "An Integrated Approach for Sustainable Supply Chain Planning", *Computers & Operations Research*, 54, 2015: 180 – 194.

要的研究对评价领域有显著的贡献。Seuring 将可持续模型划分为四类：基于生命周期评估（LCA）的模型、均衡模型、多属性决策（Multi-Criteria Decision Making，MCDM）和层次分析法（AHP）的应用[1]。Mardani 等将研究分为工程、管理、科学和技术四个领域。经过分析发现，混合模糊集成法和模糊 MCDM 方法是最常用的方法，排名分别位于第一位和第二位[2]。

在现实世界中，有许多问题需要处理模糊、不精确和不确定的信息[3]，因而难以提供数字精确的信息[4]。在处理非概率不确定性的问题中使用语言建模已被证明是合乎逻辑的，并且运用模糊理论处理模糊性和不确定性的研究已在不同领域中有成功的例子。多属性决策研究发展迅速，已成为处理复杂决策问题的主要研究领域。

最突出的 MCDM 方法之一是模糊 AHP（Fuzzy Analytical Hierarchy Process），它能够处理来自专家的不确定和不精确的语言判断变量。作为多属性决策工具或权重估计技术的模糊 AHP 已经广泛用于各种领域。Abdullah 和 Zulkifli 提出了一种混合模糊 AHP 方法与一种间隔二型模糊决策试验和评估实验室（DEMATEL）方法，用于人力资源管理[5]。Ng 应用模糊 AHP 方法来评估方案的环境绩效[6]。Kilincci 和 Onal 将模糊

---

[1] Seuring, S., "A review of Modeling Approaches for Sustainable Supply Chain Management", *Decision Support Systems*, 54 (4), 2013: 1513 – 1520.

[2] Mardani, A., Jusoh, A., & Zavadskas, E. K., "Fuzzy Multiple Criteria Decision-making Techniques and Applications—Two Decades Review from 1994 to 2014", *Expert Systems with Applications*, 42 (8), 2015: 4126 – 4148.

[3] Abdullah, L., & Zulkifli, N., "Integration of Fuzzy AHP and Interval Type – 2 Fuzzy DEMATEL: An Application to Human Resource Management", *Expert Systems with Applications*, 42 (9), 2015: 4397 – 4409.

[4] Chen, C. T., "Extensions of the TOPSIS for Group Decision-making Under Fuzzy Environment", *Fuzzy Sets and Systems*, 114 (1), 2000: 1 – 9.

[5] Abdullah, L., & Zulkifli, N., "Integration of Fuzzy AHP and Interval Type – 2 Fuzzy DEMATEL: An Application to Human Resource Management", *Expert Systems with Applications*, 42 (9), 2015: 4397 – 4409.

[6] Ng, C. Y., "Evidential Reasoning-based Fuzzy AHP Approach for the Evaluation of Design Alternatives' Environmental Performances", *Applied Soft Computing*, 46, 2016: 381 – 397.

AHP 法应用于洗衣机公司的供应商选择问题[1]。Chen 等使用模糊 AHP 来评估教学绩效[2]，Patil 和 Kant 提出了一种用于知识管理的模糊 AHP 方法[3]。

模糊 TOPSIS（Fuzzy Technique for Order Performance by Similarity to Ideal Solution）是另一种 MCDM 方法，已被广泛用于解决模糊环境中的问题。模糊 TOPSIS 基于这样的观念，所选择的方案应当最接近正理想解（PIS），并且离负理想解（NIS）最远[4]。模糊 TOPSIS 方法非常适合在模糊环境下解决现实生活中的应用问题[5]。Cavallaro 等应用模糊 TOPSIS 来评估电热系统[6]。Zyoud 等提出了一个用于发展中国家水土损失管理的模糊 AHP-TOPSIS 框架。Lima-Junior 和 Carpinetti 使用模糊 TOPSIS 进行供应商评估和管理[7]。Kusi-Sarpong 等使用集成粗糙

---

[1] Kilincci, O., & Onal, S. A., "Fuzzy AHP Approach for Supplier Selection in a Washing Machine Company", *Expert Systems with Applications*, 38 (8), 2011: 9656-9664.

[2] Chen, J. F., Hsieh, H. N., & Do, Q. H., "Evaluating Teaching Performance Based on Fuzzy AHP and Comprehensive Evaluation Approach", *Applied Soft Computing*, 28, 2015: 100-108.

[3] Patil, S. K., & Kant, R., "A Fuzzy AHP-TOPSIS Framework for Ranking the Solutions of Knowledge Management Adoption in Supply Chain to Overcome Its Barriers", *Expert Systems with Applications*, 41 (2), 2014: 679-693.

[4] Cavallaro, F., Zavadskas, E., & Raslanas, S., "Evaluation of Combined Heat and Power (CHP) Systems Using Fuzzy Shannon Entropy and Fuzzy TOPSIS", *Sustainability*, 8 (6), 2016: 556; Zyoud, S. H., Kaufmann, L. G., Shaheen, H., Samhan, S., & Fuchs-Hanusch, D., "A Framework for Water Loss Management in Developing Countries Under Fuzzy Environment: Lntegration of Fuzzy AHP with Fuzzy TOPSIS", *Expert Systems with Applications*, 61, 2016: 86-105.

[5] Patil, S. K., & Kant, R., "A Fuzzy AHP-TOPSIS Framework for Ranking the Solutions of Knowledge Management Adoption in Supply Chain to Overcome its Barriers", *Expert Systems with Applications*, 41 (2), 2014: 679-693.

[6] Cavallaro, F., Zavadskas, E., & Raslanas, S., "Evaluation of Combined Heat and Power (CHP) Systems Using Fuzzy Shannon Entropy and Fuzzy TOPSIS", *Sustainability*, 8 (6), 2016: 556.

[7] Lima-Junior, F. R., & Carpinetti, L. C. R., "Combining SCOR® Model and fuzzy TOPSIS for Supplier Evaluation and Management", *International Journal of Production Economics*, 174, 2016: 128-141.

集和模糊TOPSIS方法来评估采矿业的绿色供应链实践[1]。此外，Patil和Kant对供应链中克服知识管理障碍的解决方案进行了排序[2]。

混合模糊集成方法和模糊MCDM方法已被发现是当前最流行的方法[3]。作为FMCDM方法的混合模糊AHP-TOPSIS方法已经广泛应用于管理和商业环境中。我们的第二个目的是设计一个来评估白酒行业供应链可持续绩效的框架，使用的是混合模糊AHP-TOPSIS方法。

（三）白酒评价

中国白酒行业对国民经济发展做出了重要贡献。王艳红和周健将层次分析法（AHP）和模糊评价法结合起来，建立了白酒行业节能减排技术评价模型；并对四川某白酒企业进行实证分析，得出该企业的节能减排的技术效率，提出相应的对策和建议[4]。李明蔚等提出了包含生态经济建设、厂区空间优化、生态制度建设、生态环境建设和生态文化建设5个方面34项指标的白酒企业生态文明评价指标体系，为白酒企业开展生态文明建设提供参考[5]。李琛等以品牌生态学理论为基础，运用AHP法从系统活力、组织结构和系统弹性三个层次构建白酒品牌生态系统评价指标体系[6]。黄妍和戴新民建立了一套科学的企业财务竞争力

---

[1] Kusi-Sarpong, S., Bai, C., Sarkis, J., & Wang, X., "Green Supply Chain Practices Evaluation in the Mining Industry Using a Joint Rough Sets and Fuzzy TOPSIS Methodology", *Resources Policy*, 46, 2015: 86 - 100.

[2] Patil, S. K., & Kant, R., "A Fuzzy AHP-TOPSIS Framework for Ranking the Solutions of Knowledge Management Adoption in Supply Chain to Overcome its Barriers", *Expert Systems with Applications*, 41 (2), 2014: 679 - 693.

[3] Mardani, A., Jusoh, A., & Zavadskas, E. K., "Fuzzy Multiple Criteria Decision-making Techniques and Applications—Two Decades Review from 1994 to 2014", *Expert Systems with Applications*, 42 (8), 2015: 4126 - 4148.

[4] 王艳红、周健：《白酒企业节能减排技术评价实证分析》，《酿酒科技》2014年第9期。

[5] 李明蔚、张俊娥、王永刚等：《白酒企业生态文明评价指标体系构建》，《中国人口·资源与环境》2016年第1期。

[6] 李琛、曾祥凤、凌泽华：《白酒品牌生态系统健康评价指标体系设计与评价方法》，《企业经济》2015年第8期。

评价体系，并提出提升企业财务竞争力的可行性措施①。崔风暴等对白酒产业价值链结构及价值创造方式进行了分析和评价②。张春国采集2009—2011 年 14 家白酒行业上市公司的样本数据，构建了 DEA 模型，对白酒行业的技术有效性和规模有效性进行分析③。

　　Yao 和 Liu 指出白酒行业的竞争日趋激烈，白酒企业要想在激烈的竞争中生存，就必须具备足够的竞争力，并认为提高自身竞争力是白酒企业现在的主要任务④。Ma 根据利益相关者理论将白酒企业环境社会责任分为股东、员工、政府、消费者和企业自身五个方面；然后从环境保护法、消费者权利、绿色生产和社区影响四个维度运用层次分析法进行评价；结果表明，环境保护法律制度具有明显的敦促白酒企业履行环境社会责任的效应，而绿色生产和消费者权利正成为环境保护新的手段，但是社区影响的维度权重较低⑤。Guo 等指出白酒产业相关的污染问题逐渐对环境造成恶化，并对当地社区产生不利影响；为解决这些问题，文章提出了一系列的清洁生产方案和评估方案，对白酒行业清洁生产技术的应用和可持续发展的广泛应用提供了理论和实践支持⑥。Huang 等认为中国白酒企业应采取相应的改革策略，以降低用水，提高水的利用效率，改善副产品的回收利用，减少污染物排放，提高废弃物处理效

---

　　① 黄妍、戴新民：《应用因子分析模型评价白酒行业上市公司财务竞争力》，《酿酒科技》2013 年第 7 期。
　　② 崔风暴、蒲岚、冉华森：《中国白酒产业理性认知——产业价值创造方式评价》，《酿酒科技》2014 年第 5 期。
　　③ 张春国：《基于 dea 模型的白酒行业上市公司经营绩效评价》，《会计之友》2013 年第 3 期。
　　④ Yao, J., & Liu, T., "Evaluation of the Competitiveness of China's Liquor Enterprise Based on Factor Analysis Method", In AASRI International Conference on Industrial Electronics and Applications (IEA 2015). Atlantis Press.
　　⑤ S N. Ma, "The Connotation and Evaluation of Liquor Enterprise's Social Environment Responsibility——Based on the Stakeholder Perspective", 2015: 726 – 730.
　　⑥ Guo, H. C., Chen, B., Yu, X. L., Huang, G. H., Liu, L., & Nie, X. H., "Assessment of Cleaner Production Options for Alcohol Industry of China: A Study in the Shouguang Alcohol Factory", *Journal of Cleaner Production*, 14 (1), 2006: 94 – 103.

率，并发现对中国白酒生产的环境评价进行研究的文章并不多[1]。Zeigler探讨了贸易协定与烈性酒管制政策的关系，并研究了烈性酒工业对贸易政策方面的影响作用[2]。Zhu等探讨了烈性酒与自我选择效应的关系[3]。Yan-Ping等选择14家酒类上市公司的10个主要财务指标。使用主成分分析法，提取反映企业盈利能力、偿债能力和拓展能力的三个主要组成部分，然后计算总分并对其进行排名；为了进一步分析，将这些公司在分层聚类方法下聚类为四种类型；对数据结果进行了综合评价，得出位于第一类和第二类的高收入公司都适合投资，第四类低收入公司，因短期财务状况不佳，不适合投资，第三类拥有或多或少的问题，因此居于中间[4]。Ariyoshi对一家日本报业公司实施了酒精依赖预防措施，通过案例研究，明确了职业健康护理干预的有效性[5]。Fang和Chen通过对美国葡萄酒和烈酒行业的现实投资来研究股票策略，为对美国葡萄酒和白酒企业感兴趣的国内投资者提供决策参考[6]。

据我们所知，很少有文章将研究白酒供应链管理可持续性评价与三重底线方法整合在一起，而且对白酒供应链管理的评估文章很少。因此，可以得出结论，目前白酒企业的可持续供应链研究还没有建成系统的评估框架，在白酒可持续供应链研究领域还没有足够的集成度

---

[1] Huang, Y. L., Sun, W., & Su, Q. Q., "Environmental Issues for the Chinese Strong Aromatic Liquor Industry: An Assessment for the Brewing System", *Environmental Modeling & Assessment*, 19 (2), 2014: 153-165.

[2] Zeigler, D. W., "The Alcohol Industry and Trade Agreements: A Preliminary Assessment", *Addiction*, 104, 2009: 13-26.

[3] Zhu, J., Tews, M. J., Stafford, K., & George, R. T., "Alcohol and Illicit Substance Use in the Food Service Industry: Assessing Self-selection and Job-related Risk Factors", *Journal of Hospitality & Tourism Research*, 35 (1), 2011: 45-63.

[4] Yan-Ping, N., Ya-Nan, S. U., & Xin, W., "Investment Risk Evaluation of Liquor Listed Companies Based on Cluster Analysis", *Journal of Hebei University of Science and Technology (Social Sciences)*, 2015.

[5] Ariyoshi, H., "An Evaluation of Alcohol Dependence Prevention Measures at a Japanese Newspaper Company", *AAOHN journal*, 58 (10), 2010: 433-436.

[6] Fang, Q., & Chen, Y., "Stock Portfolio Analysis Based on Margin of Safety and Competitive Edge Evaluation in the American Wine and Liquor Industry", In 2016 IEEE International Conference on Big Data Analysis (ICBDA), 2016: 1-7.

和成熟度[1]。

第一，现有研究中大多数的供应链可持续评价文献重点关注一个或两个维度，很少同时考虑三个维度[2]。在白酒企业的评价中，有的文献评价了白酒企业的环境维度[3]。有的文献考虑了白酒企业的环境和社会可持续维度[4]。有的文章研究了白酒企业的经济维度[5]。可以看出已有研究集中在经济维度和环境维度，而忽视了社会维度。这可能是因为社会维度是最难评估的，因为社会指标很难量化，而且往往倾向于主观化[6]。

第二，在白酒供应链研究中，几乎没有文献同时考虑经济、环境和社会的可持续指标体系[7]。在白酒企业的供应链中，常规指标已不足以准确评估可持续供应链的绩效，因为它们主要关注单一维度[8]。

---

[1] Seuring, S., Müller, M., "From a Literature Review to a Conceptual Framework for Sustainable Supply Chain Management", *Journal of Cleaner Production*, 16 (15), 2008: 1699 – 1710; Boukherroub, T., Ruiz, A., Guinet, A., & Fondrevelle, J., "An Integrated approach for Sustainable Supply Chain Planning", *Computers & Operations Research*, 54, 2015: 180 – 194; Chardine-Baumann, E., & Botta-Genoulaz, V., "A Framework for Sustainable Performance Assessment of Supply Chain Management Practices", *Computers & Industrial Engineering*, 76, 2014: 138 – 147.

[2] Seuring, S., "A Review of Modeling Approaches for Sustainable Supply Chain Management", *Decision Support Systems*, 54 (4), 2013: 1513 – 1520; Eskandarpour, M., Dejax, P., Miemczyk, J., & Péton, O., "Sustainable Supply Chain Network Design: An Optimization-oriented Review", *Omega*, 54, 2015: 11 – 32.

[3] Guo, H. C., Chen, B., Yu, X. L., Huang, G. H., Liu, L., & Nie, X. H., "Assessment of Cleaner Production Options for Alcohol Industry of China: A Study in the Shouguang Alcohol Factory", *Journal of Cleaner Production*, 14 (1), 2006: 94 – 103; 李明蔚、张俊娥、王永刚、王旭、王媛媛：《白酒企业生态文明评价指标体系构建》，《中国人口·资源与环境》2016 年第 1 期；Huang, Y. L., Sun, W., & Su, Q. Q., "Environmental Issues for the Chinese Strong Aromatic Liquor Industry: An Assessment for the Brewing System", *Environmental Modeling & Assessment*, 19 (2), 2014: 153 – 165。

[4] S. N. Ma, "The Connotation and Evaluation of Liquor Enterprise's Social Environment Responsibility-based on the Stakeholder Perspective", 2015: 726 – 730.

[5] Yao, J., & Liu, T., "Evaluation of the Competitiveness of China's Liquor Enterprise Based on Factor Analysis Method", In AASRI International Conference on Industrial Electronics and Applications (IEA 2015), 2015.

[6] Beske-Janssen, P., Johnson, M. P., & Schaltegger, S., "20 Years of Performance Measurement in Sustainable Supply Chain Management—What has been Achieved?", *Supply Chain Management: An International Journal*, 20 (6), 2015: 664 – 680.

[7] Seuring, S., Müller, M., "From a Literature Review to a Conceptual Frame-work for Sustainable Supply Chain Management", *Journal of Cleaner Production*, 16 (15); 2008: 1699 – 1710; Seuring, S., "A Review of Modeling Approaches for Sustainable Supply Chain Management", *Decision support systems*, 54 (4), 2013: 1513 – 1520.

[8] Seuring, S., Müller, M., "From a Literature Review to a Conceptual Framework for Sustainable Supply Chain Management", *Journal of Cleaner Production*, 16 (15), 2008: 1699 – 1710.

第三，大多数评价主要关注企业本身，很少有文献是评估整个供应链的[1]。但是，要全面考查白酒企业的可持续发展，从供应链管理的角度进行综合评估就显得越来越重要[2]。因此，在全球经济竞争越来越激烈的今天，建立一套全面、系统、可操作性强的白酒行业可持续供应链评价体系势在必行[3]。

考虑到中国白酒行业的现状，在白酒供应链管理中很有必要建立一个合适的可持续绩效评估框架[4]。从当前的可持续供应链研究来看，绩效评估指标、方法和管理体系对可持续供应链来说都是必不可少[5]。通过为中国白酒行业可持续供应链绩效评估制定框架，可以丰富相应贡献。该框架要满足可持续发展的三个维度。我们的第三个目的是确定白酒供应链管理的具体可持续性指标，对其他研究可以提供有用的参考。很明显，这种可持续性维度、评估方法和绩效测量指标是白酒可持续供应链管理的重要组成部分。

二　框架研究

到目前为止，为中国白酒行业供应链可持续研究确定指标和排序，并提供相应评估框架的研究还很少。在很多情况下，信息是模糊的、不准确的和不确定的，因此很难提供精确的数字信息。MCDM 已经被证明是一个功能强大的工具，广泛用于解决多个经常冲突的指标

---

[1] 王艳红、周健：《白酒企业节能减排技术评价实证分析》，《酿酒科技》2014 年第 9 期。

[2] Seuring, S., Müller, M., "From a Literature Review to a Conceptual Frame-work for Sustainable Supply Chain Management", Journal of Cleaner Production, 16 (15): 2008: 1699 – 1710; Seuring, S., "A Review of Modeling Approaches for Sustainable Supply Chain Management", Decision support systems, 54 (4), 2013: 1513 – 1520.

[3] Boukherroub, T., Ruiz, A., Guinet, A., & Fondrevelle, J., "An Integrated Approach for Sustainable Supply Chain Planning", Computers & Operations Research, 54, 2015: 180 – 194; Chardine-Baumann, E., & Botta-Genoulaz, V., "A Framework for Sustainable Performance Assessment of Supply Chain Management Practices", Computers & Industrial Engineering, 76, 2014: 138 – 147.

[4] Linton, J. D., Klassen, R., & Jayaraman, V., "Sustainable Supply Chains: An Introduction", Journal of Operations Management, 25 (6), 2007: 1075 – 1082.

[5] Beske-Janssen, P., Johnson, M. P., & Schaltegger, S., "20 Years of Performance Measurement in Sustainable Supply Chain Management—What has been Schieved?", Supply Chain Management: An International Journal, 20 (6), 2005: 664 – 680.

问题[①]。在这里，模糊 AHP 用于确定绩效标准的可持续性权重，模糊 TOPSIS 应用于可持续选择方案的排序。

（一）框架结构

这里提供一个三阶段方法，用于评估白酒企业的可持续指标和可持续选择方案，如图 6.1 所示。

阶段 1：由文献分析结果和专家意见确定相关可持续指标。

阶段 2：使用模糊 AHP 方法确定指标的优先级，为白酒企业的供应链综合可持续性评估制定一个决策支持框架，其中将经济、环境和社会维度结合起来，以帮助决策者纳入不同的可持续性标准偏好，以便确定最可持续的选择。

阶段 3：使用模糊 TOPSIS 方法，对白酒企业供应链可持续性评估相关的选择方案进行排序以提高其效率和有效性。

（二）指标确定

可持续供应链管理是现代管理重视可持续发展的关键措施之一[②]。用 TBL 理论中的经济绩效、环境保护和社会责任来区分供应链可持续发展评估的三个维度[③]。受已有研究和专家意见的启发，这里建议的模型在三个维度上有 15 个指标，其中经济维度、环境维度和社会维度各有 5 个，如图 6.2 所示。

[①] Seuring, S., Müller, M., "From a Literature Review to a Conceptual Framework for Sustainable Supply Chain Management", *Journal of Cleaner Production*, 16 (15), 2008: 1699 – 1710; Mardani, A., Jusoh, A., & Zavadskas, E. K., "Fuzzy Multiple Criteria Decision-making Techniques and Applications—Two Decades Review from 1994 to 2014", *Expert Systems with Applications*, 42 (8), 2015: 4126 – 4148.

[②] Boukherroub, T., Ruiz, A., Guinet, A., & Fondrevelle, J., "An Integrated Approach for Sustainable Supply Chain Planning", *Computers & Operations Research*, 54, 2015: 180 – 194.

[③] Linton, J. D., Klassen, R., & Jayaraman, V., "Sustainable Supply Chains: An Introduction", *Journal of Operations Management*, 25 (6), 2007: 1075 – 1082; Chardine-Baumann, E., & Botta-Genoulaz, V., "A Framework for Sustainable Performance Assessment of Supply Chain Management Practices", *Computers & Industrial Engineering*, 76, 2014: 138 – 147.

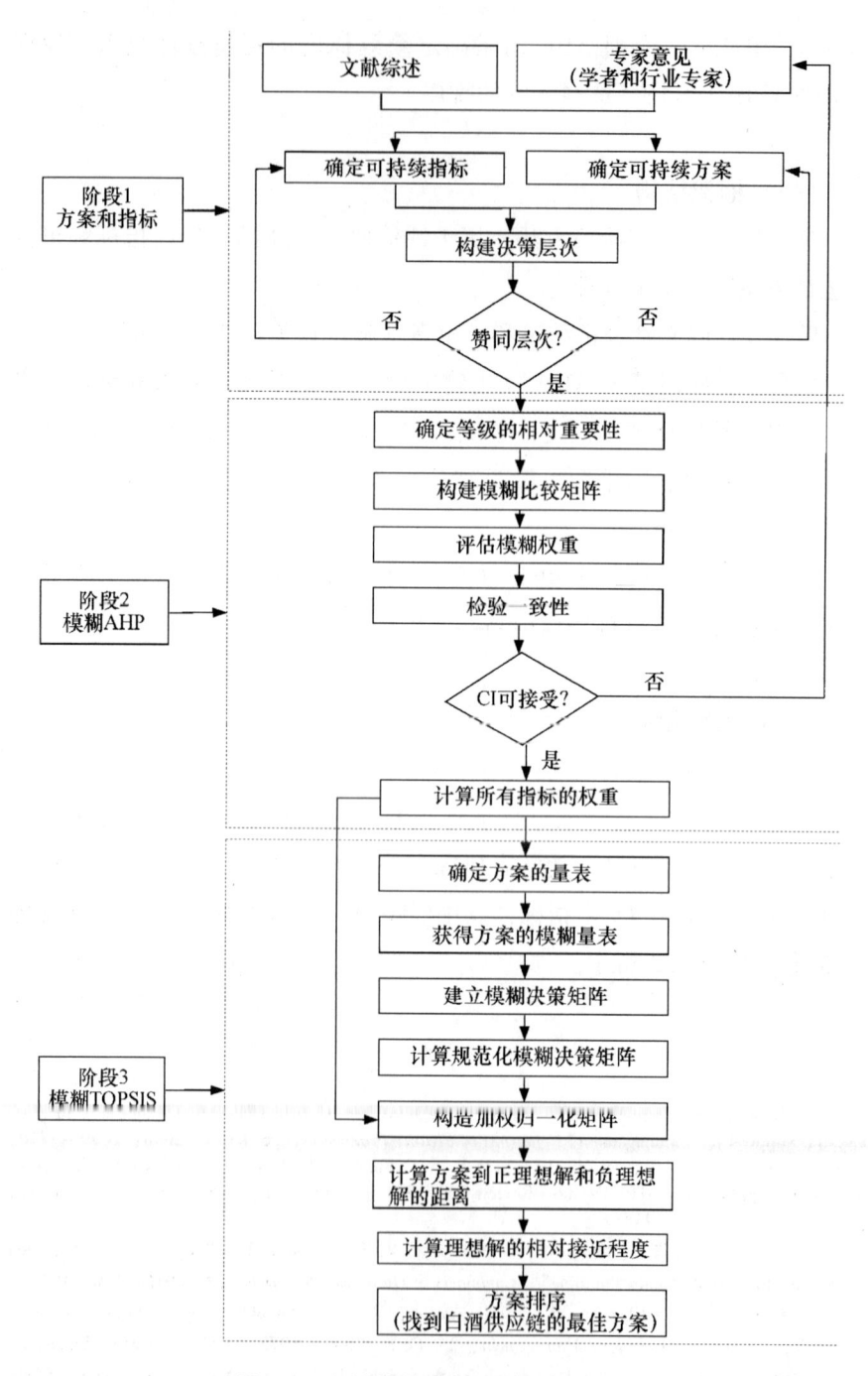

图 6.1 可持续供应链评价方法阶段图

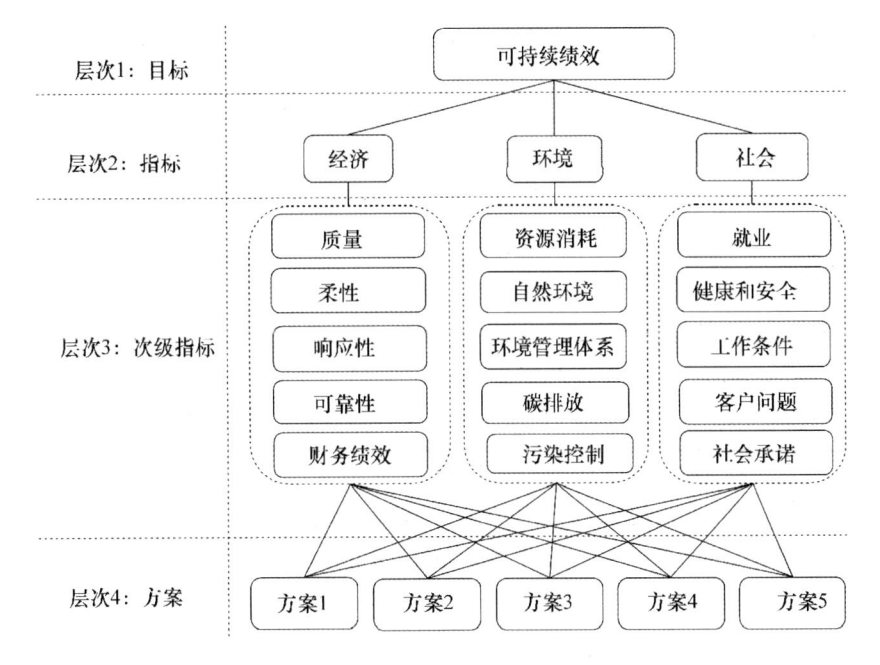

图 6.2　基于三重底线方法的可持续绩效评价层次结构

1. 经济维度

虽然已经开发了许多工具来评估供应链管理实践，但是供应链运作参考模型（Supply Chain Operations Reference Model，SCOR）的 5 个度量常常用来评估经济绩效[1]。世界上大约有 800 家公司已经验证了该模型的参考价值[2]。由于经济绩效是商业活动成功的衡量标准，它可能严重影响白酒企业的供应链发展。对供应链经济绩效测量的研究通常包括 5 个指标，

---

[1] Chardine-Baumann, E., & Botta-Genoulaz, V., "A Framework for Sustainable Performance Assessment of Supply Chain Management Practices", *Computers & Industrial Engineering*, 76, 2014: 138–147; Boukherroub, T., Ruiz, A., Guinet, A., & Fondrevelle, J., "An Integrated Approach for Sustainable Supply Chain Planning", *Computers & Operations Research*, 54, 2015: 180–194; Council, S. C., "Supply Chain Operations Reference Model", *Overview of SCOR Version*, 5 (0), 2008; Schöggl, J. P., Fritz, M. M., & Baumgartner, R. J., "Toward Supply chain-wide Sustainability Assessment: A Conceptual Framework and an Aggregation Method to Assess Supply Chain Performance", *Journal of Cleaner Production*, 131, 2016: 822–835.

[2] Boukherroub, T., Ruiz, A., Guinet, A., & Fondrevelle, J., "An Integrated Approach for Sustainable Supply Chain Planning", *Computers & Operations Research*, 54, 2015: 180–194; Council, S. C., "Supply Chain Operations Reference Model", *Overview of SCOR Version*, 5 (0), 2008.

即质量（Quality，*Eco*1）、柔性（Flexibility，*Eco*2）、响应性（Responsiveness，*Eco*3）、可靠性（Reliability，*Eco*4）和财务绩效（Financial performance，*Eco*5）[①]。

质量是客户—供应商关系的一个重要方面[②]。不良的质量影响着核心公司的财务表现，以及它的声誉。在白酒行业，质量用产品质量和服务质量来衡量。供应链质量就是供应链的适用性，即供应链能成功地满足用户需要的程度。

柔性是供应链对市场变化做出反应或获得或维持竞争优势的能力[③]，即快速响应环境变化的能力，是一种战略性资源。在这里，柔性意味着白酒企业的供应链必须随着环境的改变而不断发展和改善[④]。

响应性定义为白酒行业供应链向客户提供产品的速度[⑤]。从白酒行业供应链的角度来看，响应性是指物流、信息流和资金流从原产地到消费地的效率[⑥]。

可靠性一般是指顾客对供应链的满意程度或对企业的信赖程度。为了对供应链可靠性做出具体和定量的判断，可将供应链可靠性定义为在规定的条件下和规定的时间内，供应链稳定完成其任务的功能。可靠性主要是指白酒供应链的交货性能，包括供应商服务、顾客服务、预测的可靠性和库存的可靠性。也就是说在适当的时间将适当的产品放置在适当的位置，在适当的条件下，将适当的文件以适当的质量包装送到适当的

[①] Boukherroub, T., Ruiz, A., Guinet, A., & Fondrevelle, J., "An Integrated Approach for Sustainable Supply Chain Planning", *Computers & Operations Research*, 54, 2015: 180-194.

[②] Council, S. C., "Supply Chain Operations Reference Model", *Overview of SCOR Version*, 5 (0), 2008.

[③] Sarkis, J., & Dhavale, D. G., "Supplier Selection for Sustainable Operations: A Triple-bottom-line Approach Using a Bayesian Framework", *International Journal of Production Economics*, 166, 2015: 177-191.

[④] Gunasekaran, A., Patel, C., & Tirtiroglu, E., "Performance Measures and Metrics in a Supply Chain Environment", *International Journal of Operations & Production Management*, 21 (1/2), 2001: 71-87.

[⑤] Council, S. C., "Supply Chain Operations Reference Model", *Overview of SCOR Version*, 5 (0), 2008.

[⑥] Eskandarpour, M., Dejax, P., Miemczyk, J., & Péton, O., "Sustainable Supply Chain Network Design: An Optimization-oriented Review", *Omega*, 54, 2015: 11-32.

客户手中。

财务绩效是一个广义术语，包括供应链管理中的成本和资产管理，例如设计成本、采购成本、生产成本、交付成本、回报成本、供应链成本、预期成本差异、标准成本或合同成本以及互补资产，以及投资回报[1]。财务绩效能够很全面地表达企业成本控制的效果、资产运用管理的效果、资金来源调配的效果以及股东权益报酬率的组成，它可以体现供应链的盈利能力、营运能力、偿债能力和抗风险能力。

2. 环境维度

环境评估判断供应链的环境保护意识[2]。然而，对于环境绩效和社会绩效应该是什么，至今没有达成共识。因为这取决于工业部门运营所在的部门和地区或者所在的国家[3]。一些国际标准，例如 OECD 指导方针（Organization for Economic Co-operation and Development Guidelines）[4]、ISO 26000（International Standard Organization 26000）[5]、ISO 14001[6]、

---

[1] Matos, S., & Hall, J., "Integrating Sustainable Development in the Supply Chain: The Case of Life Cycle Assessment in Oil and Gas and Agricultural Biotechnology", *Journal of Operations Management*, 25 (6), 2007: 1083 – 1102; Council, S. C., "Supply Chain Operations Reference Model", *Overview of SCOR Version*, 5 (0), 2008; Gunasekaran, A., Patel, C., & Tirtiroglu, E. (2001), "Performance Measures and Metrics in a Supply Chain Environment", *International Journal of Operations & Production Management*, 21 (1/2), 71 – 87; Boukherroub, T., Ruiz, A., Guinet, A., & Fondrevelle, J. (2015), "An Integrated Approach for Sustainable Supply Chain Planning", *Computers & Operations Research*, 54, 180 – 194; Sarkis, J., & Dhavale, D. G. (2015), "Supplier Selection for Sustainable Operations: A Triple-bottom-line Approach Using a Bayesian Framework", *International Journal of Production Economics*, 166, 177 – 191.

[2] Matos, S., & Hall, J., "Integrating Sustainable Development in the Supply Chain: The Case of Life Cycle Assessment in Oil and Gas and Agricultural Biotechnology", *Journal of Operations Management*, 25 (6), 2007: 1083 – 1102.

[3] Chardine-Baumann, E., & Botta-Genoulaz, V., "A Framework for Sustainable Performance Assessment of Supply Chain Management Practices", *Computers & Industrial Engineering*, 76, 2014: 138 – 147.

[4] Gordon, K., & Mitidieri, C., "Multilateral Influences on the OECD Guidelines for Multinational Enterprises", *Oecd Working Papers on International Investment*.

[5] International Organization for Standardization (ISO), "Guidance on Social Re-sponsibility", ISO: Geneva, Switzerland, 2010.

[6] Curkovic, S., & Sroufe, R., "Using ISO 14001 to Promote a Sustainable Supply Chain Strategy", *Business Strategy and the Environment*, 20 (2), 2011: 71 – 93.

SA8000 (Social Accountability 8000 International Standard)[①]、GRI (Global Reporting Initiative)[②]、SCOR 参考模型[③]和一些科学著作，提出了或多或少的可以改编的通用标准，但这些标准不包括所有可持续发展领域。白酒行业供应链管理环境维度涉及 5 个方面：资源消耗 (Resource consumption, $Env1$)、自然环境 (Natural environment, $Env2$)、环境管理体系 (Environmental Management Systems, EMS, $Env3$)、碳排放 (Carbon emissions, $Env4$) 和污染控制 (Pollution control, $Env5$)。

资源消耗是环境维度中最常用的指标之一[④]。在白酒供应链中，资源消耗通常是指在生产配送阶段使用的粮食资源、水资源以及电力、天然气、石油和煤炭等能源。

自然环境关注于生态环境、尊重生物多样性、土地利用等方面[⑤]。白酒行业需要良好的生态环境。各种白酒依赖于独特的地缘优势，以及水资源等方面的优势。

环境管理体系是一个实用的决策支持工具，旨在帮助组织实现更好的环境绩效，确保持续改进和防止不利的环境影响[⑥]。在白酒供应链

---

① Social Accountability International, Social Accountability 8000 International Standard, New York, NY, USA, 2014.

② Initiative, G. R., "Sustainability Reporting Guidelines", Version 3.0. GRI, 2006, Amsterdam.

③ Council, S. C., "Supply Chain Operations Reference Model", *Overview of SCOR Version*, 5 (0), 2008.

④ Schaltegger, S., Burritt, R., Varsei, M., Soosay, C., Fahimnia, B., & Sarkis, J., "Framing Sustainability Performance of Supply Chains with Multidimensional Indicators", *Supply Chain Management: An International Journal*, 19 (3), 2014: 242 – 257; Schöggl, J. P., Fritz, M. M., & Baumgartner, R. J., "Toward Supply Chain-Wide Sustainability Assessment: A Conceptual Framework and an Aggregation Method to Assess Supply Chain Performance", *Journal of Cleaner Production*, 131, 2016: 822 – 835.

⑤ Boukherroub, T., Ruiz, A., Guinet, A., & Fondrevelle, J., "An Integrated Approach for Sustainable Supply Chain Planning", *Computers & Operations Research*, 54, 2015: 180 – 194.

⑥ Curkovic, S., & Sroufe, R., "Using ISO 14001 to Promote a Sustainable Supply Chain Strategy", *Business Strategy and the Environment*, 20 (2), 2011: 71 – 93; Beske-Janssen, P., Johnson, M. P., & Schaltegger, S., "20 Years of Performance Measurement in Sustainable Supply Chain Management—What has been Achieved?", *Supply Chain Management: An International Journal*, 20 (6), 2015: 664 – 680.

中，环境管理体系包括诸如建立环境预算、环境认证、环境合规性和环境评估等方面[1]。要求白酒行业供应链企业通过 ISO 14000 环境管理体系标准。

由于气候变化被认为是现代社会的重点关注点[2]，因此碳排放的减少已成为过去十年缓解气候变化的一个紧迫的全球性问题[3]。在白酒供应链中，人们主要关注生产和物流配送阶段的碳排放。

污染控制涉及对空气污染、水污染、土地污染和其他污染的控制[4]。白酒行业需对生产、配送过程中产生的废气、粉尘进行收集和处理；对产生的高浓度废水进行回收循环利用；对酒糟等固体废弃物进行管理往往是工业化发展程度的代表[5]，通常指原材料和产品的回收再利用[6]。白酒供应链中的废弃物管理主要涉及黄浆水、锅底水的利用和排放，酒糟和炉渣回收利用等方面。

3. 社会维度

社会责任是用来评估公司社会绩效的全球性指标。它评估公司的活

---

[1] Boukherroub, T., Ruiz, A., Guinet, A., & Fondrevelle, J., "An Integrated Approach for Sustainable Supply Chain Planning", *Computers & Operations Research*, 54, 2015: 180 – 194.

[2] Hassini, E., Surti, C., & Searcy, C., "A Literature Review and a Case Study of Sustainable Supply Chains with a Focus on Metrics", *International Journal of Production Economics*, 140 (1), 2012: 69 – 82.

[3] Chaabane, A., Ramudhin, A., & Paquet, M., "Design of Sustainable Supply Chains under the Emission Trading Scheme", *International Journal of Production Economics*, 135 (1), 2012: 37 – 49; You, F., Tao, L., Graziano, D. J., & Snyder, S. W., "Optimal Design of Sustainable Cellulosic Biofuel Supply Chains: Multiobjective Optimization Coupled with Life Cycle Assessment and Input-output Analysis", *AIChE Journal*, 58 (4), 2012: 1157 – 1180; Varsei, M., & Polyakovskiy, S., "Sustainable Supply Chain Network Design: A Case of the Wine Industry in Australia", *Omega*, 66, 2017: 236 – 247.

[4] Beske-Janssen, P., Johnson, M. P., & Schaltegger, S., "20 Years of Performance Measurement in Sustainable Supply Chain Management—What has been Achieved?", *Supply Chain Management: An International Journal*, 20 (6), 2015: 664 – 680.

[5] Eskandarpour, M., Dejax, P., Miemczyk, J., & Péton, O., "Sustainable Supply Chain Network Design: An Optimization-oriented Review", *Omega*, 54, 2015: 11 – 32.

[6] Hassini, E., Surti, C., & Searcy, C., "A Literature Review and a Case Study of Sustainable Supply Chains with a Focus on Metrics", *International Journal of Production Economics*, 140 (1), 2012: 69 – 82.

动对其利益相关者的社会影响[1]。可持续运营需要一个可持续的员工队伍和社区。一个具有社会责任的供应链应努力改善其运营的社区，并确保其员工和客户的福祉[2]。这个维度有 5 个衡量标准：就业（Employment，$Soc1$）、健康和安全（Health and safety，$Soc2$）、工作条件（Work conditions，$Sco3$）、客户问题（Customer issues，$Soc4$）和社会承诺（Societal commitment，$Soc5$）。

就业（或创造就业机会和财富）是最重要的社会指标[3]。公司通过提供充分和稳定的就业岗位来提高员工的生活水平[4]。白酒企业的供应链中创造的职位数量和总的员工流动率被用作相应的社会指标。

健康和安全评估实践或产品影响员工和客户的健康安全[5]。公司应促进和保持员工和客户身体、精神的健康和安全，以及使社会福利达到最大化，以防止职业事故（劳动伤害），并确保客户不会受到劣质产品的伤害。

---

[1] Boukherroub, T., Ruiz, A., Guinet, A., & Fondrevelle, J. (2015). An integrated approach for sustainable supply chain planning. Computers & Operations Research, 54, 180–194.

[2] Sarkis, J., & Dhavale, D. G., "Supplier Selection for Sustainable Operations: A Triple-bottom-line Approach using a Bayesian Framework", International Journal of Production Economics, 166, 2015: 177–191.

[3] Chaabane, A., Ramudhin, A., & Paquet, M., "Design of Sustainable Supply Chains under the Emission Trading Scheme", International Journal of Production Economics, 135 (1), 2012: 37–49; G. R. Initiative, "Sustainability Reporting Guidelines", Version 3.0. Oxford University Press.

[4] Chardine-Baumann, E., & Botta-Genoulaz, V., "A Framework for Sustainable Performance Assessment of Supply Chain Management Practices", Computers & Industrial Engineering, 76, 2014: 138–147; Boukherroub, T., Ruiz, A., Guinet, A., & Fondrevelle, J., "An Integrated Approach for Sustainable Supply Chain Planning", Computers & Operations Research, 54, 2015: 180–194; Matos, S., & Hall, J., "Integrating Sustainable Development in the Supply Chain: The Case of Life Cycle Assessment in Oil and Gas and Agricultural Biotechnology", Journal of Operations Management, 25 (6), 2007: 1083–1102.

[5] Eskandarpour, M., Dejax, P., Miemczyk, J., & Péton, O., "Sustainable Supply Chain Network Design: An Optimization-oriented Review", Omega, 54, 2015: 11–32; Boukherroub, T., Ruiz, A., Guinet, A., & Fondrevelle, J., "An Integrated Approach for Sustainable Supply Chain Planning", Computers & Operations Research, 54, 2015: 180–194; Matos, S., & Hall, J., "Integrating Sustainable Development in the Supply Chain: The Case of Life Cycle Assessment in Oil and Gas and Agricultural Biotechnology", Journal of Operations Management, 25 (6), 2007: 1083–1102.

工作条件指职工在工作中的设施条件、工作环境、劳动强度和工作时间的总和。它包括与员工满意度相关的许多领域，如薪酬和其他报酬、工作时间、休息时间、假期、人力资源开发、纪律处分、解雇和生育保险等问题[1]。

客户问题是指影响每个单独客户的所有问题[2]。主要关注消费者医疗保健和安全，保护客户数据和隐私，向消费者提供市场信息以及提供其他基本服务[3]。

社会承诺是指公司向当地社区和利益相关者展示的社会责任[4]，包括教育、文化、医疗保健和技术发展的改善，以及对社会投资的贡献。

(三) 方法概述

为了实现研究的目的，使用模糊 AHP-TOPSIS 首先确定白酒行业可持续性评估标准的相对优先级，然后对白酒行业可持续方案进行排序。在白酒行业供应链管理中，由于决策问题通常是模糊的和不确定的，可

---

[1] Chaabane, A., Ramudhin, A., & Paquet, M., "Design of Sustainable Supply Chains under the Emission Trading Scheme", *International Journal of Production Economics*, 135 (1), 2012: 37 – 49; G. R Initiative, Sustainability Reporting Guidelines, Version 3.0., Oxford University Press: Oxford, UK; Boukherroub, T., Ruiz, A., Guinet, A., & Fondrevelle, J., "An Integrated Approach for Sustainable Supply Chain Planning", *Computers & Operations Research*, 54, 2015: 180 – 194.

[2] Eskandarpour, M., Dejax, P., Miemczyk, J., & Péton, O., " Sustainable Supply Chain Network Design: An Optimization-oriented Review", *Omega*, 54, 2015: 11 – 32.

[3] Gordon, K., & Mitidieri, C. (2005). Multilateral Influences on the OECD Guidelines for Multinational Enterprises. Oecd Working Papers on International Investment; International Organization for Standardization (ISO). Guidance on Social Re-sponsibility. ISO: Geneva, Switzerland, 2010; Boukherroub, T., Ruiz, A., Guinet, A., & Fondrevelle, J., "An Integrated Approach for Sustainable Supply Chain Planning", *Computers & Operations Research*, 54, 2015: 180 – 194; Matos, S., & Hall, J., "Integrating Sustainable Development in the Supply Chain: The Case of Life Cycle Assessment in Oil and Gas and Agricultural Biotechnology", *Journal of Operations Management*, 25 (6), 2007: 1083 – 1102; International Organization for Standardization (ISO), *Guidance on Social Responsibility*, ISO: Geneva, Switzerland, 2010.

[4] Sarkis, J., & Dhavale, D. G., "Supplier Selection for Sustainable Operations: A Triple-bottom-line Approach Using a Bayesian Framework", *International Journal of Production Economics*, 166, 2015: 177 – 191.

以使用模糊集合理论来表示①。可持续性维度和子标准系统具有层次结构，意味着可以使用 AHP 方法来确定维度和子标准的重要性权重②。由于使用语言判断或变量来描述专家偏好，可以应用模糊集理论来解决偏好中的固有不确定性。因此，在此选择集成模糊理论和 AHP 方法的模糊 AHP 方法来确定指标权重。

TOPSIS 是另一种多属性决策（MCDM）方法，它是基于所选择的方案最接近正理想解并且离负理想解最远的理念③。在典型的 TOPSIS 方法中，个人判断使用清晰的值来表示；然而，在现实中，使用清晰值来测量并不总是可能的。更好的方法可能是使用语言值，而不是清晰值，因此可以使用模糊集理论。为此，模糊 TOPSIS 方法适用于解决模糊环境下的现实生活中的应用问题。使用这种技术，选择方案根据一系列的指标来进行评估，而语言专家的观点是主观的，模糊的和不精确的④。因此，模糊 TOPSIS 适用于白酒企业的供应链评估并对可持续方案进行排序。这种模糊 AHP – TOPSIS 方法的细节在随后的研究中给出。

1. 模糊 AHP

AHP 是一种定量技术，由 Saaty 引入多属性决策解决方案结构⑤。

---

① Mardani, A., Jusoh, A., & Zavadskas, E. K., "Fuzzy Multiple Criteria Decision-making Techniques and Applications—Two Decades Review from 1994 to 2014", *Expert Systems with Applications*, 42 (8), 2015: 4126 – 4148.

② Abdullah, L., & Zulkifli, N., "Integration of Fuzzy AHP and Interval Type – 2 Fuzzy DEMATEL: An Application to Human Resource Management", *Expert Systems with Applications*, 42 (9), 2015: 4397 – 4409; Zyoud, S. H., Kaufmann, L. G., Shaheen, H., Samhan, S., & Fuchs-Hanusch, D., "A Framework for Water Loss Management in Developing Countries Under Fuzzy Environment: Integration of Fuzzy AHP with Fuzzy TOPSIS", *Expert Systems with Applications*, 61, 2016: 86 – 105.

③ Chen, C. T., "Extensions of the TOPSIS for Group Decision-making under Fuzzy Environment", *Fuzzy Sets and Systems*, 114 (1), 2000: 1 – 9; Cavallaro, F., Zavadskas, E., & Raslanas, S., "Evaluation of Combined Heat and Power (CHP) Systems Using Fuzzy Shannon Entropy and Fuzzy TOPSIS", *Sustainability*, 8 (6), 2016: 556.

④ Lima-Junior, F. R., & Carpinetti, L. C. R., "Combining SCOR® Model and Fuzzy TOPSIS for Supplier Evaluation and Management", *International Journal of Production Economics*, 174, 2016: 128 – 141.

⑤ Saaty, T. L., "How to Make a Decision: the Analytic Hierarchy Process", *European Journal of Operational Research*, 48 (1), 1990: 9 – 26.

模糊 AHP 方法结合 AHP 和模糊集理论来解决具有层次的模糊问题，并能够处理语言变量，包括专家不确定的不精确的判断。近年来，模糊 AHP 已被广泛用于解决其他领域中的多属性决策问题，例如人力资源管理、供应商选择和绩效评估等领域①。为了进行可持续性评价，模糊 AHP 方法如下所示。

（1）构建指标体系层次模型。使用维度和指标来建立 AHP 层次模型。（2）应用模糊概念。由于在模糊和不确定环境下决策是很困难的，模糊集理论被用来处理这些信息。（3）构建模糊成对比较矩阵。表 6.2 给出了相对重要性的模糊度量。（4）分析指标的重要性。为了确定指标的重要性权重，分析了模糊评估矩阵，并将模糊值转换为清晰值。为了实现这个目标，需要一些适当的计算过程。

表 6.2　　　　　　　相对重要性成对比较矩阵的标度

标度	语言变量	隶属函数
$\tilde{1}$	同等重要	(1, 1, 1)
$\tilde{2}$	两者重要性介于 $\tilde{1}$ 和 $\tilde{3}$ 之间	(1, 2, 3)
$\tilde{3}$	一个比另一个稍微重要	(2, 3, 4)
$\tilde{4}$	两者重要性介于 $\tilde{3}$ 和 $\tilde{5}$ 之间	(3, 4, 5)
$\tilde{5}$	一个比另一个明显重要	(4, 5, 6)
$\tilde{6}$	两者重要性介于 $\tilde{5}$ 和 $\tilde{7}$ 之间	(5, 6, 7)

---

① Kilincci, O., & Onal, S. A., "Fuzzy AHP Approach for Supplier Selection in a Washing Machine Company", *Expert Systems with Applications*, 38 (8), 2011: 9656 – 9664; Ng, C. Y., "Evidential Reasoning-based Fuzzy AHP Approach for the Evaluation of Design Alternatives' environmental Performances", *Applied Soft Computing*, 46, 2016: 381 – 397; Cavallaro, F., Zavadskas, E., & Raslanas, S., "Evaluation of Combined Heat and Power (CHP) Systems Using Fuzzy Shannon Entropy and Fuzzy TOPSIS", *Sustainability*, 8 (6), 2016: 556.

续表

标度	语言变量	隶属函数
$\tilde{7}$	一个比另一个强烈重要	(6, 7, 8)
$\tilde{8}$	两者重要性介于 $\tilde{7}$ 和 $\tilde{9}$ 之间	(7, 8, 9)
$\tilde{9}$	一个比另一个极端重要	(8, 9, 10)

模糊层次分析法的具体计算步骤见参考文献[①]。

2. 模糊 TOPSIS

TOPSIS 基于这样的概念：所选择的方案应该最接近于正理想解（PIS）并且离负理想解（NIS）最远。模糊集理论可用于呈现语言值。因此，模糊 TOPSIS 方法适合于在模糊环境下解决现实生活中的应用问题[②]。

模糊 TOPSIS 范围分析方法的基本计算步骤如文献所述[③]。

表 6.3　　　　　　　　　　语言变量的评级

语言变量	三角模糊数
很差（VP）	(0, 0, 1)
差（P）	(0, 1, 3)

[①] Patil, S. K., & Kant, R., "A Fuzzy AHP-TOPSIS Framework for Ranking the Solutions of Knowledge Management Adoption in Supply Chain to Overcome its Barriers", *Expert Systems with Applications*, 41 (2), 2014: 679–693; Saaty, T. L., "How to Make a Decision: The Analytic Hierarchy Process", *European Journal of Operational Research*, 48 (1), 1990: 9–26.

[②] Chen, C. T., "Extensions of the TOPSIS for Group Decision-making under Fuzzy Environment", *Fuzzy Sets and Systems*, 114 (1), 200: 1–9.

[③] Sun, C. C., "A Performance Evaluation Model by Integrating Fuzzy AHP and Fuzzy TOPSIS Methods", *Expert Systems with Applications*, 37 (12), 2010: 7745–7754;岳超源：《决策理论与方法》，科学出版社 2003 年版；徐玖平、吴巍：《多属性决策的理论与方法》，清华大学出版社 2006 年版。

续表

语言变量	三角模糊数
中等差（MP）	(1, 3, 5)
一般（F）	(3, 5, 7)
中等好（MG）	(5, 7, 9)
好（G）	(7, 9, 10)
很好（VG）	(9, 10, 10)

三 应用实例

基于上述混合框架，我们对中国西部极具竞争力的一家白酒企业的供应链进行了评价和选择。该企业位于四川省，是白酒发展的重要产地。近年来，由于来自客户、政府、非政府组织和日益激烈的全球竞争的压力，可持续发展在白酒供应链中发挥着越来越重要的作用[①]。面对供需不平衡、结构不合理、区域发展不平衡、环境保护和社会福利等问题，企业需要一个坚实的战略方法，以充分了解实现可持续的白酒供应链的指标和选择方案。因此，我们设计了一个决策支持框架，用于评估中国白酒企业的供应链可持续性，这可以帮助确定与白酒行业相关的可持续性指标和选择方案，并对经济、环境和社会三个可持续层面进行考评。根据文献分析结果和专家意见形成指标体系，然后用模糊 AHP 方法确定指标权重，再用模糊 TOPSIS 方法进行

---

① Seuring, S., "A Review of Modeling Approaches for Sustainable Supply Chain Management", *Decision Support Systems*, 54（4），2013：1513 – 1520；Eskandarpour, M., Dejax, P., Miemczyk, J., & Péton, O., Sustainable Supply Chain Network Design: An Optimization-oriented Review. *Omega*，54，2015：11 – 32；Boukherroub, T., Ruiz, A., Guinet, A., & Fondrevelle, J., "An Integrated Approach for Sustainable Supply Chain Planning", *Computers & Operations Research*，54，2015：180 – 194；Chardine-Baumann, E., & Botta-Genoulaz, V., "A Framework for Sustainable Performance Assessment of Supply Chain Management Practices", *Computers & Industrial Engineering*，76，2014：138 – 147.

方案排序。

（一）指标方案

在第一阶段，为了分析这个问题，成立了一个由 12 位专家组成的决策团队。其中有 2 位高级管理人员、3 位教授、3 位高级供应链管理人员、2 位环境专家和 2 位客户。所有的专家高度熟悉他们各自的领域，精通决策。在这个案例中，我们从文献综述和与决策团队的深入讨论中确定了基于三重底线方法的 15 个可持续性绩效评估指标。

在此采用四级决策层次结构。可持续绩效评估目标是第一层次；由经济、环境和社会维度构成的三重底线位于第二层次；15 个指标位于第三层次；可持续选择方案位于第四层次（见图 6.2）。

（二）绩效权重

在这一阶段，专家组被要求使用语言变量如表 6.2 进行三个可持续维度和 14 个指标的成对比较。然后使用几何平均法计算合成的成对比较矩阵元素。

$$\tilde{A}_{ij} = (\tilde{A}_{ij}^1 \otimes \tilde{A}_{ij}^2 \otimes \cdots \otimes \tilde{A}_{ij}^{12})),\text{以 } \tilde{A}_{12} \text{ 为例：}$$

$$\tilde{A}_{12} = ((2,3,4) \otimes (1,2,3) \otimes \cdots \otimes (1,1,1))^{\frac{1}{12}}$$

$$= ((2 \otimes 1 \otimes \cdots \otimes 1)^{\frac{1}{12}}, (3 \otimes 2 \otimes \cdots \otimes 1)^{\frac{1}{12}}, (4 \otimes 3 \otimes \cdots \otimes 1)^{\frac{1}{12}})$$

$$= (1.1892, 1.7151, 2.2134)$$

使用相同的计算方法确定其他矩阵元素，然后，我们可以得到表 6.4 所示的成对比较矩阵。

（1）为了计算维度的模糊权重，计算过程如下：

$$\tilde{r}_1 = (\tilde{A}_{11} \otimes \tilde{A}_{12} \otimes \tilde{A}_{13})^{\frac{1}{3}}$$

$$= ((1 \otimes 1.1892 \otimes 1)^{\frac{1}{3}}, (1 \otimes 1.7151 \otimes 1.6420)^{\frac{1}{3}}, (1 \otimes 2.2134 \otimes 2.2572)^{\frac{1}{3}})$$

$$= (1.0595, 1.4122, 1.7095)$$

表6.4　　　　　　　　　三个维度的模糊成对比较矩阵

维度	经济	环境	社会
经济	(1, 1, 1)	(1.1892, 1.7151, 2.2134)	(1.0000, 1.6420, 2.2572)
环境	(0.4518, 0.5830, 0.8409)	(1, 1, 1)	(1.0054, 1.4422, 1.9064)
社会	(0.4430, 0.6090, 1.0000)	(0.5246, 0.6934, 0.9946)	(1, 1, 1)
权重	(0.4337, 0.4546, 0.4408)	(0.3147, 0.3039, 0.3018)	(0.2517, 0.2415, 0.2574)
MSw	0.4430	0.3068	0.2502

类似地，计算其他维度的权重 $\tilde{r}_i$：

$\tilde{r}_2 = (0.7687, 0.9439, 1.1704)$

$\tilde{r}_3 = (0.6148, 0.7502, 0.9982)$

每个维度的权重使用 $\tilde{\omega}_i = \tilde{r}_i / \sum_{i=1}^{n} \tilde{r}_i$ 得到：

$\tilde{\omega}_1 = (0.4337, 0.4546, 0.4408)$

$\tilde{\omega}_2 = (0.3147, 0.3039, 0.3018)$

$\tilde{\omega}_3 = (0.2517, 0.2415, 0.2574)$

（2）采用模糊平均和扩散方法对模糊数进行去模糊化和排序：

$MS\tilde{\omega}_i = (l\omega_i + m\omega_i + u\omega_i)/3$

$MS\tilde{\omega}_1 = 0.4430$

$MS\tilde{\omega}_2 = 0.3068$

$MS\tilde{\omega}_3 = 0.2502$

用同样的方法，经济、环境和社会的标准模糊判断矩阵可以确定，如表6.5至表6.7所示。基于表6.4至表6.7中提供的成对比较矩阵的计算获得的结果呈现在表6.8中。一致性比率（CR）用于直接估计

表 6.5　经济维度的模糊成对比较矩阵

	Eco1	Eco2	Eco3	Eco4	Eco5
Eco1	(1,1,1)	(2.2134,2.9658,3.7224)	(1.8942,2.4521,3.1665)	(0.9902,1.2165,1.5131)	(0.9763,1.1126,1.2409)
Eco2	(0.2686,0.3372,0.4518)	(1,1,1)	(0.6389,0.8454,1.1210)	(0.6551,0.7923,0.9701)	(0.5571,0.6710,0.8529)
Eco3	(0.3158,0.4078,0.5279)	(0.8921,1.1828,1.5651)	(1,1,1)	(0.5706,0.7311,0.9265)	(0.5756,0.7208,0.9125)
Eco4	(0.6609,0.8221,1.0099)	(1.0309,1.2621,1.5264)	(1.0793,1.3677,1.7526)	(1,1,1)	(0.8130,0.9583,1.1713)
Eco5	(0.8059,0.8988,1.024)	(1.1725,1.4903,1.7952)	(1.0959,1.3873,1.7373)	(0.8538,1.0435,1.2301)	(1,1,1)
Weight	(0.3009,0.3020,0.2995)	(0.1307,0.1311,0.1355)	(0.1413,0.1454,0.1501)	(0.2052,0.2033,0.2030)	(0.2219,0.2182,0.2120)
MSw	0.3008	0.1324	0.1456	0.2038	0.2174

表 6.6　环境维度的模糊对比较矩阵

	Env1	Env2	Env3	Env4	Env5
Env1	(1,1,1)	(2.1211,2.7525,3.4792)	(1.2599,1.6581,2.0089)	(1.2181,1.7741,2.5534)	(0.8879,1.1697,1.5347)
Env2	(0.2874,0.3633,0.4714)	(1,1,1)	(0.8409,1.2438,1.6893)	(0.7791,1.1081,1.4282)	(0.4903,0.7418,1.1191)
Env3	(0.4978,0.6031,0.7937)	(0.5920,0.8040,1.1892)	(1,1,1)	(0.9583,1.5874,2.2232)	(0.5587,0.7937,1.1760)

续表

	$Env1$	$Env2$	$Env3$	$Env4$	$Env5$
$Env4$	(0.3916,0.5637,0.8210)	(0.7002,0.9024,1.2836)	(0.5637,0.7749,1.2272)	(1,1,1)	(0.5022,0.7002,1.0699)
$Env5$	(0.6516,0.8549,1.1263)	(0.8936,1.3480,2.0396)	(0.8503,1.2599,1.7897)	(0.9347,1.4282,1.9913)	(1,1,1)
$Weight$	(0.2546,0.2615,0.2585)	(0.1773,0.1750,0.1681)	(0.1851,0.1832,0.1811)	(0.1762,0.1706,0.1697)	(0.2068,0.2097,0.2226)
MSw	0.2582	0.1735	0.1831	0.1721	0.2130

表 6.7　社会维度的模糊成对比较矩阵

	$Soc1$	$Soc2$	$Soc3$	$Soc4$	$Soc5$
$Soc1$	(1,1,1)	(1.3466,1.7473,2.2300)	(2.3190,2.9368,3.6147)	(1.2272,1.6085,2.1646)	(2.6925,3.4040,4.0793)
$Soc2$	(0.4914,0.6424,0.8138)	(1,1,1)	(2.2671,3.1806,4.0395)	(1.2025,1.7526,2.3681)	(1.4983,2.0584,2.5891)
$Soc3$	(0.2766,0.3405,0.4312)	(0.2476,0.3144,0.4411)	(1,1,1)	(1.1956,1.6244,2.1800)	(1.8877,2.3940,3.2377)
$Soc4$	(0.4620,0.6217,0.7691)	(0.4223,0.5706,0.8316)	(0.4587,0.6156,0.8364)	(1,1,1)	(0.9668,1.3765,1.8331)
$Soc5$	(0.2451,0.2938,0.3714)	(0.3862,0.4858,0.6674)	(0.3089,0.4177,0.5297)	(0.5455,0.7265,1.0344)	(1,1,1)
$Weight$	(0.3558,0.3480,0.3402)	(0.2564,0.2663,0.2643)	(0.1536,0.1499,0.1538)	(0.1367,0.1404,0.1444)	(0.0975,0.0953,0.0972)
MSw	0.3480	0.2624	0.1524	0.1405	0.0967

成对比较矩阵的一致性。CR 通过使用公式（6.1）求得。其中 CI 是一致性指标。RI 是随机一致性指标，如表 6.9 所示，n 表示矩阵的大小。

表6.8　　　　　　　　　　　可持续供应链绩效的最终排序

维度	维度权重	CR	指标	相对权重	相对排序	全局权重	全局排序
经济	0.4430	0.0267	Eco1	0.3008	1	0.1333	1
			Eco2	0.1324	5	0.0587	9
			Eco3	0.1456	4	0.0645	8
			Eco4	0.2038	3	0.0903	3
			Eco5	0.2174	2	0.0963	2
环境	0.3068	0.0908	Env1	0.2582	1	0.0792	5
			Env2	0.1735	4	0.0532	11
			Env3	0.1831	3	0.0562	10
			Env4	0.1721	5	0.0528	12
			Env5	0.2130	2	0.0654	7
社会	0.2502	0.0754	Soc1	0.3480	1	0.0871	4
			Soc2	0.2624	2	0.0656	6
			Soc3	0.1524	3	0.0381	13
			Soc4	0.1405	4	0.0352	14
			Soc5	0.0967	5	0.0242	15

$$CR = \frac{CI}{RI} \tag{6.1}$$

$$CI = \frac{\lambda_{\max} - n}{n - 1} \tag{6.2}$$

表 6.9　　　　　　　　　随机一致性指标（RI）

	1	2	3	4	5	6	7	8	9	10
RI	0	0	0.58	0.90	1.12	1.24	1.32	1.41	1.45	1.49

因为所有矩阵的 CR 值小于 0.1，所以这些矩阵是满足一致性的。可以看出在排序中最重要的是质量，其次是财务绩效。

（三）方案排序

假设所有专家都具有同样的权重。专家组被要求使用表 6.3 中所示的语言条件建立模糊评价矩阵。备选方案 A1、A2、A3、A4 和 A5 是核心白酒企业董事会办公室给出的解决方案。5 个方案是不同的，因为上游和下游企业的数量不同。在研究中，我们考虑了一个三级供应链，其中包括供应商、核心公司和客户。

选择方案的模糊决策矩阵用 $\tilde{x}_{ij} = \frac{1}{12}(\tilde{x}_{ij}^1 \oplus \tilde{x}_{ij}^2 \oplus \cdots \oplus \tilde{x}_{ij}^{12})$ 确定，如表 6.10。使用 $\tilde{R} = [\tilde{r}_{ij}]_{m \times n}$ 对模糊决策矩阵进行规范化，如表 6.11 所示。模糊加权归一化判定矩阵使用公式 $\tilde{V} = [\tilde{v}_{ij}]_{m \times n}, i = 1, 2, \cdots, m, j = 1, 2, \cdots, n$ 来确定，见表 6.12。选择方案的最终评价排序由 $d_i^* = \sum d(\tilde{v}_{ij}, \tilde{v}_j^*), i = 1, 2, \cdots, 5, j = 1, 2, \cdots, 15, d_i^- = \sum d(\tilde{v}_{ij}, \tilde{v}_j^-), i = 1, 2, \cdots, 5, j = 1, 2, \cdots, 15$，以及 $CC_i = \frac{d_i^-}{d_i^* + d_i^-}, i = 1, 2, \cdots, 5$ 确定，见表 6.13。

表 6.10　方案的模糊决策矩阵, A1, 方案 1

	Eco1	Eco2	Eco3	Eco4	Eco5
A1	(6.5833,7.8333,8.5000)	(5.3333,7.0000,8.3333)	(5.9167,7.6667,8.8333)	(6.5000,8.0000,8.9167)	(6.7500,8.2500,9.0000)
A2	(6.5000,8.3333,9.4167)	(5.2500,6.9167,8.2500)	(5.0833,6.8333,8.2500)	(5.4167,7.1667,8.5000)	(6.3333,8.1667,9.3333)
A3	(4.8333,6.5833,8.0833)	(5.5000,7.5000,8.8333)	(4.0000,5.6667,7.2500)	(5.6667,7.5000,8.8333)	(4.3333,6.3333,8.0833)
A4	(5.0833,6.5833,7.7500)	(4.2500,6.0833,7.0833)	(4.3333,5.8333,7.0833)	(5.1667,6.7500,8.0000)	(4.1667,5.8333,7.2500)
A5	(4.0833,6.0000,7.8333)	(5.2500,6.5833,7.5833)	(4.6667,5.8333,6.9167)	(6.8333,8.5000,9.5000)	(5.8333,7.7500,9.0000)

	Env1	Env2	Env3	Env4	Env5
A1	(7.1667,8.7500,9.5833)	(4.1667,5.8333,7.3333)	(4.6667,6.1667,7.4167)	(4.7500,6.0000,7.0833)	(3.8333,5.6667,7.4167)
A2	(5.6667,7.1667,8.0833)	(4.0000,5.8333,7.5833)	(4.8333,6.5000,7.8333)	(4.6667,6.5833,8.0833)	(3.5000,5.0833,6.5833)
A3	(4.9167,6.7500,8.2500)	(2.9167,4.5000,6.2500)	(3.5000,5.3333,7.2500)	(4.0000,5.7500,7.4167)	(3.0833,4.8333,6.5833)
A4	(5.2500,7.0000,8.2500)	(4.2500,6.1667,7.9167)	(5.0000,6.9167,8.5000)	(5.0000,7.3333,8.7500)	(2.7500,4.6667,6.5833)
A5	(4.6667,6.1667,7.4167)	(2.9167,4.4167,6.0833)	(4.9167,6.5000,8.000)	(4.0000,6.0000,7.8333)	(4.0000,6.0000,7.8333)

	Soc1	Soc2	Soc3	Soc4	Soc5
A1	(5.2500,7.1667,8.5833)	(5.8333,7.6667,8.9167)	(6.5833,8.0000,8.8333)	(7.5000,8.9167,9.5000)	(5.2500,6.8333,8.0000)
A2	(5.5833,7.0833,8.1667)	(5.6667,7.2500,8.3333)	(4.7500,6.3333,7.6667)	(5.5833,7.2500,8.4167)	(4.6667,6.2500,7.6667)
A3	(5.0000,6.7500,8.1667)	(5.6667,7.5833,9.0833)	(5.2500,7.0833,8.4167)	(5.1667,6.9167,8.2500)	(4.6667,6.5000,8.0833)
A4	(3.9167,5.7500,7.4167)	(3.7500,5.6667,7.5000)	(3.9167,5.7500,7.4167)	(5.3333,7.2500,8.7500)	(4.7500,6.5000,8.0000)
A5	(4.1667,5.8333,7.0000)	(4.6667,6.3333,7.5833)	(6.3333,8.0000,9.2500)	(6.5000,8.2500,9.3333)	(4.8333,6.4167,7.7500)

表 6.11　模糊规范化决策矩阵

	$Eco1$	$Eco2$	$Eco3$	$Eco4$	$Eco5$
A1	(0.6991,0.8319,0.9027)	(0.6038,0.7925,0.9434)	(0.6698,0.8679,1.0000)	(0.6842,0.8421,0.9386)	(0.7232,0.8839,0.9643)
A2	(0.6903,0.8850,1.0000)	(0.5943,0.7830,0.9340)	(0.5755,0.7736,0.9340)	(0.5702,0.7544,0.8947)	(0.6786,0.8750,1.0000)
A3	(0.5133,0.6991,0.8584)	(0.6226,0.8491,1.0000)	(0.4528,0.6415,0.8208)	(0.5965,0.7895,0.9298)	(0.4643,0.6786,0.8661)
A4	(0.5398,0.6991,0.8230)	(0.4811,0.6887,0.8774)	(0.4906,0.6604,0.8019)	(0.5439,0.7105,0.8421)	(0.4464,0.6250,0.7768)
A5	(0.4336,0.6372,0.8319)	(0.5943,0.7453,0.8585)	(0.5283,0.6604,0.7830)	(0.7193,0.8947,1.0000)	(0.6250,0.8304,0.9643)

	$Env1$	$Env2$	$Env3$	$Env4$	$Env5$
A1	(0.7478,0.9130,1.0000)	(0.5263,0.7368,0.9263)	(0.5490,0.7255,0.8725)	(0.5429,0.6857,0.8095)	(0.4894,0.7234,0.9468)
A2	(0.5913,0.7478,0.8435)	(0.5053,0.7368,0.9579)	(0.5686,0.7647,0.9216)	(0.5333,0.7524,0.9238)	(0.4468,0.6489,0.8404)
A3	(0.5130,0.7043,0.8609)	(0.3684,0.5684,0.7895)	(0.4118,0.6275,0.8529)	(0.4571,0.6571,0.8476)	(0.3936,0.6170,0.8404)
A4	(0.5478,0.7304,0.8609)	(0.5368,0.7789,1.0000)	(0.5882,0.8137,1.0000)	(0.6286,0.8381,1.0000)	(0.3511,0.5957,0.8404)
A5	(0.4870,0.6435,0.7739)	(0.3684,0.5579,0.7684)	(0.5784,0.7353,0.8627)	(0.5238,0.7429,0.9143)	(0.5106,0.7660,1.000)

	$Soc1$	$Soc2$	$Soc3$	$Soc4$	$Soc5$
A1	(0.6117,0.8350,1.0000)	(0.6422,0.8440,0.9817)	(0.7117,0.8649,0.9550)	(0.7895,0.9386,1.0000)	(0.6495,0.8454,0.9897)
A2	(0.6505,0.8252,0.9515)	(0.6239,0.7982,0.9174)	(0.5135,0.6847,0.8288)	(0.5877,0.7632,0.8860)	(0.5773,0.7732,0.9485)
A3	(0.5825,0.7864,0.9515)	(0.6239,0.8349,1.0000)	(0.5676,0.7658,0.9099)	(0.5439,0.7281,0.8684)	(0.5773,0.8041,1.0000)
A4	(0.4563,0.6699,0.8641)	(0.4128,0.6239,0.8257)	(0.4234,0.6216,0.8018)	(0.5614,0.7632,0.9211)	(0.5876,0.8041,0.9897)
A5	(0.4854,0.6505,0.8155)	(0.5138,0.6972,0.8349)	(0.6847,0.8649,1.0000)	(0.6842,0.8684,0.9825)	(0.5979,0.7938,0.9588)

(四) 评价结果

从研究可以看出，白酒评估问题主要聚焦于白酒企业本身[1]，几乎很少有文章从整个供应链的角度进行评估。随着白酒企业的可持续供应链的发展，越来越多的企业意识到应从供应链管理的角度进行可持续评价[2]。然而，大多数的白酒供应链评估只考虑一个可持续维度[3]；很少考虑两个维度[4]；考虑三个维度的就更少了。在白酒企业的供应链中，常规指标不足以准确评估可持续供应链的绩效，因为它们主要关注经济问题或环境问题。然而，近年来，学术界和企业界对可持续供应链的研究越来越关注。本书采用了三重底线方法，从经济利益、环境保护和社会责任三个维度来评估白酒企业供应链，并确定了15个指标，这无论对公司运营，还是理论研究，都具有重要的意义和价值。

---

[1] 王艳红、周健：《白酒企业节能减排技术评价实证分析》，《酿酒科技》2014 年第 9 期；黄妍、戴新民：《应用因子分析模型评价白酒行业上市公司财务竞争力》，《酿酒科技》2013 年第 7 期。

[2] Seuring, S., & Müller, M., "From a Literature Review to a Conceptual Framework for Sustainable Supply Chain Management", *Journal of Cleaner Production*, 16 (15), 2008: 1699 – 1710; Seuring, S., "A Review of Modeling Approaches for Sustainable Supply Chain Management", *Decision Support Systems*, 54 (4), 2013: 1513 – 1520; Beske-Janssen, P., Johnson, M. P., & Schaltegger, S., "20 Years of Performance Measurement in Sustainable Supply Chain Management——what has been Achieved?", *Supply Chain Management: An International Journal*, 20 (6), 2015: 664 – 680.

[3] Guo, H. C., Chen, B., Yu, X. L., Huang, G. H., Liu, L., & Nie, X. H., "Assessment of Cleaner Production Options for Alcohol Industry of China: A Study in the Shouguang Alcohol Factory", *Journal of Cleaner Production*, 14 (1), 2006: 94 – 103; 李明蔚、张俊娥、王永刚、王旭、王媛媛：《白酒企业生态文明评价指标体系构建》，《中国人口·资源与环境》2016 年第 1 期；Jie, Y., & Tongqiang, L., "Evaluation of the Competitiveness of China's Liquor Enterprise Based on Factor Analysis Method", In AASRI International Conference on Industrial Electronics and Applications (IEA 2015), 2015, Atlantis Press; Huang, Y. L., Sun, W., & Su, Q. Q., "Environmental Issues for the Chinese Strong Aromatic Liquor Industry: An Assessment for the Brewing System", *Environmental Modeling & Assessment*, 19 (2), 2014: 153 – 165。

[4] S. N. Ma, *The Connotation and Evaluation of Liquor Enterprise's Social Environment Responsibility—Based on the Stakeholder Perspective*, 726 – 730, 2015.

表6.12　模糊加权标准化矩阵

	Eco1	Eco2	Eco3	Eco4	Eco5
A1	(0.0932, 0.1109, 0.1203)	(0.0354, 0.0465, 0.0553)	(0.0432, 0.0560, 0.0645)	(0.0618, 0.0760, 0.0848)	(0.0696, 0.0851, 0.0929)
A2	(0.0920, 0.1179, 0.1333)	(0.0349, 0.0459, 0.0548)	(0.0371, 0.0499, 0.0602)	(0.0515, 0.0681, 0.0808)	(0.0653, 0.0843, 0.0963)
A3	(0.0684, 0.0932, 0.1144)	(0.0365, 0.0498, 0.0587)	(0.0292, 0.0414, 0.0529)	(0.0539, 0.0713, 0.0840)	(0.0447, 0.0653, 0.0834)
A4	(0.0719, 0.0932, 0.1097)	(0.0282, 0.0404, 0.0515)	(0.0316, 0.0426, 0.0517)	(0.0491, 0.0642, 0.0760)	(0.0430, 0.0602, 0.0748)
A5	(0.0578, 0.0849, 0.1109)	(0.0349, 0.0437, 0.0504)	(0.0341, 0.0426, 0.0505)	(0.0650, 0.0808, 0.0903)	(0.0602, 0.0800, 0.0929)
	Env1	Env2	Env3	Env4	Env5
A1	(0.0592, 0.0723, 0.0792)	(0.0280, 0.0392, 0.0493)	(0.0308, 0.0408, 0.0490)	(0.0287, 0.0362, 0.0427)	(0.0320, 0.0473, 0.0619)
A2	(0.0468, 0.0592, 0.0668)	(0.0269, 0.0392, 0.0510)	(0.0319, 0.0430, 0.0518)	(0.0282, 0.0397, 0.0488)	(0.0292, 0.0424, 0.0549)
A3	(0.0406, 0.0558, 0.0682)	(0.0196, 0.0302, 0.0420)	(0.0231, 0.0353, 0.0479)	(0.0241, 0.0347, 0.0448)	(0.0257, 0.0403, 0.0549)

续表

	Eco1	Eco2	Eco3	Eco4	Eco5
A4	(0.0434,0.0579, 0.0682)	(0.0286,0.0415, 0.0532)	(0.0530,0.0457, 0.0562)	(0.0332,0.0443, 0.0528)	(0.0229,0.0389, 0.0549)
A5	(0.0386,0.0510, 0.0613)	(0.0196,0.0297, 0.0409)	(0.0325,0.0413, 0.0485)	(0.0277,0.0392, 0.0483)	(0.0334,0.0501, 0.0654)

	Soc1	Soc2	Soc3	Soc4	Soc5
A1	(0.0533,0.0727, 0.0871)	(0.0422,0.0554, 0.0644)	(0.0271,0.0330, 0.0364)	(0.0278,0.0330, 0.0352)	(0.0157,0.0205, 0.0239)
A2	(0.0566,0.0719, 0.0828)	(0.0410,0.0524, 0.0602)	(0.0196,0.0261, 0.0316)	(0.0207,0.0268, 0.0311)	(0.0140,0.0187, 0.0229)
A3	(0.0507,0.0685, 0.0828)	(0.0410,0.0548, 0.0656)	(0.0216,0.0292, 0.0347)	(0.0191,0.0256, 0.0305)	(0.0140,0.0195, 0.0242)
A4	(0.0397,0.0583, 0.0752)	(0.0271,0.0410, 0.0542)	(0.0161,0.0237, 0.0306)	(0.0197,0.0268, 0.0324)	(0.0142,0.0195, 0.0239)
A5	(0.0423,0.0566, 0.0710)	(0.0337,0.0458, 0.0548)	(0.0261,0.0330, 0.0381)	(0.0241,0.0305, 0.0345)	(0.0145,0.0192, 0.0232)

表 6.13　　　　　　　　　方案的最终评价和排名

选择方案	d_i^*	d_i^-	CC_i	排序
A1	14.1940	0.8167	0.0544	1
A2	14.2312	0.7819	0.0521	2
A3	14.2955	0.7225	0.0481	4
A4	14.3124	0.7049	0.0469	5
A5	14.2830	0.7316	0.0487	3

在白酒供应链研究中，多属性决策方法更适合多维问题的可持续性评估[1]。在这里发展了混合模糊 AHP-TOPSIS 方法来评估可持续性标准并选择可持续性方案，评估了白酒企业供应链可持续性指标。由于激烈的竞争和供求失衡，对中国白酒企业的供应链进行系统的可持续性评价非常重要。

如表 6.4 所示，白酒企业的供应链管理可持续发展评估标准维度排名的优先级是经济—环境—社会。经济维度为 0.4430，排名第一；环境维度为 0.3068，位居第二；社会维度为 0.2502，排名第三。Markman 和 Krause（2016）认为，环境维度应该给予优先考虑，社会维度排第二，经济维度排第三[2]。Luthra 等也认为环境维度应该排第一，经济维度排第二，社会维度排在第三[3]。因此，这里的结论与已有研究得出的结论不同。奋斗的企业不能将环境可持续性置于领先于社会和经济可

---

[1] Seuring, S., "A Review of Modeling Approaches for Sustainable Supply Chain Management", *Decision Support Systems*, 54 (4), 2013: 1513-1520; Beske-Janssen, P., Johnson, M. P., & Schaltegger, S., "20 Years of Performance Measurement in Sustainable Supply Chain Management-What has been Achieved?", *Supply Chain Management: An International Journal*, 20 (6), 2015: 664-680; 李明蔚、张俊娥、王永刚、王旭、王媛媛:《白酒企业生态文明评价指标体系构建》,《中国人口资源与环境》2016 年第 1 期。

[2] Markman, G. D., & Krause, D., "Theory Building Surrounding Sustainable Supply Chain Management: Assessing What we Know, Exploring Where to go", *Journal of Supply Chain Management*, 52 (2), 2016: 3-10.

[3] Luthra, S., Mangla, S. K., & Kharb, R. K., "Sustainable Assessment in Energy Planning and Management in Indian Perspective", *Renewable and Sustainable Energy Reviews*, 47, 2015: 58-73.

持续性的位置[①]。中国的白酒企业面临产能过剩，供需不平衡。有经营困难的企业关闭或逐步淘汰生产线，有些企业面临破产，其他企业通过重组公司以确保能继续生存。因此，由于核心公司也面临生存和发展的激烈竞争，他们需要更加关注经济维度。环境维度不被认为是第一优先的第二个原因是白酒行业用的是环境友好的材料，对环境的负面影响很小。相应维度中特定指标的优先级在表6.8中给出。我们与专家组讨论了研究结果，以更好地了解中国环境下与白酒供应链管理相关的当代问题，从而提高供应链的有效性和可持续性。

"经济维度（Eco）"是第一优先顺序，相较于其他指标维度具有最高优先级。这个维度有5个特定指标，如表6.5所示：$Eco1 > Eco5 > Eco4 > Eco3 > Eco2$。其权重如下：质量（0.3008）>财务绩效（0.2174）>可靠性（0.2038）>响应性（0.1456）>柔性（0.1324）。其中，"质量（$Eco1$）"具有最高优先级。质量问题与产品的寿命有关，其中最重要的特征之一是独特的产品功能。因此，决策者需要从逻辑上考虑质量问题。"财务绩效（$Eco5$）"在"质量（$Eco1$）"之后排名第二，这意味着有效的财务管理对经济发展和提高生活水平具有相对重要性。"可靠性（$Eco4$）"排名第三。在白酒供应链中，产品、预测、库存和客户服务应该是可靠的。排名第四的指标是"响应性（$Eco3$）"。"柔性（$Eco2$）"排在列表的最后。国际和国内白酒市场需求随环境发生了变化，企业需要通过调整现有产品或开发新产品来响应这些市场变化。

"环境维度（Env）"是三个维度中第二重要的维度，表明了提高白酒供应链的环境可持续性的重要性。这一特定维度有5个具体指标。如表6.6中所示，相应的环境指标排名为 $Env1 > Env5 > Env3 > Env2 > Env4$，表明资源消耗（0.2582）>污染控制（0.2130）>环境管理体系（0.1831）>自然资源（0.1735）>碳排放（0.1721）。"资源消耗（$Env1$）"指标是最重要的，其次是"污染控制（$Env5$）"。这种排序意

[①] Markman, G. D., & Krause, D., "Theory Building Surrounding Sustainable Supply Chain Management: Assessing What we Know, Exploring Where to go", *Journal of Supply Chain Management*, 52 (2), 2016: 3–10.

味着决策者需要在供应链运营的环境维度中优先考虑节能和减排。由于白酒生产工艺中公司要消耗大量的粮食、水、电力、天然气和煤炭。此外，由于季节性温差，冬季的能耗是夏季的两倍以上。如果功率消耗降低，则碳排放和污染相应减少。白酒企业产生的废弃物主要是酒糟和锅底水等，如果直接排放会对环境造成很严重的影响。比如酒糟经过处理之后，不但对环境没有影响，还会给企业创造一定的收益。因为它可以作为动物饲料、土地肥料等，从而为白酒企业创收。"环境管理体系（$Env3$）"在环境管理优先顺序中排名第三，白酒行业供应商企业要求通过环境管理体系，以增强其环境竞争力。自然资源（$Env2$）排名第四，"碳排放（$Env4$）"排名第五。

"社会维度（Soc）"位于优先级列表的第三位。在这一特定方面有5个具体指标。如表6.7所示，相关指标的排序是 $Soc1 > Soc2 > Soc3 > Soc4 > Soc5$，具有以下权重：就业（0.3480）>健康和安全（0.2624）>工作条件（0.1524）>客户问题（0.1405）>社会承诺（0.0967）。"就业（$Soc1$）"在这个维度下排名第一，在中国这样的发展中国家，最重要的企业社会责任被确认为促进就业。"健康和安全（$Soc2$）"排名第二，主要是因为在白酒企业的供应链中，健康和安全对于员工和客户都非常重要。"工作条件（$Soc3$）"指标排名第三，表明利益相关者越来越关注工作环境和员工生活水平。"客户问题（$Soc4$）"是排名第四的指标，排在最后的是"社会承诺（$Soc5$）"指标。

所有指标的总体排名也通过分配全局权重来确定。排名被确定为 $Eco1 > Eco5 > Eco4 > Soc1 > Env1 > Soc2 > Env5 > Eco3 > Eco2 > Env3 > Env2 > Env4 > Soc3 > Soc4 > Soc5$，如表6.8所示。根据FAHP分析，在白酒企业的供应链中，质量（$Eco1$）、财务绩效（$Eco5$）、可靠性（$Eco4$）、就业（$Soc1$）和资源消耗（$Env1$）是排名前五的最重要的可持续性指标，指标值分别是0.1333、0.0963、0.0903、0.0871和0.0792。社会承诺（$Soc5$）、客户问题（$Soc4$）和工作条件（$Soc3$）是最不重要的3个指标，各自的值为0.0242、0.0352和0.0381。从最重要到最不重要的供应链选择方案是 $A1 > A2 > A5 > A3 > A4$。因此，值

为 0.0544 的 A1 是白酒核心公司的最佳解决方案，值为 0.0469 的 A4 是最不重要的解决方案。

在本章的案例研究中，选择方案仅仅是初步建议，因为最终解决方案需要董事会进一步讨论。

四　本章小结

我们从供应链管理的角度提出了一个白酒行业供应链可持续绩效评估的框架。尽管企业界对可持续性绩效评估的兴趣日益增长，但是至今几乎没有有效的方法对白酒行业可持续供应链管理的三个维度同时进行评估。通过广泛的文献分析和听取专家意见，构建了将可持续性指标方案与白酒行业供应链管理联系起来的混合模糊多属性决策方法。为了证明方法的有效性，我们将其应用在四川的一个白酒企业案例研究中。研究结果为白酒企业的供应链管理提供了新的见解。

第一，为白酒企业的供应链管理构建了一个同时考虑经济、环境和社会维度的可持续指标体系。这些指标是专门为白酒企业供应链确定的，因此可以为未来的类似研究提供理论价值和实践参考。

第二，提出了一个模糊多属性决策框架，用于评估和选择白酒企业供应链的最优解决方案。模糊 AHP 用于确定指标的权重，模糊 TOPSIS 应用于对可持续方案排序。研究结果表明该方法是有效的。

第三，提出的方法被应用于四川一家白酒企业的案例研究中。研究结果可以为寻求平衡白酒供需的政策制定者提供决策支持，以调整行业结构，促进中国区域可持续生态环境发展。

我们设计的框架可以为白酒企业确定指标体系和提供解决方案，以实现可持续的供应链管理。在进一步的研究中，不同的多属性决策模型可以应用于相同的问题并且可以比较结果。将本书的研究扩展到中国及其他国家的相关及其他行业，也是有参考价值的。

第七章 结语

近年来，经济全球化趋势越来越明显，企业之间的竞争也越来越激烈。企业之间的竞争不仅仅是供应链的竞争，已经上升到了可持续供应链的竞争。面对重重压力，企业对可持续的三个维度，即经济绩效、环境保护和社会影响力也越来越关注，随之理论界和企业界对可持续发展都给予了充分重视。中国酒文化源远流长，四川地区是中国白酒的重要发源地。随着经济全球化，白酒企业也开始关注可持续供应链的构建。现有白酒企业面临高端固态产能不足、低端液态产能过剩，产能结构不合理的问题；全球化的到来，为国际烈性酒产品进驻中国市场提供了很好的契机，中国的葡萄酒、啤酒、果酒等产品也不断抢占白酒市场份额，中国白酒面临的竞争不断增强；国内白酒企业众多，良莠不齐，部分白酒企业存在技术设备落后、管理跟不上要求、物流成本过高、污染严重、对当地人民的生活带来诸多负面影响等问题。如何在白酒行业供应链中实现可持续发展，如何增强白酒企业的市场竞争力，如何减少经济成本，降低对环境的负面影响，为当地人民的生活做出贡献已经成为有前瞻眼光的白酒企业追求的目标。因此，研究白酒行业可持续供应链具有重要的理论意义和实践价值。

一 主要工作

结合白酒企业供应链管理的实际需要，基于可持续供应链管理的思想,关注白酒企业的优化问题,分析具体问题的背景,考虑到模糊不确定的特点,我们建立了相关概念模型。衡量可持续供应链的三个维度——经济、环境和社会,为决策者厘清其指标并制定出更加合理有效的决策方案提供参考价值。在现有的白酒行业供应链模型研究中,同时考虑所有三个可持续维度的研究还比较少。因此,我们以可持续供应链理论为指导,以多目标理论、模糊理论和随机不确定理论为主要的研究工具,对白酒行业可持续供应链问题展开了研究,为白酒行业可持续供应链研究提供了理论依据和决策方法。我们从不同角度出发,对可持续供应链进行了分析研究,并将其运用于白酒企业的具体案例中,检验了模型和算法的有效性、科学性、合理性和实用性。

第一,供应链网络设计具有举足轻重的作用。针对白酒行业供应链网络中的经济、环境和社会三个维度的现有问题提出了可持续供应链优化设计方案,建立了多目标优化模型。在随机不确定环境下,构建了白酒行业可持续供应链网络设计模型。从物料购买成本、产品生产成本、产品配送成本、修建酒厂固定设施成本、修建配送中心成本、仓储成本、废弃物处理成本、酒糟销售收入几个角度考虑最小化供应链总成本。从生产阶段的碳排放、配送阶段的碳排放和废弃物处理阶段的碳排放进行网络设计,从而最小化供应链的环境影响。从就业率和当地人均GDP来最大化供应链的社会影响力。最后,将优化模型和R语言算法应用到了四川某地的一家白酒企业的供应链网络设计中,对结果进行了分析和讨论,说明了模型和算法的有效性和实用性,为白酒行业可持续供应链网络设计提供了有益的参考。

第二,供应商选择关系着产品的质量,对企业的生存和发展具有重要的影响。考虑到白酒企业对供应商的可持续要求,建立了经济、环境和社会三个可持续维度的供应商选择指标。由于供应商选择指标的模糊性,运用模糊DEMATEL方法对白酒企业的供应商选择进行了分析。根据白酒企业对供应商的可持续要求,经济维度选用了5个衡量指标,即质量($C11$)、交货($C12$)、服务($C13$)、价格($C14$)和柔性($C15$)。环境维度分为资源消耗($C21$)、污染控制($C22$)、环境管理体系（C23）、绿色产品（C24）和环境竞争力（C25）5个指标。社会维度分为员工利益和权利（C31）、利益相关者权利（C32）、工作安全和职业健康（C33）、信息披露（C34）、尊重政策（C35）5个方面。最后，我们对四川省一家白酒企业进行了供应商选择研究，从重要性上得出质量（C11）、服务（C13）、环境竞争力（C25）、信息披露（C34）和价格（C14）分别以值20.727、20.684、20.662、20.161和20.065排在最重要指标的前五位。而柔性（C15）、环境管理体系（C23）、利益相关者权利（C32）分别以值18.953、18.837和18.650处于重要度排序的后三位。从原因度来看，资源消耗（C21）具有最高的$R-C$值2.115，意味着资源消耗（C21）对整个系统具有很强的影响力。从结果度来看，利益相关者权利（C32）以$R-C$值-2.713处于结果要素的最低点，这表示此要素受到其他要素的影响最大。而质量（C11）具有最高的$R+C$值20.727，说明这个要素是最重要的结果要素。

第三，随着企业面临的环境越来越复杂，企业越来越需要重视风险控制。针对白酒行业的可持续发展需求，我们对白酒行业供应链的风险因素进行了分析，分别识别出经济、环境和社会三个维度的30个风险因素。其中经济维度14个、环境维度8个、社会维度8个。而风险管控最重要的是事先对风险有一定的认识，并进行控制。选用进行事前风险管控的FMEA方法，对白酒企业的风险因素用风险顺序数进行风险分析，并根据风险因素给出了相应的风险控制策略。我们给出了四种风险应对措施，即风险减轻、风险规避、风险转移和风险接受。最后将模型和算法应用于四川一家白酒企业的可持续供应链风险管理中，实际应用验证了方法的有效性和科学性。

第四，企业要获得长足的发展，对企业所在的供应链进行评价则有着相当重要的作用。基于可持续供应链发展的要求，对白酒企业的供应链进行了评价。考虑到指标的模糊性，运用混合模糊AHP-TOPSIS方法对相应指标和方案进行了评价和选择。其中模糊AHP用来对指标进行权重分析，模糊TOPSIS用来对选择方案进行排序。选用的指标总共有

15个，其中经济指标5个，即质量、柔性、响应性、可靠性和财务绩效；环境指标5个，即能源消耗、自然环境、环境管理体系、碳排放和污染控制；社会指标5个，即就业、健康和安全、工作条件、客户问题和社会承诺。

最后将模型应用于四川一家白酒企业的供应链评价与选择中，得出白酒企业的供应链评价指标排名优先级是经济—环境—社会。根据模糊AHP分析，在白酒供应链中，质量（$Eco1$）、财务绩效（$Eco5$）、可靠性（$Eco4$）、就业（$Soc1$）和资源消耗（$Env1$）是前五大最重要的可持续性指标，社会承诺（$Soc5$）、客户问题（$Soc4$）和工作条件（$Soc3$）是最不重要的3个指标。应用模糊TOPSIS分析，得出方案A1是白酒企业的最优选择方案，A4是最不重要的选择方案。案例分析说明了模型和算法的科学性和有效性。

二 本书创新

随着经济全球化的发展，企业之间的竞争日渐激烈。随着人们对环境保护、社会影响和经济绩效的关注，供应链管理已经上升到可持续供应链管理的高度。本书以白酒企业案例为原型，以可持续供应链管理理论为指导，以多目标理论、模糊理论和随机不确定理论为主要研究工具，以R算法和多属性决策方法为主要技术，从经济、环境和社会三个维度对白酒行业可持续供应链问题进行了深入分析研究。构建了白酒行业供应链的网络设计优化模型、供应商选择方法、风险管控策略和供应链绩效评价框架，并在四川一家白酒企业的案例分析中进行实际应用，具有重要的理论意义和实践价值。

第一，可持续决策模型。本书构建了基于经济、环境和社会三个可持续维度的供应链决策模型。在传统的网络设计中，大多数的模型都是单目标的，一般是注重经济目标，忽略了网络布局对环境和社会的影响。我们针对白酒企业经济、环境和社会三个维度的可持续供应链配送中心的网络布局问题建立了随机多目标模型，同时优化了供应链总成本、碳排放和社会影响力，并用 R 语言来处理多目标模型。在一级配送中提供了公路、铁路和水路三种运输模式来优化路径，而且考虑到多目标的二级配送问题，运用 R 语言来计算，这种处理模式在现有文献中比较少见。在对白酒行业供应链网络布局的可持续优化深入分析的基础上，结合不确定理论，建立了经济、环境和社会三个可持续维度的目标，形成了多目标规划模型，最终找到满意的决策。同时，供应商选择、风险管控和供应链绩效评价中都构建了经济、环境和社会三个维度的可持续供应链模型。

第二，可持续指标方案。本书根据需要构建了网络设计、供应商选择、风险管控和绩效评估的可持续指标方案。无论是对企业，还是对供应链来说，评价指标的确定、评估方法的应用都是其关注的重点和难点。针对白酒行业供应链的实际情况，在参考已有文献和专家意见的基础上，给出了供应商选择的可持续指标、供应链的可持续评价指标以及风险管理相关指标，它们都是从经济、环境和社会三个维度来进行指标分析的。我们选用了模糊 DEMATEL 方法、模糊 AHP-TOPSIS 以及 FMEA 方法进行选择评价。这些框架结构的建立对于白酒行业可持续供应链研究具有重要的理论和实践意义。

第三，实际应用研究。本书将模型和算法应用于企业实际案例中，给决策者提供了一定的启示。将经济、环境和社会三维可持续环境下的多目标供应链网络设计模型、供应商选择模型、风险控制方法和供应链评价方法应用到了中国白酒企业的案例中，进行了分析和讨论，提出了科学的解决方案。这些实际案例的应用研究展示了如何将理论的模型和算法应用到实际的供应链决策问题中，给理论研究者和管理决策者提供了一定的启示和参考。同时也证实了模型和算法的有效性和实用性。进一步丰富了可持续供应链管理的案例研究方法和内容。

综上所述，本书根据实际决策问题需求，展开了对新模型的研究，进而触发了新算法的设计，并将提出的模型和算法应用到实际案例中进行可行性和有效性的验证。本书创新点是层层深入、相互联系的。本书提出的决策模型和算法对于实际白酒企业的可持续供应链优化有着一定的指导意义，对于不确定理论、多目标规划理论、模糊理论以及算法研究也有着积极的推动作用。

三 后续研究

当前对于可持续供应链管理问题的研究还处于初级阶段，而且大多数学者的研究还停留在定性分析的层面上或单一决策问题上。使用多目标决策和模糊理论等数理分析方式对可持续供应链问题进行定量分析和优化决策的研究相对较少，还有许多问题需要进一步的深入分析和探讨。后续的研究将主要集中在以下几个方面。

第一，对可持续供应链中的决策支持系统、信息共享问题、需求不确定性问题进行具体分析和研究。第二，改进或提出更有效的算法来求解白酒行业可持续供应链问题。如最优性检验、灵敏度分析、稳定性讨论等。第三，深入挖掘可持续供应链中的网络设计、供应商选择、风险控制和供应链绩效评价等类问题的个性特点，研究其具体模型的数学性质，为精确算法的设计奠定理论基础。

致　　谢

本书的写作得到了我的导师徐玖平教授的关心和指导，也得到了吴志彬研究员、赵飞数据工程师和UDML实验室的热心帮助，在此向他们表示衷心的感谢。除笔者自己的研究成果外，本书参考了国内外许多学者的论著，吸收了同行们的优秀劳动成果，谨向这些同行和专家致以诚挚的谢意。

本书的研究工作得到了以下项目的支持或资助：国家社科基金重点项目（No. 12&ZD217），国家自然科学基金项目（No. 71671118，No. 71702156，No. 71772025），四川省科技厅项目（No. 2019JDR0026），四川省教育厅项目（No. 18SB0400），四川省教育厅重点研究基地川酒发展研究中心项目（No. CJZ17－02），四川轻化工大学人才引进项目（No. 2017RCSK21，No. 2018RCSK01），教育部人文社科项目（No. 17YJC630098，No. 19 YJC630222），四川省社会科学重点研究基地项目（No. Xq18C07）。在此特向以上项目支持单位表示由衷的感谢。

由于笔者学术水平和能力的局限性，书中难免存在错误和纰漏之处，恳请广大读者和同行指正。